GARDENING FROM THE GROUND UP

GARDENING FROM THE GROUND UP

Stanley Schuler

THE MACMILLAN COMPANY, NEW YORK

COLLIER-MACMILLAN LIMITED, LONDON

Many of the photographs in this book were taken by the author for his earlier book AMERICA'S GREAT PRIVATE GARDENS.

Library of Congress Catalog Card Number: 68-18476

The Macmillan Company, New York
Collier-Macmillan Canada Ltd., Toronto, Ontario

Printed in the United States of America

Contents

List of Tables

What This Book
Is All About

Several years ago, one of my city friends who had just bought his first home in the suburbs phoned to ask what he could do to grow grass in the rubble-infested soil the builder called a lawn area. Just before we rang off, he suddenly asked: "Why don't you write a book for people like us who don't know much about gardening?

"We know what a rake is. We know how to dig with a spade. I don't think we'll have any trouble running a lawn mower—if we ever have a lawn. But what we don't know are things like what fertilizer to use where . . . how to kill insects . . . how to grow flowers from seeds . . . when we should plant trees.

"What we need is a book of fundamentals."

That is exactly what this book is. It is to my knowledge the first and only complete book of current outdoor gardening practices necessary to the planning, establishment and maintenance of an attractive garden.

I hope it makes your thumbs bright green.

GARDENING FROM THE GROUND UP

1

Landscaping

LANDSCAPING IS THE FIRST AND HARDEST job in gardening. It involves not only the selection and placement of plants but also design, engineering and construction. Because of the complexity of the work, I urge you to employ a professional landscape architect—especially for difficult and extensive landscaping projects. Nobody else (and I include nurserymen, who know plants but are rarely adept at design) has the training, skill and feeling that the landscape architect brings to this all-important gardening task.

I realize, however, that for one reason or another you may not want a landscape architect. In that case, here's what you should think about and do to landscape your property successfully (the rules and procedure are the same no matter whether you are starting with a vacant lot or an old property that has already been planted but needs to be redeveloped):

¶ *The aim of landscaping* today is to make the property functionally useful to the owners. The secondary aim is to make it esthetically pleasing.

This wasn't always so. In days past, esthetic considerations often outranked the functional. But today, lots are smaller and most people spend about as much time outside their homes as in. So your first thought in landscaping must be: How can I best make this piece of property work for me?

¶ *A lot is a single large space made up of several small spaces.* The latter include: (1) The enclosed space, which is of course the house. It is the key space around which the entire lot pivots; but this does not mean that it alone should dictate the landscaping plan.

(2) The public space. This may be the front yard if there is a front yard. But it is always the part of the property which is first encountered by the public.

(3) The automobile space. This used to be considered part of the public space. But in today's living it is so important that it must be considered as a distinct space.

(4) The living space. The area in which you and your family enjoy yourselves outdoors.

(5) The backdoor space. This used to be called the service area or sometimes the work area, but neither term is accurate today because the automatic clothes dryer and garbage disposal have pretty well eliminated two functions of the backdoor space of the past; and in many homes, the attached garage has taken over the remaining functions.

All these spaces are separated from one another to some extent by walls, shrubs, trees, hedges, flower beds, etc., but they should also be connected by walks, steps, gates, etc., so that you can move easily between them. In short, good circulation is an essential element of the landscape plan.

All the spaces—or any one or two of them—may also be subdivided into smaller spaces. The outdoor living space, for instance, may include a terrace, pool, play yard, barbecue area, etc. Similarly, the automobile space may be nothing more than a stretch of driveway or it may include a turn-around, public parking area, service parking area, etc.

In other words, a lot may be landscaped to incorporate only a few large spaces, or it may be broken up into a rather complex arrangement of small and large spaces. In either case, however, the spaces, while separate, are interrelated and work together for a common purpose—which is to give you maximum enjoyment of your *entire* property.

¶ *List the things you want to do and want to have on your property.* Take time over this: be sure you do not overlook anything

Contrasting foliage and plant shapes add to the charm of this Boston terrace. Trees with open foliage, such as this clumped birch, are especially good to use around terraces because they shade against the sun yet admit plenty of light and air.

or include something that is not realistic. Make a written list. Here are some of the things it might include:

Things we want to do
    Swim
    Cook and eat outdoors
    Sit on terrace
    Raise a few tomatoes
    Enjoy the little view to the east
    Play on jungle gym and in sandbox (children)
    Roller skate (children)
    Play badminton (adults)
    Watch birds

Things we want to have
    Adequate auto turn-around
    Parking space at least for weekly bridge group
    Small drying yard
    Greenhouse
    Tool house
    Place to compost leaves
    Big dog pen

¶ *Rough out the plan for your lot.* It is not necessary to have the exact dimensions of lot and house; but they should be good enough so that you do not waste time developing a layout which later proves completely impractical. Your main aim right now is simply to come up with a rough idea of where the various spaces you need should be placed. To do this, walk around the lot two or three times and take a close look at it. At the same time, take a look at what has happened or is likely to happen on neighboring lots. Then sit down with a pencil and sheet of paper, and start doodling. Rough in the house and garage, then the driveway and turn-around and front walk. Then rough in the terrace and other parts of the living space and the backdoor space. Examine the resulting plan closely to see how well it satisfies all your needs. Is there good circulation between the main rooms of the house and the outdoors? Is there circulation between the outdoor areas? And so forth. Then make a second rough sketch, and a third, and a fourth until you arrive at a plan that makes sense.

¶ *Now make a finished plan.* Up to this point in your planning you have been concerned only with spaces and a few major yard or garden elements that bear on the spaces. Now comes the time to start thinking about the plants, walls, fences, pools, outbuildings, etc., that should go into the spaces.

For this work you need an accurate-to-the-inch plan of the lot and where the house, trees, rock outcroppings and other fixed elements are located. The plan should also show the doors and windows in the house because they affect the placement of things in the garden. Draw this basic plan in ink on plain paper or graph paper, whichever you think will make your work easier. Then lay a sheet of tracing paper over it and draw your rough landscaping plan to accurate scale. First draw in the major elements, such as the driveway, terrace and pool; then the minor elements, such as flower beds, trees and the children's sandbox.

Once again you should examine your work critically. Make changes. Redraw the whole plan if necessary.

When you are satisfied that you have the best plan possible, there is one final step to take: Get a bundle of wood laths and a couple of balls of strong white string, and actually stake out the plan on your lot. Then "live" in it for a while in your imagination. Walk through it. Sit in it. Drive the car up and down the driveway. Go through all the motions you would go through if the landscaping work were completed.

Now are you satisfied with the plan? Then this should be it.

¶ *Draw elevations, too.* These may not be necessary, but they will help you in arranging trees and shrubs around the house for the most satisfactory effect.

As a starter, you need accurate elevations of the house. If available, use the blueprints. Otherwise, make blow-up photographs of the front, back and sides of the house. Then lay tracing paper over these and sketch in the planting as you hope it will look when full grown.

A simple but effective way to treat a walk to the front door. The opening in the white fence calls attention to the walk when you drive up. The walk is bordered by small dogwoods. The ground cover is pachysandra.

LANDSCAPING FUNDAMENTALS

It is easier to develop a landscaping plan that is successful from the functional standpoint than it is to develop one that is esthetically good. And no amount of reading is going to change the situation. Unless you have an intuitive knack for creating moods, pictures and effects with plants and other garden materials, you should stick to a number of overly simplified but sound rules for achieving an attractive landscape design.

¶ *Seven basic rules.* (1) Look at your property from inside the house as well as from outside. Don't just stand out in the street and decide what needs to be done to make your lot look well from that vantage point. You should also determine what will make it attractive when you look out at it from the living room, family room and the other rooms you occupy a large part of the time.

(2) Suit the landscape design to the site and to the style of the house.

(3) Keep all elements of the plan in scale. Surround a small house with small trees, small lawns, small pools. Save the mighty oaks, towering spruces and Olympic-size swimming pools for homes that are large enough not to be overwhelmed by them.

(4) Create focal points. In the front of the house, for example, the obvious focal point is the front door, and you should develop your planting so that the eye instantly leaps to this. Similarly you need focal points in the living space and perhaps elsewhere around the property. They help to create perspective and to attract attention away from things that don't deserve attention.

(5) Don't overplant in an effort to get an immediate effect. Your lot will turn into a jungle.

(6) Lay out and plant the property in such a way that it does not require constant upkeep. Garden work is fun—but only up to a point.

(7) Be simple and restrained. Avoid clutter and cuteness. More hard-working gardeners have spoiled their homes by placing fawns, silver balls and piles of white rocks in their front yards than I care to think about.

One of the aims of landscaping is to separate your property into different spaces yet provide good circulation between the spaces. Here a bed of roses, andromeda and viburnum visually screens the living room terrace from the backdoor area; yet circulation between the areas is not interfered with. When they grow a little taller, the virburnums will also provide more privacy for the bathrooms (small windows).

¶ *Foundation planting.* Landscape architects today hate to talk about foundation planting—and with three good reasons: Many homeowners and builders think that foundation planting is the only thing there is to landscaping. Many contemporary homes do not need extensive foundation planting but have it anyway. And most foundation planting consists of a tasteless, disorderly array of overgrown evergreens which are often trimmed into rigid, unnatural shapes.

Foundation planting (the planting around the foundations of a house) is a term that Americans use so I shall also. But please remember that when you put in foundation planting, you should use great discretion in selecting and placing the plants. Do not think that you must ring the entire house with plants; two or three used as accents or to hide objectionable features are likely to be more effective. Do not think that you must use evergreens; deciduous species which shed their leaves annually often are more attractive. Above all, do not try to attract attention to the planting itself; use the planting to enhance the appearance of the house and to blend it into the natural surroundings.

Here are some more specific suggestions for achieving the best possible effect with foundation planting:

Use low-growing plants under windows. Those that grow tall must be pruned severely, usually every year, to keep them from blocking the windows. If you want a window to be screened from the street, yard or sun, plant a medium-size tree with open foliage in front of it but well out from the house.

To make a house look longer and lower, plant low shrubs in front of it and out beyond the corners. But don't arrange the plants in a long, rigidly spaced row.

To make a house look taller, set one or two slender, columnar plants in front of it.

To direct attention to the front door, place low plants on either side and grade up from them (but not in straight lines) to tall plants at the sides of the house. The V draws the eye to the door at its apex.

Don't plant high and low plants alternately from one end of the house to the other. And don't use plants of the same height. The effect is monotonous.

¶ *Selecting plant material.* The most important rule here is to use only a few different kinds of plants and to use them over and over again. In other words, don't scatter your shots even though there may be a great many plants that you like. The result will be a restless hodgepodge. Your goal should be a relaxed, unified feeling, and this can be achieved only by using, say, white dogwoods both in front and in back of the house.

Strive for color harmony. I have yet to figure out why women—with their usually good color sense—allow such wild color combinations in their gardens. But as a trip through almost any suburban community shows, something goes wrong with people when they set out flowering plants (particularly azaleas and tulips). The effect is ghastly.

Make good but subtle use of the textures which abound in nature; they can be almost as effective in creating an interesting picture as colors. But they, too, must be arranged harmoniously—which means that, as a rule, it is advisable to set plants so that the change in leaf size is graduated from plant to plant.

When using trees or vines for shade, remember that deciduous species with high crowns which admit some sunlight are generally preferable. For one thing, they give more than enough shade for comfort. Small plants grow under them better than under specimens with dense foliage. Air movement is better. And they let the sun through to your house and garden in winter.

Beware of "dirty" trees, shrubs and vines that litter the ground with fruit, nuts, twigs, large leaves or flowers. When planted in an open area, the mess they make is unattractive and causes an unnecessary amount of cleanup. If you must use such plants, either set them in an out-of-the-way spot or plant a ground cover under them to soak up some of the litter.

¶ *Planting for immediate and long-range effect.* This is a problem that is most frequently encountered by people who are trying to develop the foundation planting around new development houses. Although there are several solutions, none is perfect. But some are more nearly perfect than others.

(1) The quickest and least expensive way to surround your house

A Florida gardener shows how to make capital of plant textures. Through thoughtful selection and intermingling of foliage plants, she created a garden of rare beauty—yet it contains very few flowering plants.

with lush greenery is to put in fast-growing plants such as hemlocks and arborvitae. The specimens offered by most nurseries are large and cheap. But unfortunately, they soon make such tremendous growth that they threaten to block your house from view. So you bring out your pruning sheers—only to discover that when plants of this type are pruned severely, their natural beauty is ruined and they often develop large leafless spots.

Clearly, this is not a good way to plant around your house.

(2) You can put in fast-growing shrubs which take more kindly to pruning but which are not so large or inexpensive to start with. Some of the shrubby yews and Japanese hollies fall into this category. To get a fairly immediate effect, you must plant the shrubs more closely than they should be (plants look better when given enough elbow-room to develop naturally). But because they can be pruned regularly without showing ill effects, they can be readily maintained in the most effective size and shape for many years.

(3) You can start with full-grown specimens of choice, slow-growing plants that are now, and will always be, "perfect" for the situations in which you use them. This of course is the ideal solution to the foundation-planting problem because you can set each plant exactly where it should grow, you can allow it to develop naturally, and you will rarely have to prune it. But there is one small fly in the ointment: choice, slow-growing plants are always more expensive than common, fast-growing types. And when you start with specimens that are full grown—

(4) You can put in small specimens of the same choice, slow-growing plants and fill in between them until they are fully grown with inexpensive, fast-growing, temporary materials. This is the best solution if you cannot afford solution number 3, because the initial cost is not high and the ultimate appearance of the planting is ideal. Admittedly, the immediate effect is somewhat less than ideal; but if you use fill-in materials cleverly, the planting should look every bit as well as if you started with cheap, fast-growing shrubs and trees.

¶ *Arranging plants away from the house.* Strive for over-all balance: it is one of the essentials of good landscaping. This does not mean, however, that for every plant you place on the right side of the garden you need a matching plant on the left side. Such symmetry is usually found only in formal gardens. Balance is possible without symmetry. It is a matter of selecting and placing plants and other garden elements so that, even though quite different in appearance, they attract attention equally.

When arranging plants in groups, use at least three or four of the same kind together. As a rule, the complete grouping should be wider than it is high.

To frame a house, first decide from what point it is most commonly viewed or from what point you want it to be viewed. Then plant small to medium-size trees slightly forward and to the sides of the house.

To gain privacy and increase the usable space in your yard, make the largest plantings of shrubs and trees along the borders of your lot. But be sure to set outspreading plants far enough inside your boundaries so that they will not encroach on neighboring property. (Plants that are athwart a property line are owned equally by the homeowners on the two sides of the line. Plants that overhang a neighboring property can be legally cut back to the property line by the neighbor as long as the action does not endanger the life of the plant.)

2

Developing Your Land

LAND DEVELOPMENT MAY BE A SINGLE, simple process in the case of some properties; a difficult, expensive process involving several operations in the case of others. Exactly what is required depends on the physical character of the land and on how you elect to land-scape it.

¶ *Clearing land.* There is nothing very mysterious about this work. But it is *work*. The best procedure is to chop down large trees and shrubs, then to have the stumps pushed or yanked out by a bulldozer. Exceptionally large stumps can be removed by a chipping machine, but the tree firms that own such gadgets charge a great deal for them. A slower but much cheaper disposal method is to saturate each stump with Ammate (see Chapter 10). For stumps less than 6 in. in diameter, mix 4 lb. of Ammate with 1 gal. of water and saturate the cut surface of the stump. For larger stumps or those with very thick bark, first make deep, slanting ax cuts around the base of the stump. The cuts must be through the bark into the wood, and they should overlap and completely encircle the stump. Saturate the stump as above. Then drop about 1/2 oz. of Ammate crystals into each of the cuts.

Small trees and shrubs—those with trunks of less than 1 to 1 1/2 in. diameter—can generally be removed by hand. A fast procedure is to have one person pull on the trunk while another pries up the roots with a crowbar.

Large rocks, and especially ledge rock, are almost impossible to remove except with a bulldozer or dynamite.

The best time of year to clear land of trees and shrubs is in spring, fall or winter, when the plants are bare and therefore easier to get at and much lighter in weight. If you allow the wood to dry for a few months, it will make a handsome fire. But green wood burns well, too, if you get a hot fire started with kerosene and use a little dry wood also.

In burning any brush pile, it is of course important to take precautions against the spread of fire. Here are several good rules to follow:

(1) Burn the pile when snow is on the ground or during a light drizzle.
(2) If burning in dry weather, keep handy a hose which is connected to a faucet. Lacking this, keep on hand a couple of buckets filled with water.
(3) Do not burn too much trash at once.
(4) Rake up dry grass leaves and other flammable material in a circle around the fire; and while burning the trash pile, keep raking this area toward the fire.
(5) Do not burn the trash under trees, for no matter how high the branches, the heat of the flames is likely to damage or kill them.

Fields of grass and weeds are safer to burn in the fall, when the grass is standing, than in the spring, when much of it is matted down, because the flames do not travel so rapidly. However, the sensible course is not to burn fields at any time, but to mow them and use the grass as a mulch.

¶ *Grading.* Grading of a large area is generally a five-stage operation: (1) The topsoil is stripped off—usually by a bulldozer or front-end loader—and piled to one side. (2) The exposed subsoil is bulldozed to the desired grade. (3) The topsoil is spread evenly over the subsoil. (4) Because the bulldozer compacts the soil and

To keep a stump from sprouting, as this one did, make a continuous frill of axe cuts around it and pour in Ammate crystals. Saturate the top of the stump with Ammate solution also.

also because the topsoil may be full of large, coarse sods, the graded area is now thoroughly cultivated with a rotary tiller. (5) The soil is raked smooth in preparation for seeding or planting.

¶ *Filling land.* Filling in low land or raising the grade of any land looks easy, but it is a job that must be taken seriously if you do not want the filled area to subside at a later date.

First consider the area to be filled. If it is swampy or if the soil is composed largely of clay, ordinary fill may literally sink out of sight when weight is applied to it. In this situation, you should start filling with rocks—the larger, the better.

A second point you should consider—whatever the nature of the area to be filled—is the composition of the fill itself. This must be stable and durable; it should not decompose or compress. Good fill materials include rock, mortar rubble (but not plaster or gypsum board), gravel, sand, hard cinders, shells and ordinary soil.

Four things to remember in filling land are: (1) If the filled area is to be paved, the fill should be compacted by a bulldozer or steam roller. On the other hand, if you are going to plant the filled area, it is advisable to keep heavy machines off it as much as possible. But the fill should be allowed to settle. This takes time unless you soak it with water.

(2) If you fill an area first with a coarse material, such as large rocks, and then with a fine material, such as screened topsoil, much of the latter will in time settle into the interstices of the former. You can prevent this by placing a material of intermediate size— say, coarse traprock—between the two layers.

(3) If large rocks are too close to the surface of a filled area, grass planted over them will burn out in summer dry spells. For this reason, you should try to cover rock fill with at least a foot of soil. Not all of it needs to be topsoil.

(4) The advantage of screened topsoil is that it is free of rocks, roots and sods (but not weed seeds). But this means more when you are top-dressing a lawn or establishing a flower bed than when filling in an area that is to be planted to grass and shrubs. In the latter instance, foreign matter in the soil does not interfere either with the plants you grew or with your growing of them. Therefore, since screened topsoil costs much more than unscreened soil, you should think twice about using it for fill.

¶ *Terracing.* The usual aim of terracing is to provide some reasonably flat spaces on sloping land. The work entails cutting away the hillside at the top and filling in below. At the front, the terrace is supported either by a retaining wall or an earth bank.

An amateur can construct a retaining wall up to about 3 ft. in height. The wall requires a footing that is 1 ft. thick and 1 ft. wider than the wall itself. Three-inch weepholes just above the ground on the downhill side of the wall should be provided at 10-ft. intervals.

Walls over 3 ft. should be designed and constructed by a professional, because they may be toppled by the pressure of the earth and water behind them.

Building a bank is easier than building a wall, but requires attention anyway. The steepness of the bank is the critical factor.

If you want to walk up and down a bank without steps and if

Originally a long, steep slope, this broad terrace was created by building a retaining wall (unseen, left) and bringing in many truckloads of coarse fill which was then covered with topsoil. Hillside was developed as a rock garden.

Steep hillside was made more manageable and also more attractive by terracing. Stone walls cost more to build than banks but require no upkeep. Because they occupy less space than banks, they also enable you to have more level area.

Stone wall extends the lines of the house and also helps to provide some flat space on this very steep Seattle property. Garden is designed to flow visually through the double doors into the study.

you want to cover it with grass which you can mow, the maximum permissible pitch is 1 ft. perpendicular for 3 ft. horizontal. A bank with a sharper pitch must have steps and be planted to a ground cover. And very steep banks—those with a pitch of 1 ft. perpendicular to 1 1/2 to 2 ft. horizontal—must also be covered with large rocks (riprap), logs or railroad ties running the length of the bank. The rocks and wood should be well embedded of course.

¶ *Draining land.* In order to grow anything other than bog plants in soggy land or in a depressed area in which rain water sometimes stands, you must carry off the unwanted water in 4-in. perforated composition drainpipes. The pipes, which are very light in weight even though they come in 8-ft. lengths, are laid with the perforations down in trenches at least 1 ft. deep (deeper trenches are needed if you aim to plant deep-rooted plants). If the wet spot is not large, a single line of pipe or a Y-shaped system is probably all you need. But for large spots you may have to arrange the pipes in a tree pattern with the branches (spaced 6 to 10 ft. apart) leading into the trunk. In any case, the entire system must be sloped gently in one direction away from the area.

If possible, the water should be drained into a stream or pond on the property or into the catch basin of a municipal storm sewer. Otherwise, you must dig a large dry well at a distance from the wet spot.

¶ *Removing excess surface water.* One of the easiest ways to carry water harmlessly off your land during heavy storms is to cut shallow waterways through the property at the points where water concentrations are heaviest. The ditches must be lined with grass to prevent erosion. Be sure that they empty into the street or some other place where the water will do no damage.

To keep water from racing down hillsides that for one reason or another you do not want to terrace, cut diversion ditches across the hillsides. The downhill side of a ditch must be high enough to contain the water. The bottom of the ditch should be kept covered with turf.

3

Improving Soil

THE FACT THAT YOU CAN GROW PLANTS in a chemical solution is evidence that you can make a garden in almost any soil if you apply enough water and chemicals of the right kind. But this obviously is an expensive and inefficient way of doing things. You will get better results at less cost by making more lasting improvements in the soil on your property.

¶ *Remove foreign matter.* It is an unfortunate fact that much of the land on which developers are building today has been filled. Often it is filled close to the surface with stuff which will not support attractive plant life—rocks, plaster rubble, mortar rubble, broken bottles, beer cans, nails, etc. Such matter must either be removed before you start a garden or it must be buried under additional soil.

¶ *Make a soil test.* This is the surest way to determine what needs to be done to your soil to grow the plants you want. To make a test, you should take samples from a number of spots throughout the garden area. Dig a shovel-size hole in the first spot, and take a thin, vertical slice of soil from the side of the hole with your shovel. Place it in a clean pail. Repeat this procedure in all other test spots. Make the soil slices as uniform in size and thickness as you can, and add them to the same pail. When all the samples have been taken, mix them together thoroughly; then put a handful of the mixture in a small box or plastic bag. Send this with your name and address and information about your garden and the plants you want to grow to either your State Agricultural Extension Service or State Agricultural Experimental Station, which is usually located at the same address at the Extension Service (see Appendix). This organization will make an analysis (usually free) of your soil and will return the facts to you with recommendations for how to treat it.

The best time for making a soil test is in either the spring or late fall. To test the soil in a lawn area you should take ten or more samples 3 to 4 in. deep from the area. For flowers, vegetables and small fruits, you also need ten or more samples, but taken from holes 6 to 8 in. deep. For existing trees and shrubs, two or three samples from holes 1 ft. deep should be taken from around the bases of each plant.

Special cartons for mailing soil samples may be obtained by writing the Extension Service or Experimental Station before making a test. The testing agency will also send you a questionnaire that you fill out about the soil to be tested. If you do not use the cartons and questionnaire supplied by the testing agency, the information to send in with your soil sample should cover the following points: (1) Size of area represented by the sample. (2) Plants you intend to grow. (3) Plants previously grown. (4) Type of soil drainage. (5) What you have done previously to fertilize, lime or acidify the soil. (6) Special features of the soil and land surface.

¶ *Improve humus content.* Soil is composed of weathered mineral matter and decayed vegetable and animal matter. The decayed matter, called humus, not only adds nutrients to the soil and nourishes important microorganisms, but also lightens the soil and helps it to hold moisture.

Humus, in short, is an essential soil constituent; but sad to say, many soils—especially sandy and clay soils—do not contain enough of it.

The most convenient source of humus is dried peat, commonly called peatmoss. Expert gardeners will tell you that there are differences between peats—which is true—but it is almost impossible to find out from a garden supply store what these differences are.

The Connecticut
AGRICULTURAL EXPERIMENT STATION
P. O. BOX 1106   123 HUNTINGTON STREET   NEW HAVEN, CONNECTICUT 06504

SUGGESTIONS IN THIS REPORT ARE MADE ON THE ASSUMPTION THAT REPRESENTATIVE SAMPLES WERE TAKEN AS SET FORTH IN THE ENCLOSED FOLDER. IN THIS FOLDER YOU WILL ALSO FIND AN EXPLANATION OF THE SYMBOLS USED AND OTHER INFORMATION HELPFUL IN INTERPRETING THIS REPORT. SHOULD YOU HAVE QUESTIONS ON THIS REPORT OR ON SPECIFIC SOIL MANAGEMENT PROBLEMS, ADDRESS YOUR INQUIRY TO: SOILS, BOX 1106, NEW HAVEN, CONNECTICUT 06504

REPORT ON
SOIL SAMPLES

Mr. Stanley Schuler
Greenwich, Connecticut 06830

Date March 5, 1967

RESULTS OF TESTS - (RED D-DEFICIENT; d-PROBABLY DEFICIENT; e-PROBABLY EXCESSIVE; E-EXCESSIVE)

LABORATORY NUMBER	2105	2106	2107		
YOUR SAMPLE	B	C	D		
CROP TO BE GROWN	Vegetables	Shrubs	Estab. Lawn		
SOIL TEXTURE	L	SL	FSL		
ORGANIC MATTER CONTENT	M	M	M		
pH	5.00	5.50	5.60		
NITRATE NITROGEN	L ^{D}	M	M		
AMMONIA NITROGEN	L	L	L		
PHOSPHORUS	M	M	L ^{D}		
POTASSIUM	L ^{D}	H	M		
CALCIUM	M	M	M		
^{D}Indicates deficient					

SUGGESTED TREATMENTS (IN POUNDS PER 1,000 SQUARE FEET)

LIMESTONE	75*	0**	50***		
FERTILIZER GRADE	(5-10-10) 35*	0	(5-10-10) 15****		

REMARKS: If a new seedbed, work lime in first (if indicated), then apply fertilizer and rake in, finally seed.   If an established lawn, apply fertilizer when grass is dry.

*apply at time of seedbed preparation. **some shrubs (not broadleaf evergreens) would be benefitted by limestone at 35 lbs. per 1000 sq. ft. ***or use 38 lbs. of hydrated lime. ****or use 5 lbs. of 10-20-20. On lawns, lime and fertilizer applications should be at least 2 weeks apart.

Interpreting the Test

Soil texture: s—sand; ls—loamy sand; sl—sandy loam; fsl—fine sandy loam; l—loam; si l—silt loam; si cl—silty clay loam; cl—clay loam.

pH test: When properly interpreted in relation to the texture and organic matter of the soil, this test is indicative of lime needs of the soil. The results are given as follows:

Below 4.4—very strongly acid

4.5—5.1—strongly acid

5.2—5.9—moderately acid

6.0—6.7—slightly acid

6.8—7.2—neutral (7.0 = exact neutrality)

above 7.2—alkaline

Organic matter and chemical tests: The results of these tests are given as: O—none detected; VL—very low; L—low; M—medium; H—high; VH—very high; EH—extra high.

Deficiencies and excesses for the crop to be grown are indicated in red as follows: D—deficient; d—probably deficient; e—probably excessive; E—excessive. These are based on soil tests, descriptions and other available information.

Important Information Supplied by Soil Tests

Nitrate tests show the immediately available nitrogen, and ammonia nitrogen indicates the nitrogen available in the immediate future, but they do not tell how much nitrogen may later be liberated from organic substances in the soil.

Phosphorus tests show the amount of phosphorus likely to become available to the plant.

Potassium available to most cultivated crops is clearly indicated. However, many crops, particularly perennial forage crops, shrubs and trees seem able to obtain considerable potash from the more difficultly soluble forms, not shown by the tests.

Calcium status of the soil is definitely revealed by the tests. Lime can correct for calcium deficiency. Liming should not be done indiscriminately, for some plants grow best in acid soils. Overliming in injurious to some crops.

Magnesium tests identify cases where magnesia treatments as dolomitic lime or as sulfate of magnesia (Epsom Salts) are likely to be beneficial. It also indicates whether or not magnesium is suitably balanced in proportion to other basic metals in the soil.

Aluminum is associated with a type of acidity that is harmful to acid-sensitive crops. Liming acid soils reduces aluminum toxicity.

Manganese also is closely tied in with soil acidity. A high manganese test on strongly acid soils may cause crop injury: it can be decreased by liming.

Correcting Deficiencies or Excesses

Suggestions for lime, fertilizer, manure, humus amendment or drainage improvement are estimates of profitable treatments under the conditions the test indicates. Other measures of similar character may be equally effective.

Fertilizer requirements vary for different soils and different crops. The principal plant nutrients in fertilizers are nitrogen (N), phosphoric acid (P_2O_5), and potash (K_2O). A fertilizer formula shows what's in the fertilizer.

By law this formula appears on the container and shows the per cent of N, P_2O_5, and K_2O in that particular fertilizer. It is always given in this order. For example, in a 5-10-5 mixture there are 5 pounds of N, 10 pounds of P_2O_5, and 5 pounds of K_2O in each 100 pounds of fertilizer.

Where manure is available, the commercial fertilizer application can usually be reduced by a third to a half assuming 10 tons or more of manure per acre (or 22 bushels (1 cu. yd.) to 1000 sq. ft.). Commercial dried manures may be used at the rate of 100 to 200 pounds to 1000 sq. ft. (50 pounds in the case of poultry manure).

Hydrated lime may be substituted for ground limestone (unless the latter is specifically required) but use only three-fourths as much.

This is typical of the soil reports supplied by state agricultural extension services or experiment stations when you send in soil samples for testing.

My own preference is for baled sphagnum peat, because it is coarser and seems to hold moisture better.

A second source of humus is leafmold—decayed leaves, grass clippings and hay. Unfortunately, it takes some time for leaves to break down into leafmold; on the other hand, leafmold costs nothing and contains more helpful bacteria than peat. Oak and pine leafmold also adds to soil acidity. To make leafmold, all you have to do is rake leaves into a pile and leave them alone until they decompose. If you wish, you may mix in a chemical, such as Adco, that accelerates decomposition somewhat.

A third excellent source of humus is compost—decayed vegetable matter of all kinds. (Strictly speaking, leafmold is compost; but the word is commonly applied to mixtures of materials such as straw, leaves, grass clippings, manure, dead flowers, discarded vegetables, etc.) Making compost used to be a tedious, noisome, time-consuming chore; but University of California sanitary engineers have devised a method that takes only 14 days. The first step is to grind up the material to be composed by running a rotary mower through it. Then pile the material into a heap 4 to 5 ft. wide and from 4 to 6 ft. high (no more, no less). If the material contains a lot of woody matter, mix in 1 lb. of high-nitrogen fertilizer. As you build the pile, sprinkle it with water so that it is damp throughout but not saturated. Turn over the pile with a fork on the fourth, seventh and tenth days. Be sure to mix the material on the sides into the center so that decomposition in uniform.

(An important side-note on making leafmold or compost: Never, never, never use leaves, vegetables, etc., that have been infected with disease. This simply perpetuates the disease. Such material should be burned.)

How much peat, leafmold or compost should be mixed into soil depends on the character of the soil. Sandy soils and clay soils require the most as a rule. But there is no neat formula that says, "Mix this amount of humus with this kind of soil; this amount with this kind of soil." I recommend that you start out by mixing 1 in. of humus with each 4 in. of soil. You can increase or decrease this ratio as seems necessary.

Another excellent but quite different source of humus is a cover crop or, better still, a succession of cover crops. Use these in large gardens or lawn areas that would require more peat than you can afford.

A cover crop is usually a grain crop that is sown on bare, plowed land or over an existing crop. You can sow rye in the fall, oats in the spring, millet in early summer, Sudan grass in late summer. The seeds are broadcast at the rate of about 5 lb. per 100 sq. ft. When the grain is a foot tall, cut it down and plow it under. The roots and tops decompose quickly and enrich the soil.

If your soil is deficient in nitrogen, using cowpeas, vetch or clover instead of the grains mentioned above will put nitrogen into the soil in addition to humus. The roots of these plants are covered with nodules containing bacteria which change the nitrogen in the air in the soil into the nitrogen compounds that plants need to grow. This process is called nitrogen fixation.

¶ *Improve soil drainage.* When soil is waterlogged, the plants growing in it die for lack of oxygen. They are, quite literally, drowned.

Occasionally soil is so badly waterlogged—usually because of the presence of springs—that it can be drained only with pipes that lead the water away (see Chapter 2). Most soil drainage problems, however, are caused either by the density of the soil or by the presence of an impervious layer of subsoil (hardpan) or rock. The only way to correct this condition is to lay drainlines on top of the impervious layer or to dig deep into the layer (or through it) and fill the cavity with a 6-in. layer of coarse gravel or crushed rock.

Soil which contains too much clay is a somewhat more difficult problem. When the soil is dry, the surface is so hard that water runs off faster than it sinks in. When the soil is wet, it is a sticky mess that takes forever to dry out. The only solution is to mix it thoroughly to a depth of 2 ft. or more with coarse builder's sand or crushed gravel. How much of this you use depends on the density of the soil and also on whether you mix in humus, which also improves drainage. As a rule of thumb, I suggest that you start by adding one heaping spadeful of sand or gravel to each cubic foot of soil. But you may have to increase this amount considerably.

¶ *Improve soil water-holding capacity.* Adding clay and/or humus helps a great deal. But sometimes soil is so exceedingly sandy or gravelly that its water-holding capacity is extremely poor: in a dry spell your plants die unless you water them constantly.

Two agricultural scientists from Michigan State University have come up with an ingenious solution to this problem. All you have to do is lay a 1/8-in. layer of asphalt 2 ft. below the surface of the soil. This sounds more complicated than it is. The job is done with a specially equipped tractor which has a rear blade that digs down into the soil parallel to the surface. While the blade raises the soil about 5 in., asphalt is sprayed under it. This hardens in the few seconds before the soil drops back into place.

¶ *Lighten heavy soil.* This familiar gardening phrase simply means to make soil more porous, less dense. It is done by mixing in sand and humus.

¶ *Aerate soil.* To encourage root growth and the activity of the micro-organisms and chemicals in the soil, all soil must be able to breathe. In short, it must be reasonably loose and porous.

Sandy and gravelly soils are almost always in this happy state and therefore require little attention. But heavy soils, especially those containing a lot of clay, need to be worked over constantly. There are several things you can do: (1) Mix in coarse sand and humus. (2) Cultivate the soil regularly and dig or plow it deeply when you have the opportunity. (3) Rent a gasoline-powered aerator to spike the lawn in the spring. (4) Plow up the vegetable garden in the fall in order to give the frost a chance to break down the clods of earth.

One thing you should not do is to work heavy soil when it is very wet. An even more important "don't"—don't roll or tamp a lawn heavily, and don't let neighborhood dogs or children wear a path across your lot.

¶ *To change the pH of soil.* pH is the symbol used to describe the acidity or alkalinity of soil (and also of water and other liquids). Soil with a pH of 7 is said to be neutral. If the pH is much below 7, the soil is acid; above 7, it is alkaline.

Most soils in the United States have a pH of 6 to 7, which is just right for the great majority of plants. But some soils, notably those in wet and forest areas, are quite acid; while others, especially those in the desert, are quite alkaline. Similarly, a number of plants—particularly rhododendrons, azaleas and other broadleaf evergreens prefer an acid soil while a few, such as delphiniums, lilacs and cacti, prefer (tolerate is a better word) an alkaline soil.

You can determine the pH of your garden soil by having a soil test made in the manner previously outlined. You then can do one of two things:

(1) Leave the soil as is and grow only those plants that tolerate soil of that kind. This is the easiest course to follow, but it is sensible only if your soil is nearly neutral (in which case you have thousands of different plants to choose among) or if you live in a city like Phoenix. There, both the soil and the water are excessively alkaline; and even though it is possible to make the soil less alkaline, the water soon changes it back to its original condition. Consequently, like it or not, Phoenix gardeners are limited to about 200 kinds of plants.

(2) You can change the pH of the soil in some spots, leave it as is in others. This is a better course because it allows you to grow any kind of plants you please. But extra work is required.

There are two ways to lower the pH (increase the acidity) of soil. If you want to plant only a few acid-soil plants here and there, you can mulch the soil around the plants with oak leaves or pine needles, both of which are acid. On the other hand, if you want to increase the acidity of a large area, the best method is to apply finely ground sulfur at the rate of 1 lb. per 100 sq. ft. This will lower the pH figure of loam soil about 1 point. To lower it more, make additional 1-lb. application, at intervals of two to four weeks. The sulfur can either be mixed with the soil or spread on top. Water it in well.

To raise the pH of soil (sweeten it) apply ground limestone or agricultural hydrated lime every three or four years. This, too, should be mixed into the top few inches of soil or scattered on the surface. Ground limestone has a longer-lasting effect; hydrated lime works faster. Table I shows how many pounds you need to raise the pH of 100 sq. ft. of soil to 6.

TABLE I
Pounds of Lime Needed to Raise the pH of 100 Sq. Ft.
of Soil to 6

Original pH	In light, sandy soil		In average soil		In clay loam	
	Ground limestone	Hydrated lime	Ground limestone	Hydrated lime	Ground limestone	Hydrated lime
4.0	9	6	17.2	11.5	21.7	14.5
4.5	8.2	5.5	15.7	10.5	20.2	13.5
5.0	6.7	4.5	12.7	8.5	15	10
5.5	5.2	3.5	9.7	6.5	12	8

One point to note about liming soil is that you should not apply more than 5 lb. of ground limestone or hydrated lime per 100 sq. ft. at one time. If soil requires more than this, make several 5-lb. applications at six-week intervals.

¶ *To sterilize soil.* Treating soil to kill weed seeds, insects, fungi and other micro-organisms is simpler today than in the past because of the development of so many new chemical fumigants. Use of these is discussed in Chapter 12. You can also sterilize small batches of soil by baking in a 200°F. oven for two hours.

¶ *To prepare soil for planting.* The procedure varies somewhat, depending on what is being planted. But generally the aim is to turn over the soil and mix it so that the topsoil, which contains most organic matter, is at the bottom of the planting bed and the poorer subsoil is at the top. This puts the best soil closer to the plant roots and in time produces a deep layer of excellent soil.

If you turn the soil over with a spade or spading fork, drive the blade straight down to its full depth (about 12 in.); turn the clod of earth upside down, and chop it well. This is hard work, but it produces the deepest planting bed. Using a power-driven rotary tiller is much easier but be careful to yield a planting bed only 8 in. deep at most. If sand, peat, etc., must be added to the soil, it can be mixed in during the initial digging or tilling step, or later. Final step in soil preparation is to pulverize and smooth the surface soil with a steel rake.

Easiest and fastest way to prepare an area for planting is to go over it with a rotary tiller. Tiller should be adjusted to dig as deeply as possible. For a still deeper bed, use a spade or fork. (TORO MANUFACTURING COMPANY)

Soil in flower beds and vegetable gardens should be turned over once a year. During the summer it also needs to be cultivated lightly with a hoe, pronged cultivator or rotary tiller to keep out weeds and to let in air and moisture. Soil in other garden areas is rarely disturbed once it is planted, but may need occasional aerating with a spading fork or power-driven spiker.

4

Fertilizing

FIFTEEN CHEMICAL ELEMENTS are essential to plant growth. Oxygen, carbon and hydrogen are obtained from air and water. The rest come from the soil.

You can find out which elements your soil is deficient in by making a soil test (see Chapter 3), but you are probably safe in assuming that it needs the "Big 3"—nitrogen, phosphorus and potassium. These are usually in short supply.

¶ *When to fertilize.* Plants need fertilizer when they display signs of nutrient deficiency. If they appear stunted and have small leaves that are pale green or yellowish, they probably lack nitrogen. If they are stunted and have dark-green or purplish leaves, they probably lack phosphorus. If they are small and have lower leaves that are mottled or yellowing and with dead tips, they probably lack potassium.

As a rule, the time to fertilize plants is when they start to grow in the spring (or whenever they actually start to grow) and while they are making vigorous growth. You should usually not feed trees and other woody plants after about July 15, because this stimulates new growth which may not survive autumn frosts.

¶ *How to fertilize.* Side-dressing is the name of the method used to feed shrubs, vines, flowers and vegetables. You simply spread fertilizer on the ground around a plant and scratch it in. Then water thoroughly to dissolve the fertilizer; unless it is in solution, the plant roots cannot absorb it.

In top-dressing, the fertilizer is scattered evenly on top of a lawn or ground cover and then watered in. The easiest way to top-dress a lawn is with a wheeled spreader that automatically releases fertilizer gradually as you walk back and forth. When using a spreader, you must first adjust the size of the opening to the size of the fertilizer granules (the fertilizer bag carries directions). You must also take care not to overlap the strips of fertilizer; otherwise the grass will grow unevenly.

Except in orchards, where the trees are fertilized by side-dressing, trees are usually fed through holes punched in the ground with a crowbar or auger (see Chapter 16).

Foliar feeding is generally used for smaller plants (though it is not limited to them) and is particularly good for those with restricted root systems. It is also particularly recommended for plants growing in porous soil, where leaching (percolation of water down through the soil) is a problem. In this feeding method, a concentrated fertilizer is diluted in water and sprayed on the leaves until they drip. (To save work, you may mix the fertilizer in with the insecticide or fungicide you spray on plants. There are also foliar-feeding applicators that attach to a hose.) The nutrients are quickly absorbed through the leaves and diffused through the entire plant.

¶ *What fertilizer to use: a few preliminary words.* Note these three points:

(1) When you buy 100 lb. of fertilizer, you do not buy 100 lb. of plant nutrients. Only a part of the material in the bag has food value; the rest is an inert filler used to give even distribution of the nutrients. The nutritious chemical part is expressed in a percentage. For instance, nitrate of soda contains about 16% nitrogen (the exact percentage varies with the brand). This means that if you buy a 100-lb. bag of nitrate of soda, you actually are getting 16 lb. of nitrogen and 84 lb. of filler.

(2) In a complete fertilizer, the formula is represented on the bag by three hyphenated numbers. The first number indicates the percentage of available nitrogen contained in the mixture. The sec-

ond figure indicates the percentage of available phosphorus. The third figure indicates the percentage of available potassium, or potash. The total of the three figures is the amount of nutrients in the bag. Thus a 100-lb. bag of 5-10-5 fertilizer contains 20%, or 20 lb., of nutrients—5 lb. of nitrogen, 10 lb. of phosphorus and 5 lb. of potash.

(3) The speed with which fertilizers make their nutrients available to plants varies. Some are fast-acting; others, slow-acting.

A fast-acting fertilizer works something like a shot of adrenalin. It is quickly dissolved in water and taken up through the plant roots. But its effect is short-lived; consequently, you may have to make repeated applications during the growing season. One other problem with many (not all) fast-acting fertilizers is that, if they remain for very long in contact with plant stems or leaves, they are likely to cause burning. This is another reason why you must water plants well soon after feeding them.

Slow-acting fertilizers do not cause burning; neither do they dissolve very quickly. Instead, they release their nutrients gradually over a period of weeks or even months. This means that they have a less dramatic effect on plants than fast-acting fertilizers. But you do not need to make so many applications.

¶ *What fertilizer to use: getting down to facts.* If soil is especially deficient in one of the three major elements, the best way to correct the problem is to apply a limited-purpose chemical fertilizer that is rich in the missing element. For *nitrogen* you can use any of the following:

Bone meal contains up to 4% nitrogen and also contains phosphorus. It is slow-acting.

Cottonseed meals contains 7% nitrogen. It is especially recommended for rhododendrons, azaleas and other acid-soil plants. It is slow-acting.

Dried blood contains 12% nitrogen. It is slow-acting. One of its incidental virtues is that it helps to keep rabbits away from plants.

Dried sludge from sewage-treatment plants contains up to 6% nitrogen and is fairly slow-acting. It also contains a little phosphorus.

Urea contains up to 42% nitrogen. It is slow-acting.

Nitrate of soda (sodium nitrate) contains about 16% nitrogen. It is extremely fast-acting, effective for only a short time.

Ammonium sulfate contains about 20% nitrogen. It is rather slow-acting and makes soil acid.

Calcium cyanamid contains 21% nitrogen, and is recommended for lawns because it kills weed seeds. (It is, in fact, used primarily for this purpose and is generally classified as a herbicide, not a fertilizer.)

For *phosphorus*, you can use either superphosphate, which contains up to 44% phosphorus and is fast-acting, or bone meal, which contains up to 30% phosphorus and is slow-acting.

For *potash* the choice is between muriate of potash and sulfate of potash, both of which contain about 50% potassium and are fast-acting. Wood ashes also contain potassium (about 5%) as well as lime, but they are rather messy.

The alternative to using the above limited-purpose fertilizers is to use a complete fertilizer containing all three major elements. Most home gardeners follow this practice because they know that, even though their soil may be seriously deficient in only one element, it probably will be improved by the addition of the other two elements.

But choosing the right complete fertilizer is a confusing task because there are so many types and formulations.

Manure is the original complete fertilizer and a good one when it is well rotted (fresh manure burns plants badly and often kills them). True, it does not contain as high a percentage of nitrogen, phosphorus and potassium as other fertilizers, but it makes splendid humus. The only manure that is widely available today is in dehydrated form. However, this has all the value of ordinary manure, as well as the same aroma. In addition, it is free of weed seeds and can be applied directly to plants without danger of burning.

Much more popular than manure and more widely available are the man-made fertilizers containing high percentages of the three essential elements. These are available in five forms:

(1) Powdered. The most common form of fertilizer today, this does an excellent job but has several disadvantages: it blows on a windy day; may stick to foliage; and if stored in a damp place, is likely to cake.

(2) Pelleted. These fertilizers are essentially the same as the powdered forms but do not have the powders' drawbacks. They are easy to spread in a spreader. Pelleted lawn fertilizers which contain insecticides and/or weed killers are also available.

(3) Concentrated tablets. These are used almost entirely for house plants. They can be dissolved in water and applied as a liquid; or they can be stuck into the soil and allowed to dissolve gradually as the plant is watered.

(4) Concentrated liquids. These are exceptionally good for and most often used on seedlings and potted plants; but they may be used for all fertilizing chores. Because they are diluted considerably when they are applied, they can be sprayed directly on foliage without doing any damage (some are designed for foliar feeding). And since they are liquid, they are immediately available to plants. They do not, however, have a long-lasting effect.

(5) Concentrated powders. Like the liquids, these are diluted in water and then applied to the plant roots or foliage.

All five kinds of complete fertilizer come in different formulations. Some, such as 5-10-5 and 10-6-4, are rather loosely referred to as all-purpose mixtures; others, such as 4-7-5 and 2-12-12, serve special purposes. The mixtures you use depend on the chemical content of your soil and the needs of the plants you are growing. For instance, if your soil is of average fertility, you might use 5-10-5 or 4-12-4 for annuals, perennials, bulbs, conifers and deciduous shrubs; 10-6-4 for deciduous trees and lawns; 8-8-8 for roses; 8-16-8 for vegetables; and 10-8-8 for broadleaf evergreens. (Would it do any harm to use just one kind of fertilizer on all kinds of plants? No harm. You just would not help the plants as much as you should.)

Another point you should consider in buying fertilizer is the relative price of the different types and mixtures. Here are several guidelines:

(1) Special-purpose fertilizers are generally more expensive than all-purpose types.

(2) Fertilizers containing a high percentage of nutrients generally cost less than those with a low percentage. Example: 1 lb. of 10-20-10 fertilizer equals 2 lb. of 5-10-5, yet a bag of the former may cost only one-third more than a comparable bag of the latter.

(3) As a rule, fertilizer cost goes up as the nitrogen content increases.

(4) Slow-acting fertilizers generally cost more than fast-acting types.

(5) Powdered fertilizers are cheaper than pelleted types or concentrates.

(6) As with every other kind of product, small packages of fertilizer are more expensive per pound than large packages.

(7) It is usually cheaper to buy insecticides and weed-killers separate from fertilizers than to buy combinations.

¶ *How much fertilizer to use.* It is impossible to be specific about this, and the reason, again, is that soils and plant needs differ. For instance, you need to apply more fertilizer to a porous soil than to a dense one because the nutrients are more quickly leached out. Similarly, you need to give rapid, rank-growing plants more fertilizer than slow-growing types.

In the chapters dealing with the growing of various types of plants, however, I have tried to make some general suggestions about fertilizing. If you have reason to believe the application rates given do not apply to you, contact your State Agricultural Extension Service.

¶ *Supplying other elements.* There is generally no reason for the home gardener to worry about the minor elements that plants need because they are available in sufficient supply in most soils in the country. But this is not always the case. In Florida, for instance, citrus fruits often do badly because they are not getting enough magnesium, manganese or copper. That is why it is a good idea to test your soil before you start a garden and whenever plants—for no explainable reason—begin to look as if they are growing badly.

One minor element, however, causes frequent problems: iron. Even though this may be present in soil in goodly amounts, it frequently is present in the form of insoluble iron compounds and as a result cannot be taken up by the plants growing in the soil.

When plants are suffering from an iron deficiency, they develop an ailment called iron chlorosis. This is characterized by the paling or yellowing of the leaves between the veins, which remain dark green. To cure chlorosis, apply iron chelates in powder form to the soil around the sick plants. Follow the manufacturer's directions on the package. (Iron chelates may also be applied as a foliar spray.)

¶ *Additional points about plant nutrition.* (1) Vitamin B$_1$ is sometimes recommended for plants and is still contained in a few concentrated fertilizers on the market. Its value, however, has never been proved.

(2) Some people are almost vehement in their belief that gardeners should use nothing but organic fertilizers. Certainly there is a great deal of good in such materials. But to say that they are much better than inorganic fertilizers or that there is anything seriously wrong with inorganic fertilizers is nonsense. The fact that almost all the fruits and vegetables that are raised commercially in the U.S. are fed with inorganic fertilizers is, I think, some proof that these have a great deal of value, too.

5

Where and How
to Acquire Plant Material

ALL PLANTS HAVE PREFERENCES as to soil, moisture, light, atmosphere and temperature. None grows just anywhere in the world. There are, in fact, relatively few that grow everywhere in the United States. This is important to remember when you are buying plants for your garden. If you don't want to waste money and effort, you must first determine which species grow well in your general area and under the conditions that prevail on your particular property.

The quickest way to do this is to ask some local gardening authority, such as a nurseryman, for a short list of good trees, shrubs, vines, flowers, etc., that thrive in your community. You can then look up each of these species in a garden encyclopedia to determine whether they would be at home on your lot. Do you have the sun or shade that the encyclopedia says the plants like? Do you have the right kind of soil? And so forth.

Once you have compiled a list of plants that are well adapted to your garden, your next step is to find them. Here are the various places where you might look:

¶ *Local nurseries.* These are certainly the best sources for trees, shrubs and vines; and they may be good sources for many other kinds of plants. The average nurseryman knows more about plants than other local dealers. He is the only source of really large specimens. He has grown much of his material himself, locally. He has some knowledge of landscaping. And upon request, he will plant the plants you buy from him and give you a year's guarantee on them (the premium you pay for this service amounts to about one-third to one-half the price of each plant).

The worst thing about nurseries is that most of them price their plants higher than other dealers. And more and more of them today are reducing the number of different species they carry (they are not unusual on this score, however).

¶ *Local garden supply stores.* These include the so-called retail garden centers that have been springing up in recent years, especially along main highways. Most of them are aggressive merchandisers and for this reason generally charge lower prices than nurseries and often put on special sales. As a rule, their stock is composed primarily of seeds, bulbs, annuals, perennials and other small plants. The shrubs and trees they carry are limited in size and variety. They grow almost nothing themselves. And their sales people do not know very much about gardening.

¶ *Door-to-door salesmen.* I doubt that itinerant plant salesmen are any more untrustworthy than other breeds of door-to-door salesmen. But their record is far from good. I advise buying only from those who carry their stock with them on a truck, so you can inspect it.

¶ *Mail order firms.* These include some of the biggest and best sources of plant material in the country. A few firms sell a wide range of plants. Others specialize in a few kinds of plants, notably roses. Some sell only seeds and bulbs. But in all cases, they usually carry many more varieties than local sources.

The prices charged by mail order companies range from low to high. Except for roses, the living plants they sell are well grown but necessarily pretty small (you may be able to purchase an 8-ft. tree, but it will be a pretty skinny specimen). Since the plants you buy may come from a distance through the mails, they may not be in first-class condition upon arrival; and they may very well arrive at a time when you are not prepared to plant them. Usually, however, the plants are guaranteed.

In addition to selecting plants that will thrive in your climate, you must also select them for their particular location in the garden. In this Phoenix garden, for example, the plants in the foreground do well in full sun; but those under the roof will live in Phoenix only because they are well shaded. (ARIZONA PHOTOGRAPHIC ASSOCIATES)

The most serious charge that can be made against the mail order companies is that *some of them* are high-pressure promoters. These can usually be recognized by the grossly exaggerated claims they make for poor species and by their use of beguiling made-up names to advertise familiar plants. They also sell runty, poorly grown specimens. They are, in short, not to be trusted.

¶ *Friends and neighbors.* Over the years I have given away a good many plants and I have been given a good many. I know of no nicer way to plant a garden.

¶ *How to tell a good buy.* SEEDS. Old seed packets should be avoided if you want good germination; but I must confess that I have not seen any old seed packets for sale in recent years. Far more common are packets containing only a tiny pinch of seeds; but although you may feel cheated, there is nothing wrong—these are new or rare varieties which happen to be in short supply.

BULBS. If you can see and feel what you're buying, you know what you are getting. Bulbs should be firm and of good size if they are to produce good-size flowers. If you buy by mail, you must simply trust to luck, because bulb dealers have no standard way of describing the sizes of bulbs they offer. However, as noted before, mail order firms specializing in bulbs generally carry more varieties than local sources.

ANNUALS, PERENNIALS, BIENNIALS, HOUSE PLANTS AND OTHER SMALL WOODY PLANTS. Ideally, these should come with a small ball of soil around the roots; but those shipped from a distance have bare roots wrapped in plastic film. If plants are sold in flats, they should be fairly evenly spaced in the flat so that you can remove each plant with a clump of soil. If the soil is hard and dry, chances are that the plants have not been well grown.

In all cases, the plants must have good root systems and well-branched tops (they should not be spindly). The color should be a fresh green. Avoid plants that look limp or wilted.

ROSES are sold in two ways. Mail order firms ship dormant, bare-root plants sealed in plastic film to hold in moisture. Local stores offer either bare-root plants or so-called pot plants (though they may actually be in tin cans or roofing paper containers). The one type of plant is as good as the other, although pot plants are slightly more expensive. The main difference is that bare-root plants must be planted within a few weeks after the frost is out of the ground whereas pot plants need not be set out until June.

Roses vary considerably in quality, but it is difficult to tell this without examining them closely. The roots and tops of the best roses are much larger and better developed than second-rate plants. To some extent, this is reflected in the prices of the two types; however, first-class plants of varieties that have been favorites for many years may cost little more than second-class plants of newer varieties.

TREES, SHRUBS AND VINES. Those that you buy from mail order houses are small, rather wispy, bare-root specimens shipped in plastic film or plastic-coated kraft paper. The plants are covered by a guarantee, however, and are a good buy if you are willing to wait several years for them to fill out.

Plants bought locally should be balled and burlapped—that is, well-developed roots should be enclosed in a sizable ball of solid, moist soil that is wrapped in burlap or in containers of steel or cardboard (these are usually called cans). The tops of the plants should, of course, be well filled out and shapely. If a plant was root-pruned regularly while growing in the nursery, its top should need little if any pruning when you buy it (but ask the dealer about this).

To guard against loss, all trees, shrubs and vines should be dormant when you plant them. This means that you should buy deciduous plants either before they leaf out in the spring or after they drop their leaves in the fall. Similarly, you should buy evergreens in the spring before they make new growth or in early fall after growth has stopped. However, if you are dealing with a good nurseryman, it is usually safe to buy and move plants when they are growing—*provided* they were balled and burlapped or canned when they were dormant. It is also fairly safe to buy plants that were balled and burlapped or canned after they started growing—*provided* they are thoroughly covered at the time of purchase with a plastic spray that retards transpiration and thus helps to prevent wilting.

¶ *Growing small plants from seeds.* If you are not in a hurry for large plants, you can save money and get a good deal of satisfaction out of raising your own. This is called propagating, and there are two basic ways of doing it. You can raise plants from seeds —this is sexual reproduction. Or you can raise plants in various ways (discussed further on) without seeds—by vegetative reproduction.

The plants most easily grown from seeds are the annual, biennial and perennial flowers and vegetables. It is best to start with fresh seeds produced by a commercial seed house. But you can collect seeds from your own garden simply by allowing the seed capsules and seeds inside to dry on the plants and then shaking the seeds into envelopes. Note, however, that the flowers you raise from seeds taken from hybrid varieties will probably revert, or fail to come true (meaning that, instead of resembling the parent plant, they resemble one or more of their earlier ancestors).

Most vegetable seeds are sown outdoors in the garden where the plants are to grow; and many annual flower seeds should be or may be handled in the same way. But numerous other annual flower seeds and a few vegetables, such as tomatoes and peppers, are started under glass (indoors or in a cold frame, hotbed or greenhouse) and later transplanted. Seeds of perennials and biennials are started outdoors and also transplanted.

Tables VII (page 187) and XXI (page 275) tell when and where to sow seeds. As a rule, seed packets also give this, plus additional, information. One point not to be overlooked—whether or not it is contained on the seed packet—is the fact that all seedlings are subject to a deadly fungus disease called damping-off The fungi attack the seedlings and cause the stem to rot at ground level. To help prevent this, put a pinch of Spergon or similar seed disinfectant in the packet with the seeds and shake until the seeds are coated.

When starting seeds outdoors where the plants are to grow, dig the soil deeply; mix in humus and manure or a complete fertilizer; pulverize thoroughly, and rake smooth. Water well if the soil is dry. If sowing seeds in rows, take the time to spread them out as much as possible so they don't come up in clumps. For an informal effect, flower seeds may be scattered casually over the soil surface.

Follow the seed-packet directions for the depth to plant the seeds. Vegetable seeds, as a rule, are planted about 1/2 in. deep; but the largest seeds (peas, corn, beans, squash, etc.) are planted between 1 and 1 1/2 in. deep. The largest flower seeds (nasturtiums, marigolds, zinnias, etc.) should be covered with soil equal to their own diameter; small seeds should merely be pressed into the soil. After the seeds are covered, tamp the soil lightly with a rake or board.

Keep the soil damp by gentle sprinkling while the seeds are germinating and the seedlings are starting to grow. Thin the seedlings as soon as they get their second set of leaves. Plants that grow close together in rows (peas, bush beans, carrots, etc.) can be thinned immediately to their ultimate spacing. Thin out other plants gradually so that you can be sure of keeping the best of the lot. Start fertilizing with fast-acting fertilizer at the time of thinning.

Seeds that are started outdoors in flats, cold frames or hotbeds are handled in the way just described. Thin the seedlings to stand 1 to 1 1/2 in. apart.

Seeds that are started indoors in flats, pots or other containers may be sown in soil, sand, vermiculite or shredded sphagnum peat. They may also be sown in the special mixtures of sphagnum peat, vermiculite and fertilizer that are now sold under the names of Jiffy-Mix, Redi-Earth, Cornell Mix, etc.

The advantage of soil as a growing medium is that it usually contains enough nourishment to satisfy the seedlings as they develop. The disadvantage is that you must treat the seeds to prevent damping-off (the alternative is to sterilize the soil in an oven). Sand, vermiculite and sphagnum have the reverse advantage and disadvantage. Since they are sterile, they do not contain damping-off fungi; so you don't have to treat the seeds. On the other hand, as soon as the seedlings start to grow, you must water them regularly with a balanced nutrient solution. Eventually you should transplant them into soil.

Mixtures of sphagnum, vermiculite and fertilizer combine the best features of soil and the sterile mediums. You don't need to treat the seed against damping-off, and you don't have to feed the seedlings as they grow. No wonder these mixtures are growing in popularity.

The flats or other containers in which seeds are sown should have bottom drainage holes which are covered with small stones or shards before soil is added. They should also be well scrubbed with soap and water before they are filled.

Spread your soil mixture (whatever it is) evenly in a flat and press it down. Sow the seeds on the surface; cover as necessary, and firm the soil. Then place the flat to half its depth in a tub of water until the soil surface is damp. (If the flat is too large to fit in a tub, water thoroughly with a watering can an hour or two before sowing the seeds. Do not water with a watering can after seed sowing because this is likely to dislodge the seeds.)

Cover the flat loosely with wax paper or transparent plastic to prevent loss of moisture, and set it in a light but not sunny spot. When the seeds germinate, remove the covering, set the flat in a sunny window and turn it every day to keep the seedlings from growing toward the sun. Start to thin the seedlings as soon as you are sure they will survive. If you are going to transplant them into soil in individual pots or a cold frame before you set them out in the garden, you can allow only about 1/2 in. between seedlings. But if you intend to move the little plants directly from the flat into the garden, space them at least 1 in. apart. (Plants going directly into the garden are considerably larger than those that are transplanted into pots or a cold frame and therefore need more space in the flat.)

¶ *Growing trees and shrubs from seeds.* This is a rather uncertain undertaking because there is no set procedure that works for all woody plants. The following procedure applies to a great many common species, however.

Commercial seed is available but difficult to find, as a rule. So collect your own when it ripens on the plants. Here is the schedule of ripening for a few plants:

Seeds ripen in	Species
Spring	River birch, cottonwood, elm (except Chinese), red and silver maple, poplar willow
Summer	Cherry, Douglas fir, elder, alpine larch, magnolia, mulberry, plum, shadbush, California syacmore
Fall	Ash, beech, birch (except river), box elder, buttonwood, catalpa, cherry, Chinese elm, elaeagnus, fir, hickory, juniper, larch, magnolia, maple (except red and silver), osage-orange, pecan, pine (most species), plum, spruce, walnut

Winter	Ash, yellow birch, box elder, buttonwood, catalpa, osage-orange, black spruce, Norway spruce, walnut
Any season	Pine (aleppe, bishop, jack, lodge-pole, Monterey, pond, sand)

Once you collect the seeds, there are two ways of handling them. Try both: it should improve your chances of securing healthy seedlings.

Sow some of the seeds outdoors in a bed that will not be disturbed. If seeds have a pulp covering (examples: dogwood and barberry), it is a good idea to remove it, but not necessary. The seed bed should be a well-dug mixture of loam, humus and sand. Sow small seeds about 1/4 to 1/2 in. deep; larger ones, such as acorns, 1 in. deep. Watering and fertilizing are not necessary: for the moment, nature takes care of such things. When winter comes, mulch the bed with leaves, hay, etc.; but remove this in the spring.

The second way of handling woody plant seeds is to separate them from their fruits, clean them thoroughly and dry them in the sun. Some seeds are then poured into a dry, sealed container and kept in the fresh-food compartment of the refrigerator until spring. Other seeds are stratified—mixed with about three times their volume of moist sand or peat, and stored in a container in the fresh-food section of the refrigerator. Still other seeds are simply placed in bags or envelopes and stored anywhere in the house. Familiar species that are stored in these ways are listed below. Some can be held in storage for a couple of years; but a shorter storage period is usually better.

Store in dry, sealed containers in refrigerator	Apple, arborvitae, ash, barberry, birch, blackberry, buttonwood, ceanothus, cypress, Douglas fir, elder, elaeagnus, elm, fir, hackberry, hemlock, honeylocust, juniper, larch, black locust, maple (but not silver), mountain ash, osage-orange, pine, poplar, raspberry, eastern redbud, redwood, sassafras, giant sequoia, spruce, sweet gum, symphoricarpus, tulip tree, witch hazel

| Stratify in sand or peat in refrigerator | Beech, chestnut, chinquapin, filbert, hickory, horse chestnut, silver maple, oak, tanoak, tupelo, walnut, yew |
| Store at room temperature | Acacia, caragana, Kentucky coffeetree, eucalyptus, fremontia, lilac, linden, pear |

Sow the stored seeds outdoors in the spring as soon as the soil is workable.

Whether seeds are sown after winter storage or immediately after collection, water the seedling plants regularly during their first spring and summer. Fertilize lightly once or twice after they are well established. And until the plants are about 4 in. tall, protect them against the broiling sun with a lath screen or the equivalent. It usually takes a number of years for a tree or shrub that is started from a seed to attain any size.

For precise directions for growing some 450 common species of trees and shrubs, see the *Woody-Plant Seed Manual* prepared by the U.S. Forest Service (Misc. Pub. No. 654; available from the Superintendent of Documents in Washington; $4).

¶ *Propagating plants by division.* To divide a plant means simply to separate it into two or more pieces, each with roots and tops. In the case of small plants, you can do the job either with your fingers or a sharp knife. On large plants use a sharp spade. Occasionally, when a plant has a thick mat of fibrous roots, you may have to thrust two spading forks back to back through the roots and forcibly pry them apart.

Perennial flowers and ferns are the plants most often propagated by division. Most perennials are divided right after they bloom; but autumn-bloomers should be divided in the spring. Ferns are divided in early spring or late fall.

Plants growing from tubers (example: dahlias) or rhizomes (example: iris) are also propagated by division. Use a knife and cut through the fleshy root so that each section contains one or more buds or eyes. Dust powdered sulfur on the cut surfaces to prevent rot.

¶ *Propagating plants by suckers.* The suckers referred to here are the new plants that shoot up from an old plant's roots. Lilacs and locusts are plants that sucker freely. To propagate such plants, dig up a sucker, cut it off with a good piece of the root, and plant it anywhere you like. Cut the top of the sucker back somewhat to compensate for the loss of root. (Note that some lilacs are grown on grafted rootstock. These should not be propagated by the suckers, because the suckers will not turn out like the top of the lilac plant.)

¶ *Propagating plants by offsets.* An offset is much like the suckers found on some plants (in fact, suckers may be called offsets). It is a small plant attached to the parent plant by a short root. The house-leek is one of several species making offsets. To raise new plants, simply cut off the offset and plant it.

A few plants that produce plantlets on the leaves (example: tolmiea) or on runners (strawberry geranium) are propagated like offsets.

¶ *Propagating plants by bulblets, bulbils and cormels.* These are the small bulb-like parts that form around old bulbs or corms or in the leaf axils of some bulbous plants. Detach them from the parent plant when it has died down. Plant them separately in well-dug soil at the time the parent bulbs or corms are planted. It takes several years for plants of flowering size to develop.

Propagating plants by layering. In layering, a section of a young, vigorous plant stem is pinned or weighted to the ground and covered with soil until it takes root. Then the new plant is cut off from its parent.

Layering is best done in the spring. The following ways of doing it are the most practical from the home gardener's standpoint:

For plants that put out runners from which plantlets grow (example: strawberries), just pin the runner and plantlet to the soil. Trailing, climbing and ivy-like plants such as English ivy, periwinkle and wisteria are handled similarly. The stems should be covered with soil at a leaf node.

Some arching plants—notably forsythia and blackberries—take root when the tips of the stems touch the ground. You can encourage the development of new plants by tying down the branch tips and covering with soil.

How to divide a rhizome or tuber. Each piece must contain one or more buds or leaves.

To layer a small, pliable plant such as Daphne cneorum *or a vine, simply pin a portion of the stem down to cultivated soil and cover with soil.*

Various large shrubs, such as rhododendrons and witch hazel, can also be encouraged to make new plants by layering. Make a diagonal cut partway through a bottom branch about 18 in. from the tip; stick a toothpick in the cut to hold it open; bend down the branch and cover the cut area with several inches of soil; then weight down with a rock. Root formation may take several years.

¶ *Propagating plants by air-layering.* Use one of the air-layering kits available at garden supply stores. Cut a notch in or take a sliver of bark and wood from a one-year-old plant stem. Dust a rooting hormone (which comes with the kit) on the wound. Then soak sphagnum moss in water, squeeze as dry as possible, and wrap it around the wound. Over this wrap plastic film and seal the joint and ends with cellulose electrical tape. As soon as roots are well formed (you can unwrap and inspect the wound occasionally), cut off the stem below the roots and plant it.

¶ *Propagating plants by leaf cuttings.* Method 1: Cover a water-filled jar with a piece of wax paper with a slit in the center. Remove a young leaf with a 2-in. stem from the parent plant and stick the stem through the wax paper into the water until roots form.

Method 2. Remove a young leaf with about 1 in. of stem from the parent plant. Stick the stem in moist sand or vermiculite. Don't let the rooting medium dry out. Cover the leaf loosely with plastic film to maintain humidity around it.

Method 3. Cut large leaves into sections and insert them in moist sand or vermiculite right end up.

¶ *Propagating plants by greenwood (softwood) stem cuttings.* Such cuttings are taken from young, vigorous stems usually late in the spring or in summer when the plants are making strong growth. Half-hard cuttings are similar except that the stems used are a little more mature.

Make the cutting by slicing diagonally through the stem about 1/2 in. below the sixth or seventh (from the tip) leaf. Remove all but

To layer large plants, such as magnolias or rhododendrons, make a slight cut in a low-hanging branch and insert a toothpick to keep it open. Then bend the branch to the ground, weight down with a rock and cover the cut portion with soil.

To make a greenwood cutting, remove all but a few top leaves on the selected stem; wound the base of the stem and dip it into a hormone powder; then insert the stem in a mixture of moist sand and peat in the bottom of a plastic freezer bag, and tie the mouth of the bag tightly. In the humid atmosphere of the bag (right), cutting should soon develop roots.

the four top leaves. You can now proceed in either of two ways:

A few plants, such as begonia, geranium, ivy and philodendron, take root if you simply stick the stems in a jar of water. To hasten rooting, place the cutting about 18 in. under a 60-watt light for 18 hours a day.

The other way to root cuttings is to mix two parts of finely shredded peat with one part of sand. Wet the mixture just enough to give off a couple of drops of water when tightly squeezed. Then pour a 4-in. layer in the bottom of a large plastic freezer bag. Now "wound" the base of the cutting stem (make a slight cut through the bark from the bottom of the stem up 1 1/2 in.) and dip it in a rooting hormone. Then insert the stem in a pencil-size hole made in the peat-sand mixture and firm well.

Sprinkle with water just to dampen the leaves, and close the bag tightly with a rubber band. Try not to let the plastic touch the cuttings. Keep the cuttings in a light but not sunny spot. Thanks to the plastic bag, it should not be necessary to water the rooting medium; but if this should show signs of drying out, moisten it at once. Watch out also for fungus on the cuttings or peat-sand. If it appears, open the tent and spray with Captan or other fungicide.

As soon as cuttings have developed roots about 1/2 in. long, transplant them into soil, gradually expose them to more sun, and fertilize lightly.

Cacti and succulents are propagated by plump cuttings of stems (or leaves) taken when the plants are in active growth. Dust the cut surface on the plant (but not on the cutting) with sulfur to prevent disease. Store the cutting for ten days in a dim, cool, airy place. Then set it, cut end down, on 3 in. of almost-dry sand. Do not bury the cutting more than a small fraction of an inch. If it is tall, tie it to a stake to hold it upright. Keep out of direct sun in a warm, ventilated place, and water very sparingly until roots form and growth begins. Then shift the plant to its permanent location.

¶ *Propagating plants by hardwood stem cuttings.* Hardwood cuttings are taken from pencil-size, six-month-old shoots of some deciduous shrubs and trees after the leaves drop in the fall. The cuttings should be about 6 to 10 in. long and have three or four leaf buds. The bottom cut, made at right angles to the stem, should be about 1/2 in. below a leaf joint. The top cut is made above a leaf joint and should be on an angle so that you can tell top from bottom. In the case of most plants, you can use one long shoot to make several cuttings; however, weigela and rose of sharon cuttings must include the terminal buds (which means that you can make only one cutting from a shoot).

Bundle 10 or 12 of the cuttings together and store in sand at a temperature of about 40°F. If you have a cool garage or basement, you can store the cuttings in a box. Otherwise, lay them in a trench with a sandy bottom and cover with 12 in. of sand topped with a thick mulch of leaves or hay. The sand should not be allowed to dry out.

In the spring, separate the cuttings and set them vertically, flat end down, in a trench in a partially shaded spot. (Don't let them dry while doing this; stand in a pail of water or starter solution.) Fill around them with a mixture of sand and peat, or soil, sand and peat. Only the top pair of leaf buds should be above the surface.

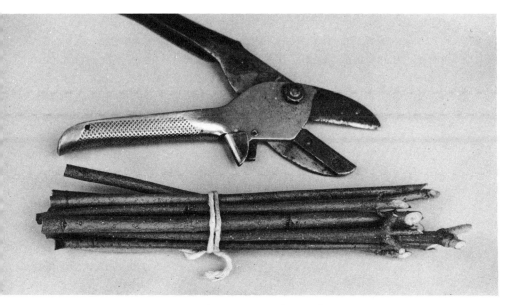

Hardwood stem cuttings are made from pencil-size shoots cut into 6 to 10 in. lengths. These are bundled together and stored in sand over the winter; then separated and planted upright in a shady place. Cut the cuttings flat at the lower end and on a slant at the top so that you will know which end should be up when you plant them.

Keep the rooting medium moist throughout the summer. The cuttings should be well rooted and ready to plant come autumn.

Hardwood cuttings of conifers are handled more like greenwood cuttings. The cuttings are taken in late fall from six-month-old shoots. They should be 6 to 8 in. long. Remove the bottom 3 to 4 in. of leaves; wound the base of the cuttings, and dip in a rooting hormone; then insert the cuttings in moist sand or sand and peat and place the rooting container over mild heat. It is not necessary to keep the tops of the cuttings covered with plastic film. Rooted plants should be ready in the spring.

¶ *Propagating plants by grafting.* The grafting process consists of uniting a shoot of the plant desired with the rooted stem of a second plant. The former is called the scion; the latter is the understock. The union is accomplished by making a cut in both plants and then placing the cambium layer (green inner bark) of one against the cambium layer of the other, and binding the two together until they are joined.

In grafting plants, it is essential to select a vigorous understock of a variety or species that is closely related to the scion. For instance, apple is grafted to apple, dogwood to dogwood, birch to birch. One of the rare exceptions to this same-to-same rule is the lilac, which is often grafted to a privet understock (both are members of the olive family).

The graft is made in late winter when the scion and understock are dormant. Both pieces should be about the diameter of a pencil. The stock should be well rooted and established in a small pot. The scion is cut from a terminal or lateral shoot and should have two or preferably three buds (some plants grow better from terminal shoots; others from laterals. A book on grafting will be of some help in learning which is better. But in many cases you'll have to learn from experience).

To make a side graft, scion is cut in a long wedge shape (left); *set into cleft in the side of the stock* (center), *and then tied in place* (right). *Top of stock is cut off* (exaggerated here) *several weeks after graft is initiated.*

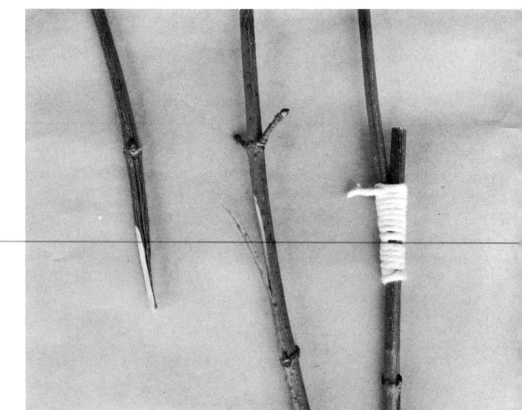

Several types of grafts are used in propagating work, but the side graft should serve your purposes. In this, long, flat slivers of bark and wood are cut from opposite sides of the bottom end of the scion. A cut of about the same length is made in one side of the understock an inch or two above the soil line; but the sliver is left attached at the bottom end. The scion is then inserted in the cut in the understock (between the sliver and the stem); the cambium layers are aligned; and the pieces are tied together with strong cotton twine dipped in copper naphthenate wood preservative. This keeps the twine from rotting before the graft is complete.

As soon as the graft is made, set the plant-to-be in a deep box and pour a 50-50 mixture of moist sand and peat around it and over it until the graft is completely covered. (Any number of pots can be set in the same box.) Cover lightly with a tent of plastic film to maintain humidity around the plant. Place in a warm, light (but not sunny) spot for six to eight weeks. Then remove the sand and peat, but continue to maintain the humidity around the plant for two or three days. About two weeks later, cut off the top growth of the understock just above the graft. Gradually move the grafted plant into more light and then, when the weather is mild, transfer it outdoors. Remove the twine from the graft occasionally so you can inspect the union, and remove it permanently as soon as the union looks and feels firm. As the new plant develops, be sure to remove from the understock any branches or shoots that may develop. This is, of course, particularly important if the stock and union were taken from different varieties or species of plants.

TABLE II
How to Propagate What

The list below includes many popular plants. The only important ones that are omitted are the annual flowers and vegetables, which are raised from seed; perennials, which are propagated by division or by seed; and a few miscellaneous plants, such as hyacinths, which are difficult for the amateur to propagate.

The methods of propagation given for the different plants are not complete. They are meant merely to get you started in the right direction. Since each variety of plant is a small law unto itself, you may find that the propagating method used for one is slightly different from that used for another. This is, perhaps, one of the annoying things about propagating, but it is also one of the things which makes propagating interesting.

In the case of several broad categories of plants—perennials, cacti, succulents, ferns and palms—I have not attempted to list individual genera or species since the propagating methods are essentially the same for all. To find how to propagate a particular kind of cactus, say Mammillaria or Zygocactus, look under the heading "Cactus." For a particular kind of palm, look under the heading "Palms." And so forth.

The key to the abbreviations in the list is as follows:

> GS—greenwood stem cutting
> HHS—half-hard stem cutting
> HS—hardwood stem cutting
> L-1, L-2, L-3—leaf cutting by Methods
>   1, 2, or 3 (see p. 52)
> div.—division
> graft—grafting

Abelia—GS
Abutilon—seed
Acalypha—HHS
Acanthus mollis—div.
Achimenes—div., GS
Actinidia—HHS, layer
Agapanthus—div.
Ailanthus—seed
Ajuga—div.
Akebia quinata—GS
Albizzia julibrissin—seed
Alder (*Alnus*)—seed
Allamanda—GS
Allium—bulbil
Alocasia—sucker (include part of rhizome)
Alpinia—div.
Alternanthera—GS
Amaryllis—bulblet
Amorpha—GS, layer
Ampelopsis—GS, layer
Andromeda (*Pieris japonica*)—layer, GS
Anemone—div.
Anthurium—sucker
Antigonon leptopus—GS, div.
Apple (*Malus*)—graft
Apricot (*Prunus*)—graft

Arborvitae (*Thuja*)—HS
Ardisia crispa—HHS
Aristolochia elegans—seed
Ash (*Fraxinus*)—seed
Aspidistra—div.
Aucuba japonica—GS
Avocado—seed, graft
Azalea—GS
Bamboo—div.
Barberry (*Berberis*)—seed, GS or HS
Bauhinia—seed
Beech (*Fagus*)—seed
Beauty bush (*Kolkwitzia*)—GS
Begonia—GS, L-2
Benzoin aestivale—layer
Bignonia capreolata—GS
Birch (*Betula*)—graft
Bird of Paradise (*Strelitzia reginae*)—div.
Bittersweet (*Celastrus*)—GS
Blackberry (*Rubus*)—sucker
Boston fern (*Nephrolepis exaltata bostoniensis*)—layer
Boston ivy (*Parthenocissus tricuspidata*)—layer, GS
Box (*Buxus*)—div., HS (but handle cuttings like greenwood cuttings)
Box elder (*Acer negundo*)—seed

Brunfelsia—GS
Buddleia—GS
Buttonwood (*Platanus occidentalis*)—
    seed
Cactus—GS, L-2
Caladium—div.
Calla lily (*Zantadeschia*)—div.
Calliandra—air layer
Callicarpa—GS
Callistemon—seed
Camellia japonica—GS
Camellia sasanqua—HS
Canna—div.
Cape honeysuckle (*Tecomaria
    capensis*)—layer
Caragana—seed
Carissa—layer
Carolina jasmine (*Gelsemium
    sempervirens*)—GS
Carpenteria californica—layer
Caryopteris incana—GS
Catalpa—seed
Ceanothus—layer, seed
Cedar (*Cedrus*)—graft, seed
Cherry (*Prunus*)—graft
Chestnut (*Castanea*)—seed
Chionanthus—layer
Chionodoxa—bulblet
Chives (*Allium*)—div.
Chokeberry (*Aronia*)—layer
Cissus—GS
Cistus—GS
Clematis—layer
Clerodendron—GS, seed
Clethra alnifolia—div.
Cleyera—GS
Clivia—div.
Cobaea scandens—seed
Coleus—GS
Corylopsis—layer
Costus—div., GS
Cotoneaster—layer, GS
Crabapple (*Malus*)—graft
Crape myrtle (*Lagerstroemia*)—GS
Crocus—bulblet
Crossandra infundibuliformis—GS
Croton (*Codiaeum*)—air layer

Cryptomeria—graft, seed
Cuphea—GS
Cypress (*Cupressus*)—graft, seed
Dahlia—div., seed
Daphne—layer, GS
Deutzia—GS, layer
Dogwood (*Cornus*)—seed
Douglas fir (*Pseudotsuga taxifolia*)—
    seed
Dove tree (*Davidia*)—GS
Doxantha unquis-cati—GS, seed
Dracaena—L-3 (lay flat on sand)
Dumb cane (*Dieffenbachia*)—GS
Dutchman's pipe (*Aristolochia
    durior*)—layer
Elaeagnus—GS
Elder (*Sambucus*)—GS, sucker
Elm (*Ulmus*)—seed
Enkianthus—GS
Eranthemum nervosum—GS
Escallonia—GS
Eucalyptus—seed
Eugenia—seed
Euonymus—GS, seed
False cypress (*Chamaecyparis*)—HS
Fatshedera—GS
Fatsia japonica—GS
Fern—div.
Ficus pumila—GS
Fiddleleaf fig (*Ficus lyrata*)—air layer
Fig (*Ficus*)—HS
Filbert (*Corylus*)—graft
Fir (*Abies*)—seed
Flowering quince (*Chaenomeles*)—
    GS
Forsythia—layer
Fothergilla—seed
Franklinia—HS
Fremontia—seed, GS
Fuchsia—GS
Galanthus—bulblet
Gardenia—GS
Genista—layer
Geranium (*Pelargonium*)—GS
Ginkgo—GS
Gladiolus—cormel
Gloriosa—div.

Gloxinia—L-1, div.
Goldenchain tree (*Laburnum*)—seed
Goldenrain tree (*Koelreuteria*)—seed
Grape (*Vitis*)—graft
Grapefruit (*Citrus*)—seed, graft
Hackberry (*Celtis*)—seed
Halesia—seed
Hazelnut (*Corylus*)—seed
Heath (*Erica*)—GS
Heather (*Calluna*)—GS
Heliconia—div.
Hemlock (*Tsuga*)—seed
Hibiscus rosa-sinensis—HHS
Hoffmannia—GS
Holly (*Ilex*)—GS or HS
Holodiscus discolor—layer
Honeylocust (*Gloiditsia*)—seed
Honeysuckle (*Lonicera*)—GS, layer
Hornbeam (*Carpinus*)—seed
Horse chestnut (*Aesculus*)—seed
Hoya carnosa—layer, GS
Hydrangea—layer, GS
Iris—div.
Ivy (*Hedera*)—layer, GS
Ixora—GS
Jacaranda—HHS
Jacobinea carnea—GS
Japanese hop (*Humulus japonicum*)—
    seed
Jasmine (*Jasminum*)—layer
Jatropha—seed
Juniper (*Juniperus*)—HS
Katsura tree (*Cercidiphyllum
    japonicum*)—GS
Kentucky coffeetree (*Gymnocladus
    dioica*)—seed
Kerria japonica—GS, div.
Kudzu (*Pueraria thunbergiana*)—div.
Ladyslipper (*Cypripedium*)—div.
Lantana—GS
Larch (*Larix*)—seed
Leatherleaf (*Chamaedaphne
    calyculata*)—layer
Lemon (*Citrus*)—seed, graft
Leptospermum—seed
Leucothoe—GS
Lilac (*Syringa*)—GS, sucker

Lily (*Lilium*)—scales of bulbs, bulbils
Lily-of-the-valley (*Convallaria*)—div.
Linden (*Tilia*)—seed
Lippia canescens—div.
Liriope—div.
Locust (*Robinia*)—sucker
London plane tree (*Platanus
    acerifolia*)—seed
Lycium—layer
Magnolia—GS
Mahonia aquifolium—layer, GS
Malvaviscus—GS
Maple (*Acer*)—seed
Mandevilla suaveolens—GS
Manettia—GS
Mockorange (*Philadelphus*)—layer,
    GS, seed
Monstera—GS, air layer
Moonseed (*Menispermum canadense*)
    —GS, seed
Mountain ash (*Sorbus*)—seed
Mountain laurel (*Kalmia*)—seed
Mulberry (*Morus*)—graft
Muscari—bulblet
Myrica—seed
Myrtle (*Myrtis communis*)—HHS
Nandina domestica—seed
Narcissus—bulblet
Necklace vine (*Muehlenbeckia
    complexa*)—GS
Neillia—GS
Nelumbo—div.
Oak (*Quercus*)—seed
Oleander (*Nerium oleander*)—layer,
    HHS
Ophiopogon japonicus—div.
Orange (*Citrus*)—seed, graft
Osage orange (*Maclura pomifera*)—
    seed
Oxydendrum arboreum—seed
Pachistima—layer
Pachysandra—GS, div.
Palm—seed
Pandorea—GS
Paper mulberry (*Broussonetia
    papyrifera*)—seed

Partridgeberry (*Mitchella repens*)—layer

Passion flower (*Passiflora*)—layer

Paulownia—seed

Peach (*Prunus*)—graft

Pear (*Pyrus*)—graft

Periploca—layer

Persimmon (*Diospyros*)—graft

Philodendron—GS

Photinia—GS, layer

Pineapple (*Ananas*)—cut through fruit just below leaves and place on soil

Pine (*Pinus*)—seed

Pittosporum tobira—HHS

Plum (*Prunus*)—graft

Plumbago—GS, seed

Plumeria—GS

Podocarpus—GS

Poinciana—seed

Poinsettia (*Euphorbia pulcherrima*)—GS

Polygonum aubertii—GS

Pomegranate (*Punica granatum*)—sucker

Poplar (*Populus*)—HS

Privet (*Ligustrum*)—GS

Pyracantha—layer, GS

Quince (*Cydonia*)—graft

Raphiolepis—HHS

Raspberry, black (*Rubus*)—layer

Raspberry, red (*Rubus*)—sucker

Redbud (*Cercis*)—seed

Rhododendron—layer, GS

Rhodotypos—GS

Rosemary (*Rosemarinus officinalis*)—GS

Rose of Sharon (*Hibiscus syriacus*)—seed, GS, graft

Rubber vine (*Cryptostegia grandiflora*)—GS

Sand myrtle (*Leiophyllum*)—layer

Santolina—GS

Sassafras—seed

Schefflera actinophylla—air layer

Schizostylis coccinea—div.

Scilla—bulblet

Seagrape (*Coccolobis uvifera*)—seed

Senecio—div., GS

Serissa foetida—HHS

Shadbush (*Amelanchier*)—seed

Shrimp plant (*Beloperone guttata*)—GS

Skimmia—GS

Smoke tree (*Cotinus*)—seed

Solandra—GS

Sophora—GS, layer

Sorbaria—sucker

Spathifyllum—div.

Spiraea—GS

Spruce (*Picea*)—GS or HS

Star jasmine (*Trachelospermum jasminoides*)—layer

Stephanandra—GS

Stephanotis floribunda—HHS

Stewartia—layer, seed

Strawberry (*Fragaria*)—layer

Streptocarpus—L-2, seed

Strobilanthes—GS

Styrax japonica—layer, seed

Succulents—GS, L-2

Sweet fern (*Comptonia aplenifolia*)—layer

Sweet gum (*Liquidambar*)—seed

Sweet olive (*Osmanthus fragrans*)—GS

Sweet shrub (*Calycanthus*)—layer, sucker

Symphoricarpus—seed

Tamarisk (*Tamarix*)—GS

Tanoak (*Lithocarpus densiflora*)—seed

Teuchrium chamaedrys—GS

Tibouchina—HHS

Trandescantia—GS

Trumpet creeper (*Campsis*)—layer

Tulip tree (*Lireodendron tulipifera*)—seed, graft

Tupelo (*Nyssa*)—seed

Umbrella pine (*Sciadopitys verticillata*)—seed

Viburnum—layer

Vinca—layer

Virginia creeper (*Parthenocissus quinquefolia*)—layer, GS

Vitex—GS

Walnut (*Juglans*)—graft

Water lily (*Nymphaea*)—div.

Weigela—GS

Willow (*Salix*)—GS

Wintersweet (*Chimonanthus praecox*)
—layer

Wisteria—GS

Witch hazel (*Hamamelis*)—GS

Yellow oleander (*Thevetia nereifolia*)
—HHS

Yellow root (*Zanthorhiza simplicis-
sima*)—div.

Yellowwood (*Cladrastis lutea*)—seed

Yew (*Taxus*)—HS

Yucca—div.

6

Managing Cold Frames
and Hotbeds

You can be a magnificent gardener without either a cold frame or a hotbed. But you will get more pleasure if you have them because they allow you to raise almost all your own plants from seed and to have them ready for planting out in the garden just as soon as winter has run its course.

COLD FRAMES

A cold frame is a bottomless box used primarily for propagating plants. It may also be used for protecting plants in winter. I have had one ever since I started gardening, and have a strange attachment that is hard to explain even to myself. Cold frames are very unglamorous gardening devices—not to be compared with greenhouses. But to me they mean that spring is coming—and what is nicer than that?

¶ *Location.* Since the main purpose of a cold frame is to permit you to get small plants off to an extra-early start in the spring by warming up the soil and protecting the plants against the cold, the frame should be located in a spot that gets all-day sun or that is shaded for no more than a couple of hours.

¶ *Construction.* A cold frame can be any size you like but 3 x 6 ft.

63

is nearly perfect. For one thing, this is the size of standard cold frame sash. More important, it is large enough to hold a good many plants, but not so wide that you cannot easily work in it from one side.

Two 3 x 6 ft. frames set side by side or one 6 x 6 ft. frame are also a good size because you can reach to the middle from either side. Anything wider than this, however, is unmanageable.

The frame should be placed on a north-south axis so that it receives the maximum sunlight. To help matters further, the glass top should be slanted toward the south. (Frames with tops that slant toward the north are built for propagating conifers and protecting certain plants in winter, but they are rare.)

The frame can be built of redwood, cypress or any wood treated with a wood preservative; brick, concrete block or other masonry materials. I personally like the permanence of a masonry frame, but a wood frame is much easier to build and can be readily moved if nearby trees grow up to shade it.

Whatever your construction materials, the front of the frame should be about 9 in. above ground level; the back about 15 in. above ground level. If the frame is of masonry, the walls should extend at least 12 in. below ground level—and preferably deeper in cold climates—to prevent frost-heaving and cracking of the walls. Wood frames need not extend more than 1 in. below ground level; but to guard against heaving, they should be nailed at the corners to 2 x 4's that are driven down a foot or so.

The best sash is one made to be used on a cold frame—if you can find it. Unlike an ordinary window sash, it has vertical mullions only, and the panes of glass between these overlap like shingles. Thus rain runs right off.

In economical moments, I have also used ordinary window sash and glass doors bought from junkyards. From the standpoint of letting in light, these are about as good as a proper cold frame sash (except that the end and bottom rails may be so wide that they cast shadows around the inside edges of the frame). But water does not run off completely, with the result that the putty and wood do not last very long. There is also a danger that, if the rain water impounded above the cross mullions has not evaporated by the time the sun comes out, it may act as a magnifying glass and cause burning of the plants underneath.

A third type of sash—which you can make yourself—is a lightweight wooden frame to which you tack polyethylene film or celloglas. (Wires should be stretched across the frame or up and down to support the film when snow accumulates on top.) This, too, is a perfectly adequate cover from the light-introducing standpoint; and because of its low poundage, it is easily handled. But for this same reason, it can easily blow away in a strong wind.

Hinging a film-covered sash to the frame may be advisable simply to keep it in place. But I am opposed to hinging a glass sash because of the difficulties of propping it safely open while you are working

A bank of permanent cold frames. The sash, made especially for cold frames, can be lifted completely off in warm weather. Small metal cleats hold them secure on windy days. Step-shaped piece of wood allows gardener to prop sash open at different heights.

in the frame, and also because you will probably want to remove it completely when summer comes.

The only other equipment needed with a cold frame is something to prop up the sash on warm days and something to cover it on cold days. For a prop, a sturdy stick is good enough; but a more convenient prop is a 12-in. length of 2 x 4 cut in the shape of a stairway so that you can open the sash in 3-in. increments. For a cold-weather covering, use a slab of exterior-grade plywood, planks, or a quilt made of burlap or canvas stuffed with straw, etc.

¶ *Soil.* To produce vigorous plants, the cold frame soil should be the best in your garden. Dig the bed at least a foot deep and put in 2 or 3 in. of coarse gravel or crushed stone if the drainage is poor. The soil that is placed on top of this should have plenty of humus and sand mixed in for consistency. Add bonemeal, Milorganite or dried manure for enrichment.

Fumigate the soil the first year to kill weed seeds and soil insects and fungi (see Chapter 10). It may not be necessary to repeat this treatment in subsequent years, but if you can, do so.

The soil should be leveled off in the cold frame at the same level as the ground outside, or somewhat lower; then it will not lose heat through the cold frame walls at night.

¶ *Using the cold frame.* In the spring the cold frame is used in two ways: (1) You can sow seeds directly in it in order to have well-grown plants ready for planting out as soon as the weather and soil conditions allow. Thus it gives you a headstart on the growing season. (2) You can move into it small plants that were started indoors and that need to be hardened off somewhat before they are planted outdoors. Thus, in effect, the cold frame is a way-station between the house and garden.

In summer, the cold frame without its sash serves as a convenient seed bed and propagating frame. In fall and winter, with its sash back on, it can be used to protect biennials against severe weather; it is a good place to start certain kinds of bulbs for indoor bloom; and it can be used for propagating conifers. These uses, however, are secondary to the two spring uses.

¶ *Managing the cold frame.* Theoretically, your cold frame is ready to go to work for you whenever the planting soil is free of frost in late winter or early spring. But don't push your luck. Seeds should not be sown in the frame until about two weeks after you start them indoors. And even at that, you should sow the seeds of the hardiest varieties first, then those of tender varieties.

Small plants that have been growing indoors should not be transferred into the cold frame until the danger of very cold nights is over. The shift should be made when you are sure of at least a couple of days of above-freezing weather. Do your transplanting in the morning and cover the frame with burlap, cheesecloth or laths so that the sun will not build up heat in the frame to the point where it causes wilting of the little plants.

Whether plants are moved into the cold frame or started there, they must be given protection against too much heat on sunny days and too little heat on cold nights. The first problem is solved by propping up the sash during the day to allow excess heat to escape. Exactly how much ventilation you provide and on what days you provide it are things you must learn from experience. I have no rules myself, and I am not always consistent in what I do. However, to give you some guidance:

In late March, if a sunny day with a maximum temperature of 40°F. is predicted, I do not open the cold frame at all. But in late April, under the same conditions, I open it an inch or two. Why the difference in tactics? Because in April the sun is higher and longer in the sky and the build-up of heat within the frame is likely to be much greater.

Similarly, as the season progresses, I open the sash further and further—even on days that may not have a very high temperature—because the sun is higher, the plants are larger and it is getting closer to the time when they must be planted outdoors.

Protecting plants against nighttime cold (and also daytime cold if you happen to have very low temperatures on a cloudy day) is accomplished by closing the frame when the sun goes down and covering it with some insulating material such as wood or straw if freezing temperatures are predicted. Ordinarily, the covering should be removed the next morning so the plants will get their full quota of sunlight; but if you have below-freezing temperatures on a cloudy day, leave the covering in place. A day of darkness will not hurt the plants.

Watering plants in a cold frame is done whenever the soil surface is almost dry. If you fertilize the seedlings, use a liquid concentrate: it is easier to handle than a powder.

HOTBEDS

A hotbed is a cold frame with heat. I have seen books which said that a hotbed is a hotbed only if the soil is heated from within, and that if a frame is heated in some other way it is not a hotbed but a heated frame. But this is a nicety.

¶ *Construction.* A hotbed is located and built exactly like a cold frame except that even though you make the frame of wood, the walls should be extended about 9 in. below ground level to hold in heat as well as the soil in which the heat source is laid. In days past, the heat was usually supplied by manure layered beneath the soil. Today the best heat source is electricity.

Soil-heating cables for use in hotbeds come with either a vinyl or lead jacket. For a 3 x 6 ft. hotbed you need a cable of about 200 watts. Such a cable is approximately 40 ft. long. Lay the cable on a

Installation of an electric heating cable in a hotbed. (GENERAL ELECTRIC CO.)

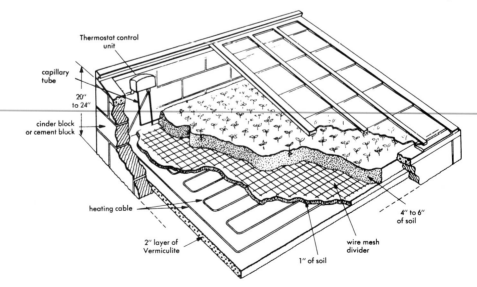

Hotbeds can also be heated with light bulbs installed on the bottom of wood strips running lengthwise along the frame. (WESTINGHOUSE ELECTRIC CORP.)

2-in. layer of vermiculite, which prevents heat loss downward, and arrange it in loops spaced 7 in. apart if you use a lead-sheathed cable, 5 1/2 in. apart if you use a vinyl-jacketed cable. Sections of the cable must not touch.

Cover with about 1 in. of soil, and on this lay a piece of 1/4- or 1/2-in. wire mesh to protect the cable from damage when you are digging. Cover the mesh with 4 to 6 in. of soil like that used in cold frames. The bulb of the thermostat capillary tube should be placed in the center area of the top soil. The thermostat itself is mounted above the soil inside the frame, and the power line runs from there to the house.

A second way to heat a hotbed is to mount eight 25-watt incandescent bulbs on a narrow, 6-ft. strip of wood which is set just under the center of and directly against each 3 x 6 ft. hotbed sash. The strip is removable. The bulbs are screwed into porcelain sockets spaced 8 1/2 in. apart; and these are wired to a thermostat (optional) and then to the house. To provide ample clearance between the bulbs and the plants, the soil surface should be 14 in. or more below the top front edge of the frame and 20 in. or more below the top back edge.

The advantage of this heating system is that the extra light from the bulbs helps to promote plant growth. The disadvantage is that the lighting strip interferes with work in the frame, and the bulbs are breakable and burn out.

¶ *Hotbed use.* An unheated hotbed can be used like a cold frame. With heat, it may be used in the spring to produce early crops of radishes and lettuce and to hasten development of dahlias, tuberous begonias and other tender bulbs so they will give a longer season of bloom. But its primary use is for producing large, vigorous plants from seed.

If you have a hotbed, in other words, you don't have to start tender plants such as tomatoes, zinnias and petunias indoors in order to have good-sized plants to set out when danger of frost is past (see Chapter 14). On the contrary, you can sow the seeds of tender plants directly in the hotbed in midwinter (even before you can sow the seeds of hardy annuals in a cold frame); and because of the warm soil and because the plants do not have to be transplanted until they are ready to go outside, the plants you wind up with will be far ahead of those started indoors or in a cold frame.

¶ *Managing a hotbed.* This is little different from managing a cold frame. You must cover the sash on cold nights. (You should also keep soil banked around the sides of the frame in midwinter.) On days when the heat in the hotbed is likely to build up too much, you must open the sash.

For tender plants, you need a soil heat of about 70°F. when the seed is sown and while the plants are still very small (hardier plants are happy with a temperature down to 50°F. or even less). This should gradually be reduced as the plants develop and the weather becomes warmer. And you should finally reach a point several weeks before the plants are set outside when the electricity is turned off entirely to allow the plants to harden off.

One problem to be alert for is an attack by fungi. These pests are encouraged by a combination of warmth and moisture. You can guard against them by watering just enough to keep the soil around the roots barely moist. Spray the plants with a fungicide if disease does set in.

7

Water Management[*]

WHEN NATURE FAILS TO SUPPLY the water gardens need, most gardeners eventually give up struggling to compensate for the shortage. And what we say in justification for our action is true: there really isn't any easy way to keep gardens going when rain doesn't fall and water tables drop and utilities fail to build adequate reservoirs and water distribution systems.

But there is much we can do to make the problem less severe by learning and applying the sciences of water management.

LEARN THE BASICS OF WATERING

¶ *Soil composition influences watering in a major way.* Irrigation experts have calculated that to wet 1 ft. of dry soil, you need to apply about 3/4 in. of water if the soil is sandy; 1 1/2 in. if the soil is a loam; and 2 1/2 in. if the soil is clay. These figures do not take into account the water that may be lost through runoff. Runoff increases in direct proportion to the density of the soil, the dryness of the surface, the hardness of the surface covering, the steepness of the slope and the rate at which the water is applied.

The speed with which soil dries out also depends on the composition of the soil as well as on the state of the weather and on how fast soil moisture is taken up by plant roots. Assuming all roots to be

---

* Reprinted from *The American Home,* © 1967, The Curtis Publishing Company.

alike, sandy soil loses moisture faster than loam, and loam loses it faster than clay. By adding humus, however, you can change the picture to some extent. In sand and loam soils, humus helps to retain moisture, but in clay it may have the opposite effect by making the soil lighter, more porous.

What do these assorted facts mean?

(1) To water plants efficiently, you must make yourself familiar with the composition of the soil in which they are growing. The easiest way to do this is to make a rough percolation test after a two- or three-week dry spell.

Place a flat-bottom glass jar on flat ground near a lawn sprinkler, turn the water on to average speed and let it run until the jar is filled to 1-in. depth. Note the time this takes. Turn off the sprinkler and wait about two hours for the water to settle into the ground. Then dig a hole next to the jar and measure the depth to which the water has penetrated. You now have a reasonably good idea of how deep 1 in. of water will wet your soil in a certain length of time. And if the soil throughout your garden is of fairly uniform composition and is not underlain in spots by ledge rock, you may safely assume that 2 in. of water will wet the soil twice as deep in twice the length of time, 3 in. will wet it three times as deep, and so on.

(2) Quite apart from whatever you do to contour the land and cover it with plants or mulches, you can minimize the loss of water through runoff by adjusting the rate of application to the composition of the soil. In other words, remember that you should not apply water as rapidly to dense soil as to porous soil. At the same time, do not overlook the fact that all soils—even the sandiest—have a saturation point, and when you exceed this by applying water too fast, some of the water is likely to run off. (Another danger in applying water too fast to porous soil is that the nutrients in the soil are lost through excessive leaching.)

(3) You can improve all soils by adding humus. The moisture-absorbing qualities of clay can also be improved by the addition of sand.

¶ *The condition of the soil indicates when you should apply water and how much.* Most of the roots on a plant lie within about

6 to 48 in. of the soil surface. If they do not have access to a fairly constant supply of moisture, the plant will not grow even though it may stay alive by sending a few roots down to tap deep water sources. It follows that in order to have a vigorous, attractive garden you must keep track of whether there is moisture in the soil around the main root mass. As soon as this supply shows signs of dwindling appreciably, you should get out the hose and apply enough water again to wet the soil down to the bottom of the main root mass and even further. Occasional deep waterings like this are infinitely better than frequent shallow waterings because they stimulate deep rooting and because the water is not lost so rapidly through evaporation. In areas where both the water and soil have a high pH, deep waterings also wash the alkali salts deep into the earth out of the reach of plant roots.

One way to check the condition of soil is to use a soil probe. Drive this into the ground, pull it out and examine the soil sample that comes up with it.

But the easiest and most accurate way of determining whether soil contains enough moisture is to install a tensiometer. This is an instrument that measures how much moisture is available to plants in any type of soil. A complete installation (which you can make at a cost of about $45) consists of two tensiometers—a short one that measures the moisture in the soil at one-quarter of the depth of the root mass, and a long one that measures the moisture at about three-quarters of the depth of the root mass. Thus, by reading the dials on the two instruments, you can tell instantly what the condition of the soil is throughout the most important part of the root zone; and when water is needed, you can tell when you have applied enough.

¶ *The space between plants also determines how much water should be applied.* Plants compete desperately for the water available in the soil. If they are close together, they need more water. If they are far apart, they need less.

You can make this fact work for you in two ways. If your water shortage is truly dire, you can reduce your use of water by increasing the space between plants. On the other hand, if you make a practice of watering plants well, you can set them much closer together than is usually recommended. The result will be a more beautiful and bountiful garden than you ever had before.

⁋ *Mulching retards the loss of water from soil through evaporation.* That's all the reason you should need for using mulches in flower beds, vegetable gardens, shrubbery borders, under trees, etc. (see Chapter 8).

⁋ *Plants need water over the entire root mass.* In addition to going deep, roots spread far out to the sides of plants. Tree roots, for example, commonly extend from the trunk to the ends of the overhanging branches and even beyond. It is obvious, therefore, that it does little good simply to empty your hose at the base of a plant. You should, instead, apply the water more or less evenly over the entire root system—or at least that part which lies under the canopy of the branches.

⁋ *Consider the timing of water application.* The time of day is not of crucial importance. But it is worth noting that you will probably

Tensiometers are installed in a covered box in the lawn, but can be left exposed in areas that are not mowed. One tensiometer measures soil moisture at one-quarter of the depth of the grass roots; the other measures it at three-quarters of the depth of the roots. (IRROMETER COMPANY)

lose less water through evaporation if you water in the late afternoon or evening when humidity tends to rise. On the other hand, you should not water so late in the day that the foliage does not have a chance to dry completely before nightfall. Plants that are wet at night are a target for fungus diseases.

The time of year that you apply water is more critical. For instance, you should supply a fairly even level of moisture when plants are flowering and fruiting. This helps to prevent various problems such as blossom drop, splitting of fruit, etc. You should also make sure that shrubs and trees are heavily watered in the fall so that they can go safely through the winter. And of course you must water plants thoroughly when you transplant them.

Soak the soil around the roots before digging up plants (you can water small plants just before lifting them; but water trees and shrubs a day or two ahead of time, otherwise the root balls are too heavy to handle). After the plants have been moved, build a collar of soil around them (above the outer ends of the roots) and fill the saucers with water. Continue watering small plants every other day until they no longer show signs of wilting. Water trees and shrubs twice a week for the next fortnight (or longer in dry weather).

DEVELOP NEW SOURCES OF WATER

It is almost impossible to predict how much water a garden will need during the growing season in addition to the precipitation that falls upon it. But suppose it totals 6 in. And suppose further that you own a quarter-acre lot of which 9000 sq. ft. are under cultivation. You would need to apply 4500 cu. ft. of water—almost 34,000 gal.!

Where is this to come from if your water utility bans watering of gardens? There are a number of water sources you can tap if you value the appearance of your property.

¶ *Dig a well.* The cost of drilling a well and putting in a pump and pressure tank varies. Competent authorities figure a range of between $200 and $2000. This may or may not seem high, but it is not excessive when you compare it with the cost of rebuilding lawns and replacing dead trees and shrubs.

Newly planted white pine is ringed by an earthen dike. The saucer thus created is filled with water twice a week for at least a fortnight after planting. A mulch of hay (or other material) keeps the soil from drying out quickly and also helps to eliminate weeds that would compete with the tree for water and nutrients.

Recent custom indicates that when a well is put in, it should be a deep one with (the FHA says) a sustained yield of 5 gal. a minute or more. Such a well supplies enough water in one hour for you to apply a 1-in. depth over an area of about 500 sq. ft. In other words, it is more than adequate for watering a 9000-sq. ft. yard and garden.

Deep wells, however, are expensive simply because they are deep and require large pumps. You may be able to save considerable money if you put in an "intermediate-storage" water system. This consists of a fairly shallow well yielding only about 3 gal. a minute. The water is pumped by a small pump over a period of 12 hours a day into a nonpressurized storage tank holding at least 2000 gal. From there it is pumped by a second small pump into a pressure tank that distributes it to the outlets.

¶ *Make fuller use of an existing well.* If you already have a well, perhaps you can get more water out of it than you are presently doing. S. G. Tomczuk, a Connecticut well driller, says that almost none of the wells that have been drilled in recent years are being used to capacity. He cites as an example one that is 195 ft. deep, has a yield of 9 gal. a minute.

Figuring that the homeowner, like most homeowners, did not want to spend more than was absolutely necessary for a water system, Tomczuk installed a 1/2-h.p. submersible pump in the well at a depth of 140 ft. "That is about as deep as a pump that size can be used," he explained to me. "It supplies more water than the family needs, but not enough for extensive irrigations. However, the well itself has plenty of water for watering the grounds from morning to night. To make use of it, all I'd have to do is put a larger pump closer to the bottom of the well."

¶ *Install a rain trap.* Farmers have for years built ponds to catch and store the rain water that runs off from the land. But the efficiency of these is impaired by the fact that a varying percentage of the rain never reaches them, and the part that does may be quickly lost through evaporation and percolation.

The new rain trap completely solves these problems, though it is not attractive enough to be used on anything but a large property, where it can be tucked behind trees. The trap is made of butyl rubber in two large sections which are laid out on a hillside. The upper section is a more or less saucer-shaped sheet that catches the falling rain and funnels it through a connecting tube to a huge storage bag that vaguely resembles a hot-water bottle and is placed in a slight depression in the ground. The water is drawn from the bag as needed by a portable pump or by gravity.

A 200 sq. ft. catchment collects roughly 1500 gal. per inch of rainfall. This fills a bag measuring 6 x 20 ft.

¶ *Why waste the water that falls on your roof?* True, your roof yields only a limited amount of water and only after a rain; but in times of shortage, even a little water can do more good in the garden than in the storm drains.

The most efficient way to use roof water is to direct it from the downspouts into a cistern from which it can be withdrawn as needed. A 10 x 10 x 10 ft. concrete cistern holds about 7500 gal.; an 8 x 13 1/2 ft. round steel tank holds about 5000 gal.

The alternative—if your soil is reasonably porous—is to distribute the rain water, as it falls, to any part of the garden through 3-in. perforated composition pipes connected to the downspouts and laid about 6 to 12 in. beneath the soil surface. To estimate how much pipe you need, measure the square-foot area of your topmost ceilings and multiply the total by the fraction of a foot of rain that falls in an average storm. This gives you the approximate number of cubic feet of water that will flow into your irrigation network. Now multiply by 20 (a 20-ft. length of 3-in. pipe holds about 1 cu. ft. of water). The answer is the number of feet of pipe you should presumably install; however, since rain does not fall all at once, you should be able to reduce the total length by about 75% without much danger of having the pipe become water logged in a hard storm.

IMPROVE DISTRIBUTION OF WATER
TO AND THROUGH THE GARDEN

The system of pipes, faucets, hoses and sprinklers used to distribute water from the meter or pressure tank to the garden is more important than the average person thinks when he dashes into a discount house to buy a cheap plastic hose and nozzle.

I once heard a man complaining that he could keep two sprinklers going at once in his yard; but because the water pipe coming into his house from the street was too small, the sprinklers turned into tricklers when the automatic washer was turned on.

Contrast the experience of a Delaware agricultural engineer. At his home he has a 1 1/4-in. pipe into the house from the pump; 1-in. pipes to the hose bibbs; and a 2-in. pipe direct from the pump to serve his vegetable garden, where he has five sprinklers, each capable of delivering 6 1/2 gal. a minute over a 1600 sq. ft. area. "What with having only three-quarters of an inch rain from late June to mid-September," he told me one time, "the payoff last year was tremendous. If you're going to keep a garden going, of course, you need water—and I am fortunate in having a good supply. But you must also design the distribution system correctly—the pipe sizes, fitting sizes, interconnections and so on."

¶ *Start in the house.* "Loss of pressure because of friction in the pipes and fittings in the house is the number one problem in the many home water systems I see," a USDA water expert told me a couple of years ago. 'The hose bibbs should be on a separate line from the other outlets in the house. They should be served by 1-in. pipe—not 1/2. And the bibbs themselves should be of a design that permits the passage of the maximum amount of water.

"Your objective should be at least 30 lb. of pressure at your sprinklers. You must insist that your plumbing contractor designs for this. The common plumbing practice of undersizing piping and then putting in a booster pump to provide pressure for lawn-sprinkling is shortsighted and creates a possible back-siphonage hazard besides."

¶ *Use 3/4-in. hoses in 50-ft. lengths.* By using longer lengths of hose, you reduce the number of connections between lengths and thus reduce friction loss. And by using a 3/4-in. hose, you are able to deliver more water at higher pressure than with smaller hoses.

¶ *You can save money with portable sprinklers, but—* Undoubtedly the cheapest way to water large areas is with hoses and portable sprinklers. And now that there are timers that turn the water off for you at the hose bibb, one of the problems of using this kind of equipment has been eliminated. But other problems—not necessarily serious, but annoying—remain:

(1) You must still move the hose and sprinkler around the garden. This is even necessary with "walking" sprinklers.

(2) Most sprinklers are useful only in open areas, such as lawns. Trees and shrubs break up the spray pattern, and so do flowers and vegetables if sprinklers are cramped in amongst them. (A partial exception is the impulse sprinkler which spits jets of water over considerable distances. These can be set high enough above the ground to water over the tops of shrubs.)

(3) Most sprinklers have a limited number of sprinkling patterns (rectangular, square or round). The gardener usually needs more variety. This means that you must make a small investment in several sprinklers and spend time thereafter detaching one and attaching another.

(4) When you buy a sprinkler, there is no way of telling—or of finding out, because the dealer does not know—at what speeds it delivers water under different pressures. Consequently, you may wind up with one that lays down more water than your soil can absorb or—less serious—that is slower than you could conveniently use.

¶ *Put water exactly where you want it with snake-like porous hoses or pipe.* These are excellent for watering long, narrow strips, including vegetable rows, steep slopes where runoff is a problem and under shrubs and trees. They operate about as well at low pressure as high. And they waste relatively little water.

The oldest watering device of this type is the canvas soaker that oozes water so slowly that most of it seeps directly into the soil; there is no appreciable waste. The soaker's great advantage is that you can place water with pinpoint accuracy. On the other hand, it wets only a very narrow strip. (Water does not move sideways in soil to any extent unless the soil is clay or is underlain by an impermeable barrier.)

A more widely useful hose is a flat, three-tube plastic hose with tiny perforations in one side. When the perforations are facing down and the water pressure is low, the hose acts much like a soaker. But when the perforations are up and the pressure is high, it soaks the soil in a strip 4 to 6 ft. wide. In this position it can be used to water flower beds, shrubbery borders and narrow grass strips; and if looped in a loose spiral around trees, it soaks a large part of the root system.

Plastic pipe fitted at about 15-in. intervals with tiny brass spray nozzles is sometimes permanently installed in shrubbery borders. Although laid on top of the soil, it is more or less hidden by the plant stems, yet there is not too much low-to-the-ground growth to interfere with the water sprays. You can easily make this type of sprinkler either out of flexible or rigid plastic type.

¶ *Water trees in various ways.* In addition to watering trees with a perforated hose, you can take care of smaller trees on flat land by encircling them with a collar of soil and then flooding the saucer with a hose. But trees on slopes and large trees with deep root zones are another matter. For these, a water-management engineer of my acquaintance recommends drilling holes with a soil auger at intervals around the periphery of the main root mass and scattered through it. The holes should be about 24 in. deep. Insert in them sections of 3-in. perforated drain pipe. You can pour water into the pipes with a hose; or if you want to save work, you can interconnect the pipes with a small plastic tube by which you can fill all the pipes at once. An added advantage of this watering system is that you can feed the trees through the pipes in the spring.

(The water lance—a long, pipe-like hose nozzle that is driven into the ground—is often recommended for watering trees, but it is only as effective as the way you use it. If you stick it into the root mass in just one spot, it does comparatively little good except for trees with very compact root systems. The reason, as noted before, is that water does not travel very far laterally through soil; it prefers to go up or down. To water large trees with a water lance, you must insert it into the root system at a number of points.)

¶ *Put in an underground sprinkling system.* Here is the ideal way to water your lawn and—if you select the right kinds of sprinklers—almost every other part of the garden. There is no moving of hoses; no changing of sprinklers. All systems on the market can be

Sprinkler heads of various designs are used: some rotate, some are stationary, some swing back and forth in a high arc. All must be carefully placed so that the entire lawn area is well watered. (TORO MANUFACTURING COMPANY)

automatically operated by a timing device that turns the sprinklers on at a preselected hour, lets them run for a preselected period, and then turns them off.

The cost is extremely variable. One automatic system described by the maker as a "complete, standard system" that will water approximately 7000 sq. ft. carries a retail price of $190. The home-owner can install it himself. The same firm, in one of its booklets, shows plans for an automatic system covering a yard of almost 27,000 sq. ft. The cost of materials for this is pegged at $1,240; installation by a professional is estimated at an additional $750.

The only sensible way to buy an underground sprinkling system is to ask several contractors handling different systems to look over your water system and garden and to give you recommendations and a price. You should worry less about the types of sprinklers, pipes and controls the contractors propose to use than about the thoroughness with which they study your problem and the sug-gestions and claims they make for solving it. Putting in a sprinkling system is not child's play. According to a California Agricultural Extension Service bulletin, it involves eight steps: (1) measuring the water pressure at your faucets, (2) making a sketch of the area to be watered, (3) selecting and locating the controls, (4) selecting and spacing the sprinklers, (5) determining the number of sprinklers on one line, (6) selecting the pipe size on the basis of friction losses in pipes and fittings, (7) installing the system, and (8) adjusting the sprinklers as needed.

¶ *You can go a step further.* Although underground sprinkling systems that are operated by automatic timers take the work out of watering, irrigation authorities maintain that they are far from per-fect. The problem is that you predetermine the times at which the system should operate and for how long; but unless you have excep-tional knowledge of your soil and plants and what the weather is going to be like, your predetermination is nothing but guesswork.

What to do? The answer is to control the sprinkling system with tensiometers which constantly measure the amount of moisture in the soil and automatically signal the sprinklers to turn on and off as necessary.

Tensiometers can be used to control any kind or make of sprinkling system. The number used depends on the soil, size of property and water requirements in different parts of the property. For a medium-size garden, one "station" with two tensiometers installed at different soil levels is usually adequate. The installation, complete with controls, adds about $125 to the cost of the sprinkling system proper. For four tensiometer stations on a five-acre piece of property, the extra cost would be about $500.

8

Using Mulches

MULCHING IS ONE OF THE MOST highly touted gardening practices—
and with good reason. Yet it is one which most gardeners ignore—
and for no reason. Here is an unparalleled labor saver. An unparal-
led water saver. And a major contributor to plant health and vigor.

Specifically, mulches

—save water and watering by retarding the loss of moisture from
the soil through evaporation.

—smother weeds.

—keep the soil friable and minimize the need for cultivating it.

—help to inhibit the spread of some diseases.

In addition, organic mulches add humus to the soil; keep the soil
from freezing and thawing repeatedly in the fall and early spring
and thus help to prevent plants from being heaved out of the
ground; keep the soil cooler than it would otherwise be in summer
and thus protect plant roots from cooking; and retard runoff of
rain water and minimize erosion.

Inorganic mulches can increase soil warmth in early spring and
thus speed plant development at this time.

From this listing, it is apparent that no one mulch does everything. You may therefore find it advisable to use different mulches
in different places around your garden. There are many to choose
from.

ORGANIC MULCHES

Almost anything that will form a thick, porous, clean blanket can be used as a mulch. But the following materials are recommended:

¶ *Leaves.* These are the most readily available and inexpensive mulch, but not always the best because when leaves are new they give off considerable heat during decomposition and they sometimes form a dense, soggy mat that prevents rain from seeping through into the soil. But oak leaves and pine needles are among the most useful of mulches because they are acid—just right for mulching rhododendrons, azaleas and other acid-soil plants.

¶ *Hay and straw.* Both are pretty untidy, but otherwise good. Hay is available almost everywhere at low cost or for nothing. It decomposes rapidly. Salt hay, on the other hand, decomposes very slowly and can be used for several seasons. It is also weed-free. Grass clippings, however, are not a desirable mulch unless mixed with some coarse material which prevents their matting.

¶ *Peat.* This is very widely used, probably because it is so widely available at reasonably low cost. It looks neat, mixes readily with the soil when you finally want to dig it in, and is very effective in smothering weeds and holding in moisture. But it also tends to form an impervious layer that keeps water from seeping into the soil. This is particularly true of baled sphagnum peat. However, this defect can be corrected by mixing the peat with sawdust and by keeping the mulch moist.

¶ *Bagasse.* A by-product of sugar mills, this is used mainly in the South. It is a pleasant light-brown color; decomposes slowly. Damp mulch may sometimes be covered in the morning with a mold, but it disappears when the sun comes up.

¶ *Buckwheat hulls* make an excellent, neat mulch. Moisture passes through them easily from above but not from below. But they are lightweight and easily scattered by wind and traffic.

¶ *Cocoa beans and pecan shells.* These do everything that buckwheat hulls do; in addition, they are fairly heavy and hard to scatter.

Vegetable garden mulched with hay to keep down weeds and hold in moisture. As the hay gradually decomposes it will add valuable humus to the soil.

Chopped fir bark is one of the most attractive and durable mulching materials. To keep down weeds, spread it 2 to 3 in. deep. A thinner layer can be used, however, if you first treat the soil with a selective pre-emergence herbicide.

They also decompose slowly, which may or may not be an advantage, depending on whether you want humus or a long-lasting mulch. To prevent cocoa bean hulls from forming a slime mold (which is the result of an oily residue in the hulls), you should mix two parts hulls with one part sawdust. You should also avoid using cocoa bean hulls around rhododendrons and azaleas since they have a high potash content which damages these plants.

¶ *Ground tree bark.* One of the newest commercial mulches and extremely good, bark decomposes more slowly than buckwheat, faster than the shells. It is neat, attractive and heavy enough to stay in place. Tree branches and twigs that are put through a chipper can be used as a mulch for shrubs and trees, but it is usually coarse and very untidy.

¶ *Ground corncobs and peanut shells.* These are not very attractive either, but good otherwise. Availability is somewhat limited, however.

¶ *Sawdust* is one of the best mulches. It may be used alone or mixed with something else, such as peat. However, before applying it, you should scatter a nitrogenous fertilizer on the soil.

¶ *Conifer boughs.* These are used for winter mulching for flower and shrub borders and small plants. They give protection against heavy snow loads and the sun. Thus they help to keep the soil from freezing and thawing alternately.

INORGANIC MULCHES

¶ *Dust.* A dust mulch is nothing more than garden soil cultivated to a depth of 1 to 3 in. It was once considered a splendid mulch, but studies have shown it really has little value. In addition, it is a lot of work to maintain.

¶ *Stones and pebbles* make handsome mulches and good ones, especially for rock garden and alpine plants. Water goes through swiftly and consequently does not stand around the crowns of these low, ground-hugging plants.

Small lettuce plants are here mulched on one side with black polyethylene film and on the other with hay. Both are excellent mulches, but not at all attractive.

¶ *Fiberglass insulation* is highly recommended as a winter mulch around delphinium, columbine, chrysanthemums and foxgloves, which are often rotted by excessive moisture around their crowns. Unlike organic mulches, fiberglass does not soak up and hold water.

¶ *Polyethylene film.* Black film is used extensively in vegetable gardens. It is either laid between rows in long stripes, or laid over the entire garden and punctured so that plants can come up through. If you lay it loosely, so that water can penetrate, it classifies as an excellent mulch. It is absolute death to weeds.

Experiments at the Connecticut Agricultural Experiment Station, however, show that white translucent film is better (except in killing weeds) because the sun shines through and raises the soil temperature in early spring. This extra warmth acts as a shot in the arm to perennial plants as well as to small woody plants, and causes much faster growth and earlier flowering and fruiting.

One problem with the films is that they are hard to anchor in place in windy locations. Another is their appearance. But a municipal park commissioner of my acquaintance solves this by covering the film with a thin layer of pebbles or chopped bark. He calls it the "best" mulch he has ever used.

¶ *How to mulch.* Mulches can be used profitably around all plants except grass and dense ground covers. Organic mulches should be used in layers 2 to 5 in. thick. Avoid covering the crowns of small plants.

If possible, it's advisable to keep plants mulched the year round. If you cannot do this, you should apply organic mulches after the soil has had a chance to warm up in the spring and growth has started. Applied too early, they check growth to some extent because they keep soil cool. In the fall, organic mulches should be applied after the soil has frozen; then they will do a better job of preventing thawing and freezing of the soil.

Ground covers are a kind of mulch, too, because they smother weeds and shield the soil from the sun and thus retard evaporation of moisture. On the other hand, since their roots draw a great deal of moisture out of the soil, they should be used for mulching purposes only in warm climates with ample rainfall.

9

Pruning and Training

PRUNING IS DONE TO IMPROVE the appearance or health of a plant, to keep it from growing too large or to develop a specific shape. Training, which usually involves pruning, is done either to control the direction of growth of a plant or to produce a specific shape.

¶ *Pruning tools*. Pruning shears of two types are used. The snap-cut has a single, straight cutting blade that comes down on a wide cutting surface suggestive of an anvil. The other type has two cutting blades, usually curved, which overlap in scissors fashion. Both types should be capable of cutting through 3/4-in. branches.

Lopping shears are also of two types and similar to pruning shears except that they have handles 24 to 30 in. long. Thus you can get more leverage with them; and because they have larger blades, you can cut through branches up to about 1 3/4 in. thick.

Pruning saws have larger teeth than carpenters' saws and chew through green wood at a much faster clip. Some pruning saws cut on the forward stroke; those with curved blades on the pull stroke. The latter are especially good for cutting branches above shoulder height.

Tree pruners consist of a long pole (up to about 12 ft.) topped with a cutter that is operated by pulling a rope. They are used to remove branches up to about 1 in. thick that are high above you.

Hedge shears or clippers are simply large scissors used for shaping hedges and other plants. The electric type, with vibrating teeth, is much faster than the old hand type.

Whatever the pruning tool, it should be of top quality. Keep it sharp. And when you use it on a sick plant, always disinfect it with alcohol before using it on another plant.

¶ *Maleic hydrazide*—sometimes referred to as MH—must be mentioned here because it is a new kind of "tool" that you will hear more about in the future. It is a chemical growth inhibitor which is sprayed on non-flowering plants to keep them from growing. Highway departments use it to keep grass along road edges short. And more and more people are using it to keep hedges of privet, pyracantha and the like trimmed to size.

¶ *How to make pruning cuts.* Whether you use shears or a saw depends on the size of the piece to be pruned and how you can get at it. In using a saw, try to make your cut so that the branch will not bind the saw, but will fall away from it. If binding does occur, push the branch away from the saw or remove the saw and make a new start. A heavy branch can twist a saw permanently out of shape.

Care must also be taken, when sawing a branch that lies close to another one, not to cut or damage the bark at the back of the saw.

When using pruning shears, cut cleanly through the branch. Don't twist the shears back and forth. If you have trouble forcing the cutting blade through a thick branch, bend the end of the branch slightly in the direction of the cut. This opens up the cut so the blade can slice on through.

If you are cutting a fairly heavy branch off at the trunk with your shears, cut from the side (with the blades parallel to the trunk) to prevent possible splitting of the wood and tearing of the bark.

¶ *Where to cut.* When cutting back a branch of any type or size, always make the cut just above a bud. The cut should be at about a 60° angle to the branch. Select the bud for the direction in which it will send out new growth; that is, remember that if the bud is on the bottom of the branch, new growth will be more or less downward, but if the bud is on the top of the branch, new growth will be upward.

The one time when you need not worry about cutting above a bud is when you are shearing a hedge or other plant. Shearing is a nonselective form of pruning which is designed to encourage dense but nondirectional growth.

When a large limb is to be removed from a tree or shrub, take pains to prevent the limb from falling prematurely and ripping off the bark below it. To do this, make a first cut a third of the way through the bottom of the limb, about 10 in. from the trunk. Then, working from the top, cut all the way through the limb about 12 in. from the trunk. Then cut off the remaining stub close to the trunk (but don't cut into the trunk) and trim the bark neatly around the wound.

When a tree is topped or when one trunk of a multistemmed tree is removed, there is also danger that the trunk will not fall in the right direction and that in falling it will tear the bark and splinter the wood below it. This is prevented by making a V-shaped cut facing the direction in which you want the tree to fall. The cut should go halfway through the trunk. Then saw or chop through the trunk from the opposite side a few inches above the apex of the V.

How to cut back a branch. First is just right. Second is too slanting. Third is too far from the side branch. Fourth is too close to the side branch.

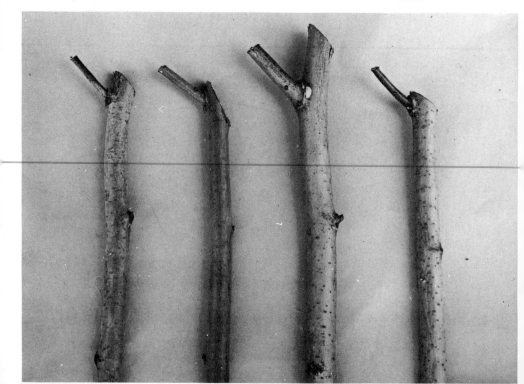

¶ *Painting wounds.* All wounds 1 in. or more across should be covered with a protective coating to prevent diseases from entering and rot from setting in. Allow the wood to dry if the sap is flowing from the wound. Then cover thoroughly with a prepared tree paint containing an antiseptic. If this is not avaliable, use shellac or oil-based house paint.

¶ *When to prune.* This is discussed at greater length in the chapters about growing different types of plants. In general, however, you should prune (by disbudding) small non-woody plants to improve their shape and/or flowering when they are making their early growth. If it seems advisable, you can prune further at intervals throughout the growing season.

When woody plants are pruned to improve shape or bloom, the job is usually done in the winter or very early spring. However, plants that bloom in early spring are usually pruned after flowering. And plants that bloom off and on throughout the year (as some tropical species do) are usually pruned after one of their flowering spurts.

Cut out dead, diseased and broken wood whenever you see it. Suckers and water sprouts should also be removed regularly.

Cut back tops of bare-root specimens of woody plants about one-third at the time they are transplanted. Balled-and-burlapped specimens and potted specimens should also be pruned at this time, if the grower has not already attended to the job (but usually he has).

¶ *How to get specific results.* There is some variation in the way different plants respond to pruning, but generally you can achieve the following results by doing the following things:

To make a multistemmed plant, such as forsythia or buddleia, more shapely and attractive, cut the old and weak stems to the ground. Do not cut back the top, because that forces new growth at the top and encourages legginess.

To make a plant bushier, remove the terminal bud and perhaps several other of the top growing points.

To keep a plant small, start pruning it when it is young, and prune it annually.

To change the direction in which a branch is growing, cut it back to where a branch, twig or side bud is headed in the desired direction. This hanging branch will now grow up.

To avoid tearing the bark on a tree trunk when you remove a large limb, make first cut part way through the bottom of the branch (small saw); then cut all the way through the branch from the top a little further out from the trunk (large saw); then remove the stub close to the trunk (in crotch).

To make a tree fall where you want it to, cut a V-shaped wedge on the side in the direction of the fall; then cut through from the opposite side slightly above the apex of the V.

To reduce the size of a plant that is too large, cut it back gradually over a period of several years. Don't cut it back all at once, if possible.

To make a branch grow larger, make a horizontal cut the width of the branch through the bark and cambium layer of the trunk just above the branch. This forces more of the sap into the branch.

To make a limb that is growing too fast grow more slowly, make a horizonal cut the width of the branch through the bark and cambium layer of the trunk just below the branch. This reduces the sap flow into the branch.

To make a branch grow in a different direction, cut back to a bud that is aimed in the desired direction.

To make a plant taller and slimmer, remove some of the branches at the bottom.

To make a tree develop a thicker trunk, allow the lower branches on the trunk to develop for several years before pruning them.

¶ *How often to prune.* One of the mistakes many gardeners make is to misjudge the speed with which woody plants grow. As a result, they sit back and do nothing until suddenly they discover the plants have outgrown their locations. But by then, unfortunately, it is usually too late to correct matters. This is because it is extremely difficult to make a material reduction in the size of most kinds of plants without ruining the appearance of the plants and possibly killing them.

Pruning of shrubs, trees and vines that grow near buildings or in other locations where their size is of critical importance should be a continuing process, and usually should involve the removal of no more wood than was produced in the previous growing season. In temperate and cold climates, once-a-year pruning (usually in the spring) is sufficient. In warm climates, you may have to prune two or three times a year after periodic spurts of growth.

¶ *Root pruning.* When you move a woody plant from one location to another, you greatly improve its chances of surviving the move if you take with it as much of the root system as possible. Root pruning helps you to do this by forcing the plant to develop many small feeding roots close to the main stem.

Pruning of roots should be done when a plant is dormant and/or in late summer a year before the plant is to be moved. Scratch a circle in the soil around the base of the plant. A circle 18 in. in diameter is about right for a smallish plant under 5 ft.; larger circles are needed for taller and better developed plants. Then go around the circle with a sharp spade, driving it straight down to a depth of 12 in. This cuts the large roots within the circle and forces them to put out small roots. (An application of fertilizer in early spring contributes to the process.) When you move the plant, the diameter of the ball of earth you take should equal or slightly exceed the size of the root-cutting circle.

If a very large plant is to be moved, the roots should be pruned over a two-year period in order to reduce the shock to the plant. Divide the circle around the plant into four equal segments. Cut the roots in two opposite segments one year; then cut those in the two remaining segments the next year.

One other purpose of root pruning is to retard the growth of certain plants (see below).

¶ *Training plants* may or may not involve pruning. But it always involves a certain amount of pulling, pushing, steering, bending and, in the end, anchoring. It is a simple job done primarily for esthetic reasons.

Training is limited to plants with stems or branches that are long and pliable enough to be guided in an unnatural direction or pattern. Young stems or branches are by far the easiest to work with, especially if they are already headed in the desired direction. Old stems, like old people, are highly resistant to change.

You can train plants in any direction except downward. Even trailing plants eventually revolt at being forced to grow in this unnatural way.

To train a plant across the ground, simply place the stems where you want them. If they refuse to stay put, anchor them with U-shaped bends of wire.

The way to train plants upwards depends on what you want to accomplish, the growth habit of the plant and the support you provide for it. Some plants train themselves if given the right kind of support. For example, pole beans and morning glory are twining plants that grow by wrapping themselves around stakes, strings, whatever is available. Grapes and gourds put out tendrils that wrap around wires and strings and anything else they can get around.

Euonymus radicans puts out little aerial rootlets that cling to rough surfaces; and Boston ivy has sucking disks that cling even to smooth surfaces. Plants like these two do not need any special support as long as they are close to a wall, post, etc.

Plants that have no natural means of supporting themselves, such as climbing roses, honeysuckle, wisteria, pyracantha, clematis and yews, require more attention. You can, however, train them on any support you like—a wall, trellis, post, wire mesh, etc. All you have to do is tie the stems and branches in place with soft string or Twist'ems (patented lengths of soft wire covered with ribbon-like green paper strips). On a wood wall, use aluminum nails as anchors. On masonry, use nails that are specially made for driving into concrete mortar (lead anchors are stronger but tedious to install).

No matter what the plant, there are several basic points you should bear in mind when training it:

(1) The size and construction of the support should be related to the size and weight of the plant. You should not, for instance, try to train bittersweet on a small doorway trellis, because it is much too large and heavy. Conversely, it would be silly to train asparagus fern on an arbor because it is not large enough to warrant such under-pinnings.

(2) Heavily foliaged plants can precipitate the disintegration of the support they are trained on because they hold in moisture. Wood and stucco are most vulnerable, but concrete mortar that was not well mixed may also be damaged. To prevent damage to a solid wall, try to provide an air space between the wall and the plant, or keep the plant thinned out. To protect a wood trellis or arbor, build it out of redwood, cypress or other wood that has been thoroughly impreg-nated with a preservative.

(3) When grown on wire mesh or a trellis with closely spaced members, twining and tendril-climbing plants often become so intertwined with the support that it takes forever to remove them when they die or grow too large. You can save yourself work by growing such plants on single stakes or wires or on open trellises.

¶ *Espaliers.* An espalier is a plant that is trained to a definite shape against a flat surface. Vines are very easy to espalier. Other plants that make fine espaliers are listed in Table III (page 102).

This pergola was built of large timbers in keeping with the design of the house and also because it is used to support several wisteria vines. Large vines like wisteria need sturdy underpinnings.

Developing an espalier requires no skill but lots of patience. Start with a small plant, preferably one that is somewhat flat and well branched, and plant it in well-dug, well-drained soil of good consistency and fertility. If the plant is to be trained on a wall, set it 8 to 12 in. in front of the wall; if it is grown against a trellis or fence, it may be set directly underneath.

Espaliers take many shapes. Once you decide on a shape, stick to it. Select the stems and branches that you want to train and tie them in place at 8 to 12 in. intervals. Cut out the others. Rub off buds that face toward the wall, because if allowed to develop, they will push the plant away from the wall. For best appearance, keep the shoots that develop between the main arms of the espalier thinned out (a good espalier has an open, airy structure; it should not form a mat). All major pruning should be done in the winter, when the plant is dormant; but to keep a vigorous espalier in shape, continuous light pruning up to the end of August is often necessary. Once the plant reaches the desired size, prune the roots every fall by cutting around them with a spade. This will slow top growth.

TABLE III
Selected Trees and Shrubs for Espaliering

Abelia	Goldenchain tree (*Laburnum*
Abutilon	*anagyroides*)
Apple (*Malus*)	Hawthorn (*Crataegus phaenopyrum*)
Barberry (*Berberis nevini* and	Holly (*Ilex*)
B. julianae)	Hydrangea quercifolia
Buddleia	Jasmine (*Jasminum*)
Camellia	Kerria japonica
Carissa grandiflora	Magnolia
Ceanothus	Mock orange (*Philadelphus*)
Citrus	Pear (*Pyrus*)
Cotoneaster	Plum (*Prunus*)
Crabapple (*Malus*)	Podocarpus
Dogwood (*Cornus florida*)	Pyracantha
Eucalyptus	Rhododendron
Feijoa sellowiana	Sorbaria
Flowering quince (*Chaenomeles-*	Tamarisk (*Tamarix*)
lagenaria)	Viburnum
Forsythia	Yew (*Taxus*)
Genista	Weigela

Closely grouped espaliered flowering crabs grace this Atlanta terrace. Espaliers are easier to make than most people think but require frequent pruning and training. Foliage generally should not be allowed to obliterate the outline of the branches. (UNITED PRESS INTERNATIONAL)

Large Magnolia grandiflora *treated as an espalier. It adds far more interest to* house wall *than a vine would.*

Three espaliers developed by Henry Leuthardt of Long Island, leading grower of dwarf fruit trees and espaliers. This page, a six-armed Palmette Verrier apple just before blooming.

A Belgian fence of apples and pears.

A fan-shaped yew.

10

Pest Control

AT THE OUTSET LET ME SAY that I disagree with the people who would ban the use of modern pesticides. These have caused problems, certainly. But they have done tremendous good—and that, too, is a certainty. In fact, the good far outweighs the bad; and for that reason, I have no hesitancy about recommending that you use them
—but with care, because they can be dangerous;
—and with discrimination.
The last thought stems from a suspicion that a great many gardeners get overly excited about bugs. A case in point was my wife's discovery last year that Japanese beetles were eating our roses. She asked me to bring out the sprayer at once. But before I did so, I took another look at the roses. The damage seemed minor—hardly worth the trouble of hauling out the sprayer, diluting insecticide in water, spraying the roses, getting rid of the excess spray solution and finally washing out the tank. But what really made me rule out the sprayer was the fact that the beetle population did not warrant it. It would be a lot easier and quicker to pick them off by hand, I thought; and that is exactly what I did—in a few minutes' time.
No, I do not think that all pest problems can be solved without modern pesticides. But let this be your first rule in waging war on pests: Before using a pesticide, ask yourself whether it is really and truly needed.

Rule number 2 is to grow your plants as well as you know how. Plant them in good soil; give them plenty of water and plant food; and so on. It's true that strength and vigor do not give protection against all pests. But they do against a great many.

Your third pest fighting rule should be: Forestall trouble by intelligent gardening practices. This covers a lot of ground. For instance:

(1) If you make a practice of sanitizing the garden—keeping garden trash picked up, destroying sick plants, cutting out and burning dead wood, tearing up wild plants, and so forth—you will make it difficult for many pests to become established and to spread.

(2) By rotating the locations of specific kinds of vegetables and flowers, you may be able to prevent some pests from multiplying to a point where you are called upon to fight an entire army rather than a platoon.

(3) By planting various kinds of plants instead of concentrating on a few of the same kind, you in effect disperse targets to such an extent that the enemy is not much interested in any of them.

(4) If you turn over your garden soil in the fall, many of the larvae in it will be killed by exposure to cold.

(5) By erecting physical barriers against certain pests, you deprive them of an opportunity to cause damage. For instance, if you enclose crocus bulbs in a wire-mesh cage, rodents are unable to eat them. Similarly, if you wrap wire mesh around young fruit trees, rabbits cannot eat the bark; if you put a stiff paper collar around cabbage seedlings, cutworms are repelled; and so on.

Pest-fighting rule number 4 is to plant varieties of plants that are resistant to common difficult diseases and insects. More and more of these are being developed.

A final rule is to take a stop-who-goes there? attitude toward all plants coming into and going out of your garden. In other words, when you buy plants from someone out of town, be sure that the firm you are buying from is a reputable outfit that sells only healthy, first-class material and that has a stake in upholding government laws about interstate shipments of plant material. When you buy plants in person from a local source, inspect them carefully to make sure there is nothing wrong with them.

In short, don't bring into your garden plants that are already infested with insects or disease. And as a kindness to others, don't give away plants that may be similarly infested; and don't make interstate shipments of plants without asking your Agricultural Extension Service about the rules.

CONTROL METHODS

¶ *Spraying* is the usual method of applying pesticides, and by and large the best. Some spray materials are in liquid from; some in tablets or powder. When you buy the last, ask for the "wettable" type which readily dissolves in water. Ordinary powders do not dissolve well, although this does not mean they cannot be used in sprays.

Several types of sprayers are used indoors. The aerosols are the most effective, but not all spray materials are packaged in this way. So you also need a good Flit gun or Larvacide-bottle sprayer.

The compressed-air sprayer is best for outdoor spraying of flowers, vegetables, shrubs and other small plants because it delivers a fine, penetrating mist, is quite maneuverable and is not wasteful of spray material. Pick the design that appeals to you most, but don't make the mistake of getting one that is too large to lug around. The 2-gal. size is about right. Even when it is only three-quarters full (you should not fill a compressed-air sprayer any more), it will give coverage of your entire garden and then some.

The type of sprayer that attaches to the end of a hose is best for spraying the lawn or large trees because it makes up to about 15 gal. of spray and can be adjusted to deliver the spray material to a distant target. Some hose sprayers, however, are very dangerous because they may allow the spray material to flow backward into the house piping system and to contaminate the drinking water. When buying a hose sprayer, therefore, make sure that it is equipped with an anti-back-siphonage device.

Spraying should be done right after a rain because diseases most often infect plants when they are wet. When using a contact poison, you must hit the insects that are giving trouble. When using a residual spray, you apply a thin mist to all plant surfaces; and you must make repeat applications after each heavy rain and as new leaves, stems and flowers develop.

Two problems in using a compressed-air sprayer arise from the fact that the nozzle clogs easily and that you cannot see into the tank very well. But these are solved by marking the inside of a bucket to show 1/2-, 1-, 1 1/2- and 2-gal. levels. When making up a spray, pour water into the bucket to the proper level. Add the spray chemical, making sure that you measure it carefully (*do not use more than the directions call for*). Mix thoroughly. Then pour the mixture through a small kitchen strainer or cheesecloth into the sprayer. This keeps out hair and other particles that might clog the nozzle.

Always make a fresh spray mixture for each application.

If the spray chemical is a powder, shake the sprayer frequently while using it in the garden. I like to keep a fine wire tied to the sprayer so that, if the nozzle does clog and I cannot free it simply by removing the cap and letting go a squirt, I can poke out the offending matter.

No matter what kind of sprayer you use, rinse it thoroughly after each use. Then force clean water through it to clean the nozzle. Hang upside down to drain and dry.

If a sprayer is used for applying a herbicide, it must be washed and washed and washed again with hot, soapy water and household ammonia before it is used for any other purpose. (The bucket in which the herbicide is mixed must also be washed thoroughly). Even then, there is a chance that a trace of the herbicide will be left and will damage or kill a plant the next time the sprayer is used. For this reason, it is advisable to invest in two sprayers—one for herbicides and the other for insecticides and fungicides.

¶ *Dusting* is the next commonest way of applying insecticides and fungicides. It is a shade faster than spraying, and does not require so much preparation or after-the-fact cleanup. But the dust detracts from the appearance of plants (especially if applied when the foliage is wet), and it does not help your shoes, clothing or lungs.

Dusting should be done after a rain when the foliage has dried. A light, even coat is just as effective as a heavy one. As with sprays, repeat applications are necessary after each heavy rain and as plants make new growth.

The effectiveness of dusting depends to great extent on the nature and quality of the equipment you use. Shaker cans are worthless except for applying herbicides to single scattered weeds. So are many of the cheap dust guns. Preferred equipment includes a cylindrical gun with a long discharge tube and nozzle and a smoothly operating plunger; a crank-type, or rotary, duster which can discharge a continuous stream of dust in large volume; or a motor-driven duster-fogger, which is capable of applying more dust over a larger area and with fewer refills.

Whichever type of duster you use, keep it in good condition. Lubricate moving parts regularly with powdered graphite. Empty a metal duster after every use. And always store the duster in a dry place.

¶ *Spreading.* This is the easiest way of applying dry chemicals to lawn areas. Use the same wheeled spreader that you use for applying fertilizer and grass seed. Be sure to adjust the spreader opening so that it lays down the chemical at the rate called for by the manufacturer. Avoid overlapping strips. Wash the spreader thoroughly after use.

¶ *Fumigating.* Fumigants should be used by the home gardener only to kill weeds, soil insects and fungi. (Commercial greenhouse operators fumigate greenhouses, but this is not a safe practice for the uninitiated.) Depending on the chemical, fumigants are applied in three ways. Some are mixed with the surface soil and then sealed in with water (that is, the treated area is wet with about 1 in. of water). Some are applied in the same way but are effective only when the wet, treated soil is covered for several days with a thick polyethylene film. Some are injected through a sharp-pointed tube that is thrust into the soil at 12 to 24 in. intervals. (Another way to kill pests is to bake small quantities of soil in an oven.)

Great care must be taken in using fumigants, because some are very poisonous to humans and animals. And you must as a rule wait several weeks before planting in the treated soil.

¶ *Trapping.* Insect traps of several kinds are used. The commonest has an ultraviolet or blue light to lure bugs of all kinds into a container from which they cannot escape. But the trouble with traps is that they attract to your garden insects which might otherwise be happy to stay next door. They also attract friendly insects as well as pests.

¶ *Baiting.* This is a good way to kill crawling insects such as ants, grasshoppers and cutworms. For ants, the familiar ant trap is effective bait. For other insects, such as cutworms, a standard bait consists of 2 tbs. of chlordane, 5 lb. of bran, 1 cup of syrup and about 2 3/4 qt. of water mixed to a crumbly mass. Spread this through the garden or around special plants.

¶ *Disinfecting* of seeds before planting is done to prevent the fungus disease called damping-off. The disinfectant is a powder. Drop a pinch into the seed envelope and shake well.

¶ *Soaking in poison* is the method used to kill borers and rot organisms in iris rhizomes. The poison is bichloride of mercury (deadly to humans and animals) or Semesan.

¶ *Systemic poisoning.* This is a method of killing insects that live in plant tissues or that suck the juices out of plants. The poison, which is applied to the soil, is absorbed by the plants through their roots. Sodium selenate is one of the best known systemic poisons but not widely used except by African violet fanciers.

¶ *Biological control* is a fancy phrase meaning insect control without chemicals. A number of methods are used. Most are of interest only to farmers. But one controls Japanese beetles in the garden. This involves use of a readily obtainable powder that is made of spores of a bacteria which causes a deadly disease in the beetles. The powder is spotted around the lawn in little piles.

USE OF PESTICIDES

Pesticides on the market contain either a single chemical or a combination of chemicals. You should use a single-chemical formula when you are trying to control a single, specific pest. Use a combination pesticide when you are trying to protect plants that are prone to attack by several pests (for example, roses, which are attacked by various insects as well as by black spot, mildew and other diseases).

You can mix your own combination pesticides; but before you do so, make certain that the chemicals you mix together are compatible. Ask your garden supply dealer about this. If you combine incompatible chemicals, they may damage the plants to which they are applied.

Plant damage may also be caused by adding a spreader-sticker to a spray. Spreader-stickers are materials designed to make a spray spread more evenly and stick to foliage longer. They should be used only if the pesticide manufacturer calls for them.

This brings up the most important thing to remember when using a pesticide: *Read the directions for its use carefully, and do what you are told.* Many pesticides are extremely poisonous when swallowed and/or spilled on the skin.

INSECTICIDES

The following are excellent single-chemical pesticides which are only moderately toxic (unless otherwise noted). Contact insecticides must be sprayed directly on insects; others kill insects when they bite into plants.

¶ *Aramite.* A mite killer used on ornamental plants. It is not compatible with some chemicals but is used in many combination pesticides.

¶ *Carbon bisulfide.* Fumigant primarily used to kill borers in trees. Poisonous and inflammable.

¶ *Chlordane.* Contact insecticide controlling a variety of insects including ants, bagworms, beetle grubs, chinch bugs, grasshoppers. Also used as a pre-emergence killer of crabgrass but not so effective as other such killers. Not compatible with some chemicals.

¶ *Chloropicrin.* Fumigant for control of soil insects, nematodes, some fungi and weeds. Extremely poisonous and unsafe to use close to living plants. It is applied to the soil by injection.

¶ *DDT.* The best known modern insecticide, it can be used to control many kinds of insect pests. But it also kills many beneficial insects which prey on spider mites, so it must not be used indiscriminately. It is incompatible with some pesticides. Household DDT must not be used on plants. Do not use on fruits and vegetables within four weeks of harvest.

¶ *Dimethoate*. Best control for scale insects on camellias. Also controls aphids, leafhoppers and mites.

¶ *Dimite*. Mite killer especially good in controlling cyclamen mites.

¶ *Dormant oil*. This is also known as miscible oil and superior oil. It is applied in early spring, after danger of freezing is past, to dormant deciduous plants for the control of scale insects, aphids and mite eggs.

¶ *Kelthane*. Kills spider and cyclamen mites. Should not be used on fruits and vegetables within two weeks of harvest.

¶ *Lime-sulfur*. A dormant spray for control of scale insects. It is also a fungicide. Not compatible with many chemicals.

¶ *Lindane*. Controls many insects but not mites and leafhoppers. Do not use on fruits within two months of harvest; do not use on vegetables that are beginning to form.

¶ *Malathion*. A leading insecticide that is effective against many insects, especially aphids and scale insects. But it also kills bees and other beneficial insects. Do not use on fruits and vegetables within a week of harvest.

¶ *Methoxychlor*. A good substitute for DDT, but it also kills beneficial insects. It is safer than DDT for use on fruits and vegetables, can be applied up to two weeks before harvest.

¶ *Nicotine*. Familiar contact insecticide for control of aphids and other sucking insects. It does not harm most beneficial insects. Can be applied to fruits and vegetables up to two days before harvest.

¶ *Para-dichlorobenzene*. Soil fumigant controls peach tree borers.

¶ *Pyrethrum*. Contact insecticide controls many insects but kills fish and therefore should not be used near pools. Can be applied to fruits and vegetables right up to harvest—one of its outstanding advantages.

¶ *Rotenone.* Another excellent contact insecticide that can be applied right up to harvest. Has some lasting, or residual, effect. Kills fish.

¶ *Sevin.* Kills many insects; especially good for Japanese beetles. Also kills beneficial insects and so indirectly helps to add to the spider mite population. Do not use on fruits and vegetables within four days of harvest.

¶ *VC-13.* Soil fumigant kills nematodes and other insects. Can be used around living plants.

HOW TO CONTROL COMMON INSECT PESTS

Insect pests are listed here alphabetically under the names by which they are most commonly known. The paragraphs describe: (1) Where the insects are generally found. (2) What they look like. (3) Some of the plants they attack. (4) The damage caused and/or the appearance of the plants attacked. (5) The best method of control. (6) Comments, if any.

¶ *Ants.* 1. Everywhere. 2. Familiar insects. 3. Lawns, flower beds. 4. Ant hills. 5. Sprinkle chlordane on and around the hills. Ant traps are also somewhat effective. 6. Ants are often seen scrambling over peony buds and flowers but do no damage. But they cause other garden problems by hoarding aphids.

¶ *Aphids.* 1. Everywhere. 2. Tiny, soft-bodied insects in many colors that suck the juices in plants. Some look wooly; some, mealy. They secrete a sticky "honeydew" which attracts ants. They are also vectors of a number of serious diseases. 3. Almost all kinds of plants, but notably apples, beans, cabbages, corn, grapes, melons, peas, pines, potatoes, roses, spruces. 4. Plants look stunted. Buds and flowers are distorted. Leaves are deformed. Some plants are covered with a sooty mold. Spruce trees have galls (more or less spherical growths) at the base of young shoots. 5. Spray or dust with lindane, malathion, nicotine, pyrethrum or rotenone. Remove galls from spruce trees as soon as possible before they open, and burn. Dust tulip bulbs with lindane. 6. The lady beetle (ladybug) is one of the natural enemies of aphids and kills many of them; so avoid using multipurpose sprays that may kill it. Since ants hoard aphids, you should make a practice of destroying them if present in large numbers.

¶ *Apple curculios.* 1. East of the Mississippi. 2. 1/4-in. brown beetles with humps on back and long, slender snouts. 3. Apples, cherries, pears, hawthorns, quinces, shadbush. 4. Fruits have grouped puncture holes, become misshapen and drop. 5. Control is same as for plum curculios (see page 126).

¶ *Apple maggots.* 1. East of the Rockies but not in the Deep South. 2. White maggots (wormlike legless larvae) produced by a small black fly with black bars on the wings and white on the abdomen. 3. Apples, cherries, blueberries, plums. 4. Fruits punctured in summer. Maggots tunnel through the fruits. 5. Spray with DDT at tenday intervals from about July 1 until mid-August.

¶ *Armyworms.* 1. Almost everywhere. 2. 1 1/2-in. smooth green caterpillars with light-colored stripes on sides and in middle of back. Travel in armies. 3. Small plants in the line of march, but cause more trouble to field crops than in gardens. 4. Plants eaten. 5. Spray or dust with DDT. Poison baits are effective. 6. Armyworms are most prevalent after a cold, wet spring.

¶ *Asiatic garden beetles.* 1. East of the Mississippi. 2. Oval 1/2-in. cinnamon-brown beetles that feed at night. 3. Many flowers, vegetables; cherry and other fruit trees; lawns, seedling trees and shrubs. 4. Eat foliage, especially near the ground. Cause brown patches in grass. 5. Dust lawns with chlordane in spring to kill grubs. Spray foliage with DDT or Sevin to kill adult beetles in summer.

¶ *Bagworms.* 1. Eastern half of the U.S. 2. 1-in. caterpillars that carry with them little silky bags covered with leaves and twigs from whatever plant they are attacking. 3. Conifers, sycamores, maples, locusts, lindens, citrus trees. Damage is more serious in the South than North. 4. Leaves eaten. 5. Pick off and burn bags. Spray in late spring with malathion, chlordane or Sevin.

¶ *Black vine weevils.* 1. Almost everywhere. 2. 3/8-in. brown wingless bugs with small lengthwise corrugations on the lower back.

3. Yews, rhododendrons, azaleas and other evergreens; also various other plants. 4. Yews slow to make growth in the spring because larvae are eating on roots. Leaves of plants eaten at night. 5. Spray or dust chlordane on soil and plants in late spring when adult insects emerge from soil. 6. A similar weevil attacks strawberries and should be handled in the same way. Or mix chlordane into the soil at planting time.

¶ *Blister beetles.* 1. Almost everywhere. 2. Slender 1/2-in. beetles, black, gray, brown, yellow or striped. 3. Many flowers, vegetables, vines, young trees. 4. Leaves and flowers eaten in summer. 5. Spray or dust with DDT. 6. Beetles can be easily picked off plants, but if bodies are crushed, they will blister your skin; so wear gloves.

¶ *Borers.* 1. Everywhere. 2. Many kinds of caterpillars and grubs that bore into plants. 3. Many plants. 4. Holes in stems and branches of plants, often with crumbs of sawdust below. Plants may be seriously weakened. 5. Spray plants with DDT when parent insects are visible. On trees and other woody plants, inject carbon bisulfide into the holes and seal with putty. 6. Several especially serious borers are treated separately in this chapter.

¶ *Boxwood psyllids.* 1. Wherever boxwood is grown. 2. Small jumping nymphs of a small green fly appearing in late spring. 3. Boxwood. 4. Leaves curled to form a cup in which the nymphs hide while they suck on the leaves. 5. Spray in early spring with DDT; in late spring with malathion to control the flies.

¶ *Cabbage caterpillars.* 1. Almost everywhere. 2. Several types are all clearly identifiable when you encounter them. 3. Cabbages, cauliflower, broccoli and related vegetables. 4. Leaves eaten. 5. Spray or dust with DDT or rotenone as soon as you see them.

¶ *Cabbage maggots.* 1. Northern states. 2. Small white maggots produced by a small gray fly that appears in mid-spring. 3. Early-planted cabbages; also cauliflower, broccoli and related plants. 4. Maggots on stems just at and below the soil line. Plants may be stunted; wilt and die. 5. Dust chlordane around the stems of newly planted seedlings.

¶ *Cankerworms* (also called inch worms and measuring worms). 1. Almost everywhere. 2. Small worms that loop themselves along and lower and raise themselves from trees on threads. 3. Apples and other deciduous fruits; oaks, elms and other shade trees. 4. Foliage badly eaten in spring. 5. Spray with DDT or Sevin as soon as leaves develop. 6. This pest is much worse in some years than in others. In a bad year it seems to attack almost everything in sight.

¶ *Carpenterworms.* 1. Almost everywhere. 2. Whitish caterpillars with brown heads up to 2 1/2 in. long. 3. Oaks, elms and other deciduous trees. 4. Large holes in wood. 5. Inject carbon bisulfide into holes and seal with putty.

¶ *Cherry fruit flies.* 1. Northern U.S. 2. Small black or black, yellow and white flies. 9. Cherries, plums, pears. 4. Leaves eaten. Young fruits punctured. Ripe fruits deformed. 5. Spray trees about the first of June with methoxychlor.

¶ *Chinch bugs.* 1. Almost everywhere. 2. Very small black and white sucking insects. The nymphs are red, but darken with age. 3. Lawns. 4. Brown patches. 5. Spray or dust with chordane, DDT or Sevin.

¶ *Codling moths.* 1. Almost everywhere. 2. Small grayish-brown moths that first appear in spring. They produce two generations of small worms—the first soon after blossoms fall, the second from late July into September. 3. Apples and pears mainly. 4. Holes in fruit. The insects can be identified by their habit of tunneling through to the center of the fruit. Some fruits fall. 5. Sevin or DDT will control this pest; but it is better to use an all-purpose fruit spray and apply according to the schedule recommended by your Extension Service.

¶ *Colorado potato beetles.* 1. Almost everywhere. 2. Wide yellow beetles with black stripes and black spots on the head. Lay pale orange eggs in clusters on undersides of leaves in spring. Grubs which emerge in spring are red, fat and humpbacked. 3. Mainly potatoes but also tomatoes, eggplants, peppers, petunias and nicotiana. 4. Foliage eaten. 5. Spray plants when young and regularly thereafter as new growth is made with Sevin or methoxychlor.

¶ *Corn earworms.* 1. Wherever corn is grown. 2. 2-in. caterpillars variously colored with striped body and yellow head. 3. Mainly corn; also tomatoes and various other vegetables, fruits and some flowers. 4. Caterpillars feed on silk, then the top kernels; leave moist castings. 5. Keeps silk sprayed or dusted with Sevin from time it appears until four days before harvest. Spray tomatoes and other plants with DDT or methoxychlor.

¶ *Cutworms.* 1. Almost everywhere. 2. Large, smooth, fat caterpillars, mainly brown but also other colors. 3. Cabbages, tomatoes, other vegetables and some flowers. 4. In some cases, stems of young plants are cut off near the ground. In other cases, leaves and buds higher up are eaten. 5. Wrap 4-in.-high collars of cardboard around seedling tomatoes or cabbage plants. The collars should extend 1 in. into the soil. Or you may work DDT dust into the soil around young plants. Another effective control is a bran bait spread in the garden on a spring evening.

¶ *Elm leaf beetles.* 1. Wherever elms grow. 2. Slender 1/4-in. yellowish beetles with a black stripe on each wing. 1/2-in. grubs are yellow with black stripes. 3. Elms. 4. Beetles eat holes in leaves in spring; grubs finish the job, leaving nothing but the leaf veins. 5. Spray with DDT when leaves are half-open and about three weeks later.

¶ *European chafers.* 1. Scattered eastern states. 2. Oval 1/2-in. tan beetles with dark bands on wings. Grubs are 3/4 in., white with brown heads. 3. Grass. 4. Brown patches in lawn. Grass pulls up easily because roots have been chewed off. 5. Dust lawn in spring with chlordane to kill grubs.

¶ *European corn borers.* 1. East of the Rockies. 2. 1-in. whitish caterpillars with dark spots. Moths are yellow-brown, fly at night. 3. Mainly corn; also beans, dahlias, hollyhocks and other flowers and vegetables. 4. Corn tassels broken; sawdust outside small holes. 5. As soon as tassels start to develop, dust or spray DDT, Sevin or rotenone down into leaves. Make three or four repeat applications at five-day intervals. 6. It is very important to burn up garden debris at the end of the year.

¶ *European earwigs.* 1. Scattered areas, mainly in the East and Far West. 2. 3/4-in. hard, brown, beetle-like insects with pincers at the end of the body. 3. Many different plants. 4. Leaves, flowers, fruits eaten. 5. Dust soil around plants that are attacked with chlordane. Apply it also next to foundations of buildings, where the pests often hide.

¶ *European pine shoot moths.* 1. Northern states. 2. Reddish-brown moths with white bands produce 5/8-in. brown larvae with black heads. 3. Scotch, red and mugo pines; sometimes other pines. 4. New shoots become crooked at the tip, turn light brown and die. 5. Remove and burn damaged shoots in winter. Spray with DDT so that the liquid drips down to the base of the needles at the ends of branches in late June.

¶ *Fall armyworms.* 1. Eastern half of U.S. 2. 1 1/2-in. smooth caterpillars, tan, green or black with three yellow stripes and a white V on the head. Travel in armies, starting in the South and working North in the fall. 3. Grass, corn, other vegetables. 4. Plants eaten from the bottom up. 5. Dust with chlordane. 6. Fall armyworms are most prevalent after cold, wet springs.

¶ *Fall webworms.* 1. Almost everywhere. 2. 1-in. hairy caterpillars, pale green with yellow stripes on each side and a dark stripe on the back. 3. Deciduous fruits and other trees. 4. Ends of branches are covered with silken tents in mid-spring and/or in late summer or fall. Foliage devoured. 5. Regular spraying for other problems takes care of this pest on fruit trees. Use DDT on other plants. Cut off and burn nests. 6. Do not burn nests in trees. This pest can be distinguished from the tent caterpillar by the location of nests at the ends of branches. The tent caterpillar makes its nests in crotches.

¶ *Flea beetles.* 1. Almost everywhere. 2. Tiny beetles that jump like fleas. 3. Many vegetables, especially young ones. 4. Small holes in leaves. 5. Spray with Sevin or rotenone.

¶ *Four-lined plant bugs.* 1. East of Rockies. 2. 1/4-in. greenish-yellow sucking insects with four black stripes. 3. Currants, chrysanthemums, mint and many ornamental plants. 4. Leaves are peppered with small depressed spots that may be white, tan or black. Damage is done in late spring and early summer. 5. Spray or dust in spring with DDT, malathion or rotenone.

¶ *Gladiolus thrips.* 1. Everywhere. 2. Tiny black insects with white on wings. 3. Gladiolus; also iris and a few other flowers. 4. Leaves streaked with silver, then turn brown. Flowers deformed— if they open at all. Corms corky. 5. Spray plants with DDT every ten days from the time leaves are 6 in. high until flowering starts. Dust corms with DDT before storing. In spring, soak infested corms in a weak solution of Lysol.

¶ *Grape berry moths.* 1. East of the Rockies but mainly in Northwest. 2. 1/2-in.-wide grayish-purple moths that produce 1/2-in. green larvae with brown heads. 3. Grapes. 4. Fruits are tied together by webs, turn dark purple and drop prematurely. 5. Spray with DDT, Sevin or methoxychlor just before vines blossom and twice thereafter at 15-day intervals.

¶ *Grasshoppers.* 1. Almost everywhere. 2. Familiar insects. 3. Various garden crops. 4. Plants eaten. 5. Dust plants with chlordane, lindane, DDT or methoxychlor when grasshoppers appear. 6. Grasshoppers are a serious pest only when present in sizable swarms.

¶ *Gypsy moths.* 1. Northeast. 2. Dark-gray 2- to 3-in. caterpillars with long hairs. 3. Many trees. 4. Leaves eaten. 5. Spray with DDT in early May to kill caterpillars

¶ *Harlequin bugs.* 1. South. 2. Flat 3/8-in. black and red sucking insects. 3. Cabbages, cauliflower, Brussels sprouts, turnips, mustard and related plants. 4. Plants wilt and turn brown. Eggs laid on undersides of leaves look like little black and white barrels. 5. Spray or dust with rotenone from spring on.

¶ *Inch Worms.* See cankerworms.

¶ *Iris borers.* 1. Almost everywhere. 2. Fat pinkish caterpillars up to 2 in. long when full grown. 3. Iris. 4. In the spring, when the borers are small, they work their way down inside the leaves, which look ragged and water soaked. In summer, the borers burrow inside the rhizomes. Leaves and rhizomes may look slimy and rotten. 5. Spray or dust with DDT or malathion from time leaves are 6 in.

long until flowering starts. When dividing rhizomes, inspect them for borers, which can be cut out with a knife. If rhizomes are attacked by soft rot, cut out diseased portions and soak the rest in a bichloride of mercury solution. Clean up and burn dead and diseased plant parts.

¶ *Japanese beetles.* 1. East of the Mississippi. 2. Beautiful 1/2-in. oval, metallic green beetles with coppery wing. Grubs are up to 1 in. long, whitish with brown heads. 3. Roses, marigolds, zinnias, other summer flowers, deciduous fruits, shade trees, shrubs, lawns. 4. Flowers and leaves eaten. 5. Dust chlordane on lawn in spring to kill grubs. To kill beetles, spray frequently in summer with DDT, Sevin or methoxychlor.

¶ *June beetles* (also called May beetles). 1. Almost everywhere. 2. Large red-brown or black beetles that hide during the day, are attracted to light at night. Grubs are like Japanese beetle grubs but larger. 3. Mainly deciduous trees; also lawns. 4. Foliage or trees eaten; roots of smaller plants eaten by grubs. 5. Grub-proof lawn with chlordane in spring. Spray with Sevin to control the beetles.

¶ *Lace bugs.* 1. Almost everywhere. 2. Various small bugs with pretty lacy wings larger than the bodies. 3. Alders, ash, azaleas, birches, ceanothus, chrysanthemums, hawthorns, lantana, oaks, rhododendrons, sycamores, willows. 4. In the spring, undersides of leaves are covered with bits of dark excrement and look mottled. Later, tops of leaves begin to look pale from a distance; show a stippled effect on close examination. 5. Spray with lindane or malathion in spring and make several applications at ten-day intervals.

¶ *Leafhoppers.* 1. Almost everywhere. 2. 1/2-in. somewhat wedge-shaped sucking insects that hop. They are of various colors. 3. Many plants. 4. Leaves become pale or brown, have a stippled look. Plants may be stunted. 5. Spray with DDT at first signs of trouble. 6. Leafhoppers are vectors of various diseases, such as aster yellows.

¶ *Leaf miners.* 1. Almost everywhere. 2. Small larvae of various insects which are rarely seen because they burrow between the two surfaces of leaves. 3. A wide assortment of plants including birch and holly. 4. Leaves spotted with pale, seemingly translucent blotches or trails. 5. Spray with DDT a couple of times in the spring when plants are making new growth and leaves are developing. This may catch the adults when they are laying eggs. Spraying with lindane as soon as you detect the young miners at work in the leaves may also help.

¶ *Leaf rollers.* 1. Almost everywhere. 2. Small caterpillars of various colors which roll up leaves around themselves when they feed. 3. Deciduous fruits and other plants. 4. Leaves rolled up and eaten. 5. Applying a dormant oil spray to fruit trees before buds break destroys egg masses of some leaf rollers. Spray with Sevin in spring before young leaves are folded.

¶ *Leaf tiers.* 1. Almost everywhere. 2. Small caterpillars which tie leaves around themselves with silk threads. 3. Celery, strawberries and other plants. 4. Leaves rolled and tied with silk. 5. Spray young plants with DDT.

¶ *Lilac borers.* 1. East of Rockies. 2. White caterpillars with brown heads, up to 1 1/2 in. long. 3. Lilacs, ash, mountain ash, privet. 4. Holes in trunks of older plants with sawdust spilling out. 5. In May, spray trunks and large branches with DDT to kill the wasp-like moths that lay eggs in rough bark and also to kill larvae. Inject carbon bisulfide into borer holes and seal with putty.

¶ *Mealybugs.* 1. Greenhouses; indoors and outdoors in warm climates. 2. Tiny, oval sucking insects covered with a white, mealy wax. 3. Many house plants; also citrus fruits, apples, filberts, grapes, yews, etc. 4. Plants ailing; white insects and cottony egg masses are seen on stems and under leaves. 5. Spray with malathion. On small house plants, pick off bugs and egg masses with a cotton swab dipped in alcohol.

¶ *Mexican bean beetles.* 1. East of the Mississippi and in the Southwest. 2. 1/3-in. beetles, quite round; yellow with eight black spots on each wing. Lay clusters of yellowish eggs on undersides of leaves in spring. Grubs are yellow. 3. Beans. 4. Leaves skeletonized. 5. Spray or dust with rotenone or methoxychlor as soon as you discover the insects or their eggs. Make a second application ten days later and continue as necessary. Be sure to hit undersides of leaves.

¶ *Mites.* 1. Everywhere, outdoors and in. 2. Microscopic sucking insects. 3. Given encouragement, they will probably eat anything. African violets, cyclamens and delphiniums are favorites. 4. Symptoms vary. Cyclamen mites cause twisted leaves and stems, general distortion and stunting of plants. Spruce mites spin webs between needles. All mites cause rusty discoloring of leaves, which often drop. 5. Spray at the first sign of trouble with Aramite, Dimite or Kelthane. 6. High temperatures seem to encourage an increase in mite populations. Widespread use of DDT, malathion and Sevin is almost certain to magnify mite problems by killing insects that feed on them. When using these chemicals, therefore, it is often advisable to apply a miticide at the same time.

¶ *Nematodes.* 1. Everywhere. 2. Microscopic insects. 3. Plants of all kinds, but mainly flowers, vegetables and other small plants. 4. Symptoms vary widely but in general include stunting and yellowing of plants and dying back. Some nematodes cause galls. 5. Sterilize soil by baking or with chloropicrin, D-D Mixture or VC-13.

¶ *Onion maggots.* 1. Northern states. 2. Small white maggots produced by gray or brown flies which appear in mid-spring. 3. Onions. 4. Seedling plants suddenly die; tunnels in older bulbs. 5. Dust onion seed with aldrin before planting, or dust the seed rows with DDT. 6. This pest causes most trouble in years with wet springs.

¶ *Orange dogs.* 1. Florida. 2. 2 1/2-in. brown and yellow caterpillars, one end looking like a dog. Parents are large yellow and black butterflies. 3. Citrus. 4. Trees defoliated in late summer and early fall. 5. Pick off insects by hand. Spray with DDT.

¶ *Orange tortrix.* 1. California. 2. Brown-headed whitish caterpillars—offspring of gray, mottled moths. 3. Oranges, lemons and miscellaneous plants. 4. Leaves rolled and webbed around caterpillars. Fruit scarred and drops. 5. Spray or dust with cryolite.

¶ *Oriental fruit moths.* 1. Where peaches grow—mainly in the East and Far West. 2. Gray and brown moths producing 1/2-in.

pink larvae. 3. Peaches, quinces and other deciduous fruits. 4. There are three or four generations a year. First larvae in spring cause tips of twigs to die. Later larvae bore into fruit through the stem (you may not see the holes). 5. DDT, Sevin or methoxychlor give good control; but use an all-purpose fruit spray according to the schedule recommended by your Extension Service.

¶ *Peach tree borers.* 1. Almost everywhere. 2. 1-in. light-yellow caterpillars with brown heads. 3. Peaches; also plums, cherries, nectarines, apricots and some ornamental shrubs. 4. Masses of gum oozing from holes near base of trunk. 5. Fumigate soil around trunks of trees with para-dichlorobenzene crystals applied in the fall. In summer, spray trunk and soil around it three times at monthly intervals with DDT.

¶ *Plum curculios.* 1. East of the Rockies. 2. 1/4-in. brown and gray beetles with long, downward-curving snouts. 3. Stone fruits, apples, pears, quinces. 4. Leaves eaten to some extent. Young fruit with crescent-shaped marks next to puncture holes. 5. Various sprays are used, but this pest is most easily taken care of with an all-purpose fruit spray applied when blossoms begin to show color; when the last petals are falling; and ten days later. Pick up and destroy fallen fruit. Many of the insects can be shaken out of the tree on to a sheet.

¶ *Rose chafers* (also called rose bugs). 1. Northeastern states mainly. 2. Light-tan beetles up to 1/2 in. with long legs. 3. Roses, grapes, peonies and miscellaneous plants. 4. Flowers, fruits and foliage eaten in mid-spring. 5. Spray in spring with DDT or methoxychlor.

¶ *Sawflies.* 1. Almost everywhere. 2. Wasp-like insects with transparent wings that produce small caterpillars of various colors. 3. Pines and other evergreen and deciduous trees; also roses. 4. Foliage eaten. 5. Spray with DDT when caterpillars appear (usually in the spring).

¶ *Scale insects.* 1. Everywhere, indoors and out. 2. Tiny, lumpish sucking insects with a hard, scaly covering. 3. Trees, vines, shrubs of many kinds; also small plants. 4. You will see the scales probably before you notice the damage they do (yellowing and loss of leaves). They cover plant stems and undersides of leaves. 5. Spray in late winter or early spring before growth begins with dormant oil or lime-sulfur. In spring when the scales start to move around (you must look hard to see this), spray with malathion once or twice. Scales can be rubbed off potted plants with a cotton swab dipped in malathion. To stop tea scale on camellias, spray in spring after bloom period with dimethoate.

¶ *Sod webworms.* 1. Almost everywhere but worst in warm climates. 2. Small, fat caterpillars produced by small yellowish millers that fly up from the grass, especially near nightfall. 3. Grass, especially bent and blue grass. 4. Grass leaves eaten. Silky tubes are found between the leaves. 5. Dust lawn with chlordane.

¶ *Spittlebugs.* 1. Almost everywhere. 2. Brown, gray or black hopping bugs that make small masses of foam on plants. 3. Strawberries, pines and other plants. 4. Plants and fruits stunted. 5. Spray strawberries with methoxychlor. Use DDT or lindane on pines.

¶ *Spotted cucumber beetles.* 1. Almost everywhere. 2. 1/4-in. slender yellowish beetles with black spots and head. 3. Cucumber family, beans, corn, other vegetables, late summer flowers. 4. Foliage eaten. Grubs burrow downward through stems. 5. Dust or spray with rotenone, pyrethrum or methoxychlor as soon as pest appears. Repeat two or three times.

¶ *Springtails.* 1. Almost everywhere. 2. Tiny black bugs, looking like a comic-strip character, that jump. 3. Mainly vegetables. 4. Leaves near ground eaten or pitted. 5. Dust malathion on the soil around young plants.

¶ *Squash borers.* 1. East of Rockies. 2. 1-in. white caterpillars with brown heads. The parent is a wasp-like moth with orange and red body. 3. Squash, pumpkins, gourds, cucumbers, muskmelons. 4. Plants suddenly wilt in early summer. Greenish-yellow frass oozes from holes in stems. 5. Spray or dust with methoxychlor starting when plants are about 8 in. high and continuing at weekly intervals.

¶ *Squash bugs* (also called stink bugs). 1. Almost everywhere. 2. 5/8-in. dark-brown sucking insects that give off an unpleasant odor when crushed. 3. Squash, pumpkins, gourds, melons. 4. Plants wilt, turn black and die when attacked in spring. 5. Apply malathion or Sevin when bugs appear and again when they lay clusters of reddish-brown eggs on undersides of leaves.

¶ *Strawberry root weevils.* 1. Northern states. 2. White, curved, legless larvae of 1/4-in. black beetles with blunt snouts. 3. Strawberries and conifers; also other plants. 4. Plants stunted, small roots eaten. Strawberry leaves bunched together. 5. Mix chlordane into soil before planting strawberries. Spray plants with malathion when weevils emerge from soil in early June.

¶ *Striped cucumber beetles.* 1. Almost everywhere. 2. 1/4-in. yellow beetles with black stripes on wings and black heads. 3. Cucumber family and some other plants. 4. Foliage eaten. Grubs work their way through stems and roots. Small plants especially susceptible to attack. 5. Spray or dust with rotenone, pyrethrum or methoxychlor as soon as pest appears. Make repeat applications.

¶ *Tarnished plant bugs.* 1. Almost everywhere. 2. Flat, oval, 1/4-in. bugs mottled in color but with a yellow mark on either side of body. 3. Many vegetables, fruits, flowers, including dahlias and asters. 4. Leaves may be deformed, fruits pitted, flower buds imperfect. Plant parts may blacken and die. 5. Spray or dust with methoxychlor or DDT as flower buds develop. Repeat application as necessary. Keep garden free of trash.

¶ *Tent caterpillars.* 1. Almost everywhere. 2. Caterpillars of several kinds easily identified by the tent-like webs they build in the crotches of trees. 3. The eastern caterpillar favors apples and wild cherries; the western likes oaks; but both attack many other kinds of fruit and shade trees. 4. Foliage chewed to bits. 5. Pick off egg clusters during winter. Pull off the tents by hand, being sure to get all the caterpillars, and burn them. Spray caterpillars and tents with DDT. 6. Burning the tents is good treatment for the bugs but very bad for the trees. Don't do it.

¶ *Thrips.* 1. Everywhere. 2. Barely visible winged insects of several colors. 3. Vegetables, flowers, many other pests. Gladiolus are a special target (see gladiolus thrips). 4. Leaves have silvery mottling. Flowers damaged. Plants may be distorted. 5. Spray or dust with DDT mixed with a miticide. 6. Thrips are worst in hot, dry weather.

¶ *Tomato hornworms.* 1. Almost everywhere. 2. Green caterpillars as long as 4 in. with eight diagonal white stripes on the body and a black horn at the rear end. 3. Tomatoes, eggplants, peppers, potatoes. 4. Foliage eaten. 5. Pick off by hand.

¶ *Tussock moths.* 1. Almost everywhere. 2. There are several kinds. Most important are the western and white-marked tussock moths. These produce colorful, hairy caterpillars with four conspicuous tufts of hair like shaving brushes on the back and long, thin tufts at head and tail. 3. Deciduous trees and fruits. 4. Foliage eaten, fruits scarred. 5. Scrape 1-in.-long white-covered egg masses from trunks and branches in late winter. Spray caterpillars with DDT.

¶ *Twig pruners.* 1. East of the Mississippi. 2. 1/2-in. grayish-brown beetles. 3. Oaks, hickories, maples, sweetgums, other deciduous trees. 4. Small twigs are piled on ground under trees in mid- and late summer. 5. Rake up and burn twigs, in which borers hibernate.

¶ *Wasps.* There are a few that cause trouble but many others do not. Some, in fact, are of great help. Since it is difficult to separate the sheep from goats, better leave them alone unless they are bothering you or other members of the family personally. In that case, spray DDT into the nests at night.

¶ *Whiteflies.* 1. Almost everywhere, especially indoors and in greenhouses. 2. Tiny, white, moth-like sucking insects. 3. Many plants, especially greenhouse plants and citrus trees. 4. Leaves speckled, covered with mold. When you brush against plants, clouds of flies appear. 5. Spray with malathion.

¶ *White fringed beetles.* 1. Southeastern states. 2. 1/2-in. gray-brown beetles with short hairs and white wing margins. 1/2-in. grubs are dirty, white, curved and legless. 3. Many plants. 4. Leaves eaten from the outer edges in. Grubs eat plant roots, causing plants to wilt and die. 5. In spring, before planting garden, work chlordane dust into soil. Spray from May on about every fortnight with DDT to control beetles.

¶ *White oak borers.* 1. Wherever white oaks grow. 2. Pale, yellow, segmented grubs up to 1 1/2 in. long produced by a large brown and white beetle with long, curving antennae. 3. White oaks, overcup oaks, hickories and walnuts. 4. Holes in tree trunks and branches exude sawdust in summer. 5. Inject carbon bisulfide into holes and plug with putty.

¶ *White pine weevils.* 1. East. 2. 1/4-in. reddish-brown beetles with white spots. 3. White pines. 4. Ends of branches turn brown and die in June and July. 5. Jar weevils out of trees on to a sheet in May. Cut off and burn damaged leaders. Spray trees, especially branch ends, when growth starts in spring with DDT.

¶ *Wireworms.* 1. Almost everywhere. 2. Thin, hard, shiny, coiled worms up to 3/4 in. 3. Vegetables and some flowers. 4. The worms work underground, kill seedlings, eat seeds before they germinate, weaken older plants. 5. Sterilize soil before planting with D-D Mixture, or work chlordane into the soil.

FUNGICIDES

The following are among the best fungicides for use in the home garden.

¶ *Acti-dione.* Controls various turf diseases as well as cedar-apple rust, cherry leaf spot, powdery mildews and white pine blister rust. Do not use on fruits and vegetables within four days of harvest.

¶ *Bordeaux mixture.* Old but still widely used fungicide useful in controlling many diseases. It may be mixed in various strengths, but probably the most common formula is 4-4-50 (4 lb. copper sulfate, 4 lb. hydrated lime in 50 gal. water). Not compatible with a number of chemicals. Do not use on fruits and vegetables within a week of harvest.

¶ *Captan.* Used for many fruit and vegetable diseases. Not compatible with some chemicals. Can be applied to fruits and vegetables up to within two weeks of harvest.

¶ *Copper compounds.* Control a variety of blights, leaf spots and downy and powdery mildews. Not compatible with a number of chemicals. Can be applied to fruits and vegetables to within a week of harvest.

¶ *Dichlone.* Controls black spot on roses, azalea petal blight and various fruit diseases. Do not use on fruits and vegetables within a month of harvest.

¶ *Dyrene.* Controls several lawn diseases, strawberry leaf spot, etc. Also used on mushrooms.

¶ *Ferbam.* Controls many diseases but not powdery mildews. Not compatible with a number of chemicals. Do not apply to fruits and vegetables within ten days of harvest.

¶ *Formaldehyde.* Soil fumigant kills damping-off fungi and other diseases. Seed can be sown 24 hours after application.

¶ *Karathane.* Controls powdery mildews on fruits, vegetables, roses and ornamental plants. Do not apply to fruits and vegetables within three weeks of harvest.

¶ *Lime-sulfur.* Used as a dormant spray to control mildews and other diseases. Also kills scale insects. Not compatible with many chemicals.

¶ *Maneb.* A many-purpose fungicide. Do not apply to fruits and vegetables within ten days of harvest.

¶ *Nabam.* For potato and tomato blights and other diseases of flowers and vegetables. Do not use on fruits and vegetables within two weeks of harvest.

¶ *Phaltan.* Controls black spot on roses and various mildews. Do not apply to fruits and vegetables after they start to form.

¶ *Spergon.* A seed disinfectant used to prevent damping-off.

¶ *Terraclor.* Applied to the soil, it controls many soil fungi.

¶ *Tersan.* Controls brown patch and dollar spot in lawns.

¶ *Vapam.* Soil fumigant. Controls many diseases as well as nematodes.

¶ *Zineb.* This is excellent for use against a long list of diseases, but not powdery mildews. Do not apply to fruits and vegetables within ten days of harvest.

HOW TO CONTROL COMMON PLANT DISEASES

The following are among the most common plant diseases. The paragraphs describe: 1. Where the diseases may be encountered. 2. Plants most likely to be affected. 3. Appearance of affected plants. 4. Recommended method of control. 5. Comments, if any.

Note that many plant ailments which are attributed to diseases may actually be caused by something else—insects, lack of essential nutrients, too much or too little water, sun scorching, etc.

¶ *Anthracnose.* 1. Everywhere. 2. Many kinds of plants. 3. White, gray, brown or black spots, often with whitish centers, on stems, leaves and fruits. Affected branches and twigs die back. Plants lose leaves and may die. 4. Spray or dust with maneb or zineb. Destroy diseased plant parts. 5. Disease is most troublesome in wet years.

¶ *Aster yellows.* 1. Almost everywhere. 2. China asters and other flowers and vegetables. 3. Leaves turn yellow. Flowers smaller than they should be. Plants stunted but have many side shoots. 4. Tear out diseased plants. Look for leafhoppers, which commonly transmit this disease, and spray plants and wide area around them with DDT.

¶ *Azalea petal blight.* 1. Southern states. 2. Mainly azaleas but sometimes rhododendrons and mountain laurel. 3. Small spots on flower petals followed almost immediately by dropping of flowers, which become slimy. 4. Spray flowers every other day with zineb from the time the buds start to open until all are open; then continue at four-day intervals until bloom ends.

¶ *Black knot.* 1. Almost everywhere. 2. Plums, cherries, apricots. 3. Long, knotty, black excrescences on twigs. 4. Cut twigs 4 in. below the knots and burn. Spray with lime-sulfur when buds start to break.

¶ *Black spot.* 1. Almost everywhere but especially in moist climates. 2. Roses. 3. Distinct, more or less circular black spots with fringed edges on leaves. Spots are up to 1/2 in. across. 4. From the time leaves develop until late fall, spray with Phaltan every week to ten days and always after a rain.

¶ *Blossom-end rot.* 1. Almost everywhere. 2. Tomatoes, peppers, squash and watermelons. 3. Irregular brown or black sunken areas develop around the blossom ends of fruits. 4. Keep plants watered. Spray with very dilute solution of calcium chloride.

¶ *Botrytis blight.* 1. Almost everywhere, outdoors and in. 2. Many flowers, vegetables and fruits. 3. Gray mold on plant parts, which rot. 4. Destroy infected plant parts. Spray with zineb or ferbam. Do not crowd plants in greenhouses or indoors, and avoid wetting foliage.

¶ *Brown patch.* 1. Warm, humid regions. 2. Almost all kinds of grass but especially bent, fescue, Kentucky blue, rye, centipede and St. Augustine. 3. Irregular brownish patches a few inches to several feet across. White filmy threads seen on grass when it is wet in the morning. Grass blades stand upright. 4. Do not overfertilize. Apply water early in the day. Spray with Dyrene or Tersan three times at weekly intervals. Lawn should be watered 48 hours before spraying. 5. Brown patch is likely to follow heavy applications of nitrogenous fertilizer.

¶ *Brown rot.* 1. Almost everywhere. 2. Peaches and other stone fruits. 3. Flowers turn brown and rot. Cankers that exude gum may form on trunks and branches. Fruits have small, circular brown spots that grow very rapidly and are covered with whitish spores. If fruits do not fall, they may become mummified. 4. Burn infected fruits and wood. Follow a spray schedule recommended by your Extension Service. This probably includes application of a dormant spray, then use of an all-purpose fruit spray when blossoms show color, when last petals are falling and every ten days thereafter until harvest.

¶ *Bud blast.* 1. Almost everywhere. 2. Peonies. 3. Small buds turn black and do not open. Flowers turn brown. Leaves are brown and spotted. 4. Burn diseased parts promptly. In fall, cut plant to the ground and burn the trash. As soon as pink shoots show in spring, spray with zineb or ferbam three times at ten-day intervals.

¶ *Camellia flower blight.* 1. Wherever camellias are grown. 2. Camellias. 3. Flowers turn brown and drop. 4. Treat soil in winter with Terraclor. Destroy diseased and fallen blooms. Buy only bare-root plants without any flower buds showing color.

¶ *Cane blight.* 1. Almost everywhere. 2. Raspberries and other bramble fruits. 3. Brown areas on canes, which wilt and die. 4. Burn all infected canes at once. Spray with ferbam.

¶ *Cankers.* 1. Everywhere. 2. Many woody plants. 3. Small lesions on stems grow larger, may girdle the stems or become so large that the wood above dies. 4. Cut out diseased wood and burn. Spray roses in early spring with lime-sulfur.

¶ *Cedar-apple rust.* 1. Wherever red cedars grow. 2. Apples, crab-apples, hawthorns, quinces, pears, mountain ash, amelanchier. 3. Leaves distorted, may have orange-red spots and be covered underneath with specks. Nearby red cedars and junipers have galls which turn red and gelatinous in the spring; or there may be swellings in the twigs and black patches on the trunks. 4. Spray with ferbam or Acti-dione in May and June. Cut down cedars that grow within one mile of diseased deciduous trees. 5. Occasionally other kinds of juniper (red cedar is a juniper) are alternate hosts for this disease; and if this proves to be the case, they should also be removed.

¶ *Chlorosis.* 1. Almost everywhere. 2. Many plants. 3. Leaves turn yellow or yellowish-green between the veins, which usually remain dark green. 4. Apply iron chelates to the soil around the plant.

¶ *Clubroot.* 1. Almost everywhere. 2. Cabbages and related plants. 3. Plants have yellowed leaves that wilt on hot days. Roots are swollen, misshapen, sometimes rotten. 4. Before planting, lime soil heavily to bring pH up to 7.2; or when setting out seedlings, water them with a solution made of 1 oz. of calomel mixed with gum arabic to 6 gal. of water.

¶ *Crown gall.* 1. Almost everywhere. 2. Fruit trees, berries, deciduous trees. 3. Large, rough, swellings just above the ground at grafts or perhaps on roots or higher up in the plant. 4. There is no cure or sure control. Inspect plants you purchase carefully for suspicious swellings.

¶ *Crown rot.* 1. Mainly in the North. 2. Delphinium, iris and other plants. 3. During humid weather, white threads form at the bottom of stems and may even spread out over the nearby ground; stems then rot or break off. 4. If you discover the disease early enough, drench the crown of the plant and surrounding soil with a solution of 1 tablet of bichloride of mercury in 1 pt. of water. If the plant is too far gone, pull it out and burn it, and apply bichloride of mercury solution to soil. If replanting a garden in which crown rot has been a problem, fumigate the soil with chloropicrin.

¶ *Damping-off.* 1. Everywhere. 2. Seedling flowers, vegetables. 3. Small plants topple over and die. 4. Sow seeds in a sterile medium, such as vermiculite or sand, or in sterilized soil. Or dust seeds before planting in ordinary soil with Spergon.

¶ *Dieback.* 1. Everywhere. 2. Many plants. 3. Twigs and branches die back from the ends. 4. This problem can be caused by various things, and it is not easy to tell what. Cutting out dead wood several inches further down and burning is a wise precaution that can do no harm and may solve the problem.

¶ *Dollar spot.* 1. Humid areas in the North, but also in the South. 2. Many grasses, mainly bent. 3. Disease occurs primarily in cool, wet springs and falls. Small spots in grass at first look black, then turn brown, finally turn almost white. Spots may merge into big spots. 4. Spray with Dyrene or Tersan.

¶ *Downy mildew.* 1. Almost everywhere. 2. Many plants. 3. Downy patches of white, gray or purple on leaves. 4. Spray or dust with zineb. 5. This problem is worst in wet weather.

¶ *Dutch elm disease.* 1. Wherever American elms grow. 2. American elms. 3. Leaves rather suddenly turn yellow and die. Sometimes this happens to individual branches; sometimes the entire tree turns at once. 4. The fungus causing the disease is usually transmitted by two small bark beetles, but also travels between trees that are planted so close together that their roots touch and form a natural graft. There is no cure, but the disease can be controlled by keeping dead wood cut out of elms and by promptly cutting down all infected trees. Every scrap of wood and foliage must be burned. Have trees sprayed in early spring with DDT to control the bark beetles. 5. This dreadful disease has been making such rapid inroads in the American elm population in recent years that effective control is no longer simply an each-man-for-himself proposition. If you live in a community with a number of elms, insist on a community-wide control program spearheaded by your town tree warden or park superintendent.

¶ *Early blight.* 1. Almost everywhere. 2. Tomatoes, potatoes, peppers, eggplants. 3. Leaves have brown spots marked with concentric lines. Spots grow together. 4. Spray with zineb. Rotate crops.

¶ *Fading out.* 1. Almost everywhere. 2. Kentucky bluegrass, bent and fescue. 3. Small, irregular, reddish-brown patches in the lawn, especially when weather is hot and humid. 4. Remove clippings. Don't fertilize too much in spring. Spray with captan or Dyrene.

¶ *Fire blight.* 1. Almost everywhere. 2. Pears, apples, quinces, cotoneasters, pyracantha, etc. 3. Young fruits, blossoms and leaves turn black and die but do not fall. Bark on twigs turns darker than usual and is slightly sunken at edge of infected areas. 4. Spray with copper compounds or Bordeaux mixture several times while trees are in bloom. Cut out infected wood at least 6 in. below dead area. 5. Overfertilization encourages this disease.

¶ *Fusarium* (also called fusarium wilt or yellows). 1. Almost everywhere. 2. Asters, gladiolus, lilies, narcissus and other plants. 3. Plants become discolored and wilt permanently. Roots are likely to be rotten. 4. Destroy diseased plants. Plant wilt-resistant varieties. Rotate crops. Sterilize soil with formaldehyde.

¶ *Grease spot.* 1. Humid areas of country. 2. Many kinds of grass. 3. Spots of grayish fungus on grass surrounded by grass blades that look black, slimy and matted. Grass soon turns brown and lies flat. 4. Water sparingly in hot, humid weather. Spray with zineb.

¶ *Helminthosporium leafspot and foot rot.* 1. Almost everywhere. 2. Kentucky bluegrass. 9. From a distance grass looks spottily brown. Leaves have small reddish-brown to purplish-black spots. Rhizomes and roots are rotten. 4. Remove clippings. Don't fertilize too much in spring. Spray with captan or Dyrene. 5. This problem occurs mainly in cool, wet springs and falls. Merion bluegrass is resistant.

¶ *Hollyhock rust.* 1. Wherever hollyhocks are grown. 2. Hollyhocks and mallows. 3. Tiny brown dots at first on leaves and stems. These turn into larger brown discs on undersides of leaves and into orange spots with red centers on top. 4. Spray with ferbam every ten days from time leaves open until autumn. Burn old stems and leaves in fall. 5. This is a difficult disease to control.

¶ *Leaf spot.* 1. Everywhere. 2. Plants of all kinds. 3. Leaves have distinct spots with brownish or whitish centers and dark edges. Spots may grow together. 4. Rarely a fatal disease; but pick off infected leaves and keep those that fall raked up. Spray with zineb or ferbam several times when you first notice the problem. 5. Disease is worst in wet weather.

¶ *Mosaic.* 1. Almost everywhere. 2. Various plants, but probably most familiar on tomatoes. 3. Leaves show a yellow and green mottling or a light-green and dark-green mottling; are often deformed. Plants may be stunted. 4. Mosaic is caused by various diseases and is difficult to control. Plant resistant varieties. Destroy infected plants. Eliminate weeds. Control aphids, leafhoppers and other insects that are vectors.

¶ *Mushroom root rot.* 1. Almost everywhere. 2. Many woody plants. 3. Clumps of toadstools at base of plants. Foliage may be yellow. Resin flows from base of conifers. 4. In the West, where this disease is a real problem, use resistant varieties of plants. Cure is very difficult; better call in a professional tree man. Fumigate soil before planting in it again. Keep plants in vigorous health.

¶ *Oak wilt.* 1. Middle West and Pennsylvania. 2. Oaks. 3. Leaves become crinkled, turn brown from the edges in. Trees lose leaves from the top down. 4. Cut out infected branches immediately; however, this probably will prolong the tree's life only slightly. Cut down infected trees and other oaks within 50 ft. 5. This has become an extremely serious disease for which no cure has been found.

¶ *Oedema.* 1. Indoors and in greenhouses. 2. Various plants. 3. Warty bumps appear on undersides of leaves. 4. This is usually caused by overwatering. Reduce the supply.

¶ *Peach leaf curl.* 1. Almost everywhere. 2. Peaches, apricots, nectarines. 3. First leaves have pronounced folds that are colored red, pink or yellow. Leaf surface is mealy. 4. Spray with lime-sulfur in early spring before buds open.

¶ *Powdery mildew.* 1. Everywhere, but least likely in areas of heavy rainfall. 2. Plants of all kinds. 3. White, powdery, felt-like blotches on leaves, which are somewhat curled. Plants stunted. 4. Spray with Karathane. 5. Mildew appears in humid, not rainy, weather.

¶ *Rust.* 1. Almost everywhere. 2. Many plants. 3. Reddish spores in powdery pustules or gelatinous lumps on leaves. Foliage yellow. Plants often stunted. 4. Spray with Acti-dione or ferbam. Remove alternate hosts, if any. 5. Several well known rusts are treated separately in this chapter.

¶ *Scab.* 1. Almost everywhere. 2. Apples, pears, peaches, pecans, citrus fruits, gladiolus and other plants. 3. Dark, discolored, scab-like lesions on leaves, fruits and other plant parts. Lesions may be raised or sunken. Leaves fall off. 4. On fruit trees use spray and spray schedule recommended by your Extension Service. Spray other plants frequently with captan or zincb.

¶ *Smut.* 1. Almost everywhere. 2. Corn. 3. Large, hideous, gray fungus growths appear in hot weather on all parts of the plant, but especially on the ears. 4. Cut off infected part at once and burn. Rotate crops every three years.

¶ *Snow mold.* 1. Almost everywhere. 2. Mainly bent grass, but also other grasses. 3. White, cottony mold on leaves, which turn tan and stick together. Patches are up to 1 ft. across. 4. In fall, keep lawn cut and avoid applying high-nitrogen fertilizers. Spray with Dyrene before first lasting snow and repeat application if snow melts in midwinter or early spring. 5. A related disease called fusarium patch or pink snow mold can occur during the growing season when humidity is high and temperature falls below 65°F. Treat with Dyrene.

¶ *Sooty mold.* 1. Almost everywhere. 2. Plants of all kinds. 3. Leaves are spotted or entirely covered with a thin black mold. 4. Sooty mold lives on the honeydew secreted by aphids, scales, mealybugs and whiteflies. To get rid of it, kill these insects.

¶ *Soft rot.* 1. Almost everywhere. 2. Irisis; also calla lilies and other flowers and vegetables. 3. Leaves look water-soaked, turn yellow or brown. Rhizomes are mushy. Infected parts have an unpleasant odor. 4. Control the iris borer which spreads this disease. Destroy infected plant parts. Cut out rotten part of rhizome and soak the rest in bichloride of mercury solution (1 tablet to 1 pt. water). Sterilize soil if possible before planting in it again.

¶ *Southern blight.* 1. Mainly in the South. 2. Flowers, vegetables, bulbs, shrubs. 3, 4. Symptoms and control as for crown rot (see page 135).

¶ *Stem rot.* 1. Almost everywhere. 2. Tomatoes, peppers, various flowers. 3. White, cottony mold on stems, which rot. 4. Cut out and destroy infected parts. Dust with sulfur or Terraclor.

¶ *Stunt.* 1. Almost everywhere. 2. Dahlias, chrysanthemums and some other plants. 3. Plants dwarfed; foliage distorted and often discolored. 4. This is a virus disease which is transmitted by insects or dodder. There is no cure. Destroy infected plants.

¶ *Tulip fire.* 1. Almost everywhere. 2. Tulips. 3. Leaves, stems and flowers develop spots, become distorted and develop a brown-gray mold. 4. Do not plant bulbs that have yellow lesions on the outer white skin. Dig up and destroy infected plants. If you have diseased plants, sterilize soil before planting new bulbs, and spray foliage of remaining bulbs at ten-day intervals with ferbam.

¶ *Verticillium wilt.* 1. Almost everywhere. 2. Plants of various kinds. 3. Plants yellow and wilt, starting from the lowest branches or leaves and working upward. Sometimes only part of a plant wilts.

Watering does not bring it back. 4. This is an enigmatic and difficult disease. Destroy small plants. Cut out infected tree limbs. Rotate crops.

¶ *White pine blister rust.* 1. Wherever white pines grow. 2. White pines. 3. Ends of branches swell, exude an orange liquid. The next year, white blisters appear on the bark and these later discharge orange spores. 4. Cut out infected wood and spray with Acti-dione. Remove currants and gooseberries, which are the alternate host for this disease, within 900 ft. of the pines, 5. Some states control the planting of currants and gooseberries.

¶ *Wood rot.* 1. Everywhere. 2. Woody plants. 3. Wood damaged, stained, usually becomes soft. 4. Cut off infected branches well below the rotten area. With a chisel, clean out rotten spots in trunks and cover with tree paint.

HERBICIDES

Before we get too deeply into the subject of these exciting weed-killers, let me remind you of several good old manual weeding methods that will never become obsolete: (1) Mulching. (2) Pulling weeds by hand. This is easier when the soil is damp. Use a three-pronged hand cultivator, trowel, old penknife or asparagus knife to get out deep-rooted weeds. (3) Hoeing—which is easier when the soil is dry. Don't try to dig up the weeds; simply cut through them at the crown. (4) Cultivating with a long-handled or wheeled culti-vator. This is more work than hoeing, but gets rid of weeds entirely. Do the job after a soaking rain when the soil is no longer sticky.

Herbicides are best used for wide-scale weed-killing and for eradicating undesirable plants which are difficult to cope with manu-ally. Some of these chemicals are known as selective herbicides because they kill certain plants without damaging others alongside; others are nonselective and kill everything in sight. Soil sterilants and soil fumigants are nonselective herbicides that render the treated soil incapable of supporting plant growth of any kind. Pre-emergence herbicides are for the most part selective herbicides that kill weed seeds before they germinate. Contact and translocated herbicides are either selective or nonselective herbicides used to kill growing weeds.

Here are a number of herbicides. All should be handled with care and in the exact way prescribed by the manufacturer.

¶ *Amiben.* A selective pre-emergence herbicide that keeps a dozen kinds of weeds out of flower gardens and shrubbery borders. Unlike other herbicides, it is also safe to use around a few vegetables.

¶ *Ammate (AMS).* A potent nonselective herbicide that is especially recommended for poison ivy, poison oak and poison sumac. It kills tree stumps, and is the only soil sterilant recommended for use in home driveways, walks, terraces, etc.

¶ *Bandane.* A pre-emergence herbicide for killing crabgrass in established and seedling grass.

¶ *Betasan (Bensulide).* A selective pre-emergence herbicide to control crabgrass and several other weeds in lawns, flower beds, ground covers and around some shrubs and trees.

¶ *Cacodylic acid.* Nonselective contact herbicide useful for quick removal of almost all plant growth from a lawn area that needs rebuilding. You can sow grass seeds within two days.

¶ *Calcium cyanamid.* A pre-emergence killer of various weeds applied before a lawn is made. Do not sow grass seed for six weeks. The chemical is also a good source of nitrogen.

¶ *Casoron (Dichlobenil).* Selective pre-emergence herbicide used around about 30 shrubs and trees. It controls a dozen and a half weeds.

¶ *Chloropicrin.* Very poisonous soil fumigant that also kills soil insects. Do not sow seeds for three weeks.

¶ *Dacthal (DCPA).* A selective pre-emergence herbicide widely used to kill crabgrass in lawns. It also controls a wide variety of weeds in flower beds, ground covers, shrubbery borders and around some trees.

¶ *DMA.* A post-emergence crabgrass killer used on all lawns except those containing bent grass or St. Augustine grass. Two or three applications are usually necessary.

¶ *Mylone (DMTT)*. A soil fumigant that also controls soil fungi and nematodes. Treated soil should not be planted for at least three weeks.

¶ *PMA*. A post-emergence crabgrass killer applied at weekly intervals to lawns.

¶ *Silvex*. A selective translocated herbicide similar to 2, 4, 5-T and often combined with 2, 4-D. It controls many weeds including ground ivy.

¶ *Treflan (Trifluralin)*. A selective pre-emergence herbicide used around various flowers, shrubs and trees to control almost 30 kinds of weeds.

¶ *2, 4-D*. Granddaddy of the selective herbicides, this kills a great many undesirable plants and also, if not used with care, a good many desirable plants.

¶ *2, 4, 5-T*. Another selective translocated herbicide to control many weeds. Often combined with 2, 4-D. It gives excellent control of poison ivy, poison oak and poison sumac.

¶ *Tupersan (Siduron)*. A pre-emergence crabgrass killer for use on most lawns except those containing Bermuda grass and some bents. It is unusual in that it can be applied safely to newly seeded areas.

¶ *Vapam (SMDC)*. Soil fumigant. It also kills soil insects, nematodes and fungi. Wait two to four weeks before planting in treated area.

¶ *Zytron (DMPA)*. A pre-emergence crabgrass killer also effective against several other weeds. Used only in established turf.

HOW TO CONTROL WEEDS AND OTHER PLANT PESTS

¶ *To sterilize soil for a long time*. You probably want to do this only to keep weeds out of areas paved with gravel, bricks laid in sand, etc. Use Ammate.

¶ *To sterilize soil for a short period.* This is done when you wish to free an area of weeds and other plants preparatory to establishing a lawn, starting a cold frame or planting ground covers, flowers, vegetables, etc. Use chloropicrin, Mylone or Vapam.

¶ *To kill woody plants, including poison ivy, poison oak and poison sumac.* Ammate kills almost everything in sight, bad and good, and sterilizes the soil temporarily. 2, 4-D combined with 2, 4, 5-T is somewhat more selective but does not give positive kill in my estimation. On the other hand, it does not sterilize the soil.

¶ *To kill crabgrass in established lawns.* To kill the crabgrass seeds before they germinate, apply Bandane, calcium cyanamid, or one of the other pre-emergence crabgrass killers. To kill growing crabgrass (which is more difficult), spray with DMA or PMA. The younger the crabgrass when it is sprayed, the better luck you will have.

¶ *To kill growing broad-leaved weeds.* Spray or dust with 2, 4-D, 2, 4, 5-T, Silvex or a combination of these chemicals.

¶ *Dodder.* This is a group of parasitic vines that cause stunting and death of small plants. The vines are orange or yellow in color; leafless; but have dense clusters of white, pink or yellow flowers in summer. They twine around plants and have no connection with the ground once they are established. The only way to get rid of the pests is to remove every speck of them from the plants under attack; then burn.

¶ *Mistletoe.* This evergreen parasite found in many parts of the country can injure, deform and even kill the trees in which it becomes established. To control it, cut off a sizable section of the branch that it is attached to.

¶ *Moss* appears in lawns and elsewhere for several reasons: lack of fertility, high soil acidity, poor drainage, etc. Rake it out with a steel rake or kill it with Ammate. Then correct whatever condition allowed it to become established in the first place.

¶ *Mushrooms.* If these become a nuisance in lawn or garden, the USDA recommends punching holes 6 to 8 in. apart and 6 to 8 in. deep around them. Then drench the area with a solution of Dyrene, making sure it seeps into the holes.

HOW TO CONTROL ANIMAL PESTS

¶ *Armadillo.* Grub-proof the soil by applying chlordane in the spring. Or place bombs recommended by your Extension Service in the burrows.

¶ *Birds.* To keep them from eating grass seed before it germinates, cover the seed with a little soil and perhaps with a sprinkling of chopped straw (see Chapter 13). To keep birds away from berries, cover the plants loosely with cheesecloth when the fruit begins to ripen.

Other bird controls include: Firing a shotgun at intervals during the day over the area you are trying to protect (the purpose is to make a lot of noise, not necessarily to kill the birds). Installing automatic noisemakers in the garden. Stringing around and over the garden any kind of device that will move in the breeze; for example, the display decorations used by gas stations.

¶ *Chipmunks.* These are bulb-eaters. Sprinkle Cyanogas in their burrows and seal tight (Cyanogas is deadly to humans and pets). You may also use a Havahart animal trap, which captures but does not kill.

¶ *Deer.* One defense—but an expensive and unsightly one—is an 8-ft. fence. A better idea is to plant plants that deer generally do not eat. Your Agricultural Extension Service should be able to give you a list. If not, write to the California Agricultural Extension Service.

¶ *Dogs.* Various ways to keep your own and neighboring dogs from beating paths across your lawn are discussed in Chapter 13. None is very effective. And I have yet to find an effective way to keep dogs from killing your favorite shrubs. Probably the best is to throw a pail of water over them or to beat them with a rolled newspaper when they offend. You can also surround the plants with wire mesh, though this adds nothing to the beauty of the garden.

¶ *Earthworms* are considered beneficial because they presumably help to increase soil fertility. But if their burrowing spoils the appearance of lawn or garden, they can be eliminated by applying chlordane dust to the soil.

¶ *Gophers.* Properly called pocket gophers because of the pouch-like pockets on both sides of the snout; also known in the South as salamanders. These are widespread, subterranean rodents that throw the soil out of their labyrinthine burrows into large, loose, unsightly mounds. They eat roots, bulbs, tubers and underground stems primarily. Control methods are with traps and poisoned baits.

The best traps are those designed especially for gophers. To use them, dig a narrow trench between two fresh mounds and at right angles to the probable course of the burrow between them. Usually a trench 1 ft. deep and 3 to 4 ft. long will cut the burrow. To be sure of catching a gopher, place one trap in the burrow on one side of the trench. Attach wires to the traps, bring them up out of the trench and tie them to a stake so that, if a gopher is not killed at once, it cannot escape with the trap. Leave the trench open but cover it with a board to keep out dogs. The light and air entering the burrow should bring the gopher running to repair the burrow.

Baits used in poison-control are sweet potatoes, Irish potatoes, carrots, turnips and beets. Cut these into pieces about 1/2 in. across and 1 in. long. Dust powdered strychnine alkaloid or thallium sulfate evenly on the baits. Then open the burrow as when using traps and place a few baits well back in the hole on both sides of the trench. Refill the trench. If fresh earth mounds appear several days after you bait a burrow, try again but with a different vegetable.

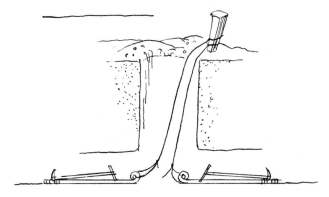

How to trap gophers. Place two traps in runway on either side of the trench you dig across it. Be sure to tie the traps to a stake above ground.

¶ *Ground squirrels* are a western pest that eats the seeds of some vegetables and that may eat fruits and nuts in trees. They live in burrows and can be controlled like gophers.

¶ *Land crabs* are sometimes a pest in Florida. The U.S. Fish and Wildlife Service reports that the most successful control method is to encircle small garden plots with a 12- to 14-in.-high fence of metal flashing above ground and attach to this poultry wire that is buried at least 14 in. under ground. The crabs are unable to burrow under the mesh or to climb over the smooth flashing.

¶ *Mice* sometimes eat the bark of young trees (especially those closely surrounded by a mulch in which the mice can hide), and they also work underground, where they feed on bulbs and succulent roots. They can usually be held in check, however, with poison baits, traps or a cat. To protect bulbs in areas where the mice are running wild, enclose them in wire cages (see Chapter 15).

¶ *Moles* are troublesome enough by themselves; but when you have a dog or cat that likes to dig them out of their runways, trouble is compounded. But you can make your life much easier simply by grub-proofing your lawn every spring with chlordane. Steel traps placed in the runways are another means of control, but not so reliable.

¶ *Muskrat.* Use muskrat traps or put out Warfarin baits, a common rat poison.

¶ *Rabbits.* To protect young trees, circle the trunks loosely with chicken wire which is high enough to keep the rabbits away when snow is deep and which extends about 2 in. below the soil line. The same kind of fencing can also be built around vegetable gardens.

Prepared rabbit repellents and naphthalene flakes scattered around plants are of some help, but not much. A gun and a hungry cat are a lot better.

¶ *Raccoons.* These characters can wreck your corn or berry crops in a single night, and they are wiley enough to elude you for years on end. Try lying in wait for them at night with a flashlight and gun.

¶ *Slugs and snails.* These slow, crawling mollusks—the first without shells; the second, with—are night-workers that chew holes in flowers, vegetables and various other plants. They indicate their presence by leaving silvery trails of mucus. Since they like to hide in damp places under debris during the day, one of the best ways to discourage them is to keep your garden clean. You should also scatter prepared baits containing metaldehyde around the garden. Place the baits under boards, which are attractive to the pests as hiding places and which also keep the poison away from dogs and children.

¶ *Squirrels*, in addition to eating nuts, occasionally go on corn-eating binges that will quickly wreck a crop. Control them by shooting or luring into Havahart traps.

¶ *Woodchucks.* I recommend my pair of Golden Retrievers—or the equivalent—to dispose of these large, burrowing, vegetable-eating pests. Or use a rifle. Or put Cyanogas in the burrows, making sure that you seal *all* the entrances.

TABLE IV
Common Pests of Some Garden Plants

ANDROMEDA: Andromeda lace bug; mites.

APPLE: Tent caterpillar; codling moth; apple curculio; apple maggot; scales; fire blight; scab.

ARBORVITAE: Bagworm; mites; scales; strawberry root weevil.

AZALEA: Lace bug; mites; mealybugs; whitefly; petal blight.

BEAN: Mexican bean beetle; leafhoppers; downy mildew (on lima beans).

BIRCH: Birch leaf miner; cankerworms; aphids.

BOUGAINVILLEA: Caterpillars; scales; leaf spot.

BOXWOOD: Leaf miner; boxwood psyllid; mites; nematodes; canker.

CAMELLIA: Scales; camellia flower blight; dieback.

CHINA ASTER: Leafhopper; aphids; tarnished plant bug; yellows; wilt.

CHRYSANTHEMUM: Aphids; lace bug; nematode; leaf spot; verticillium wilt; powdery mildew.

CITRUS: Aphids; scales; whitefly; orange dog; orange tortrix; scab.

CLEMATIS: Clematis borer; rust; leaf spot; stem rot.

CORN: Corn earworm; European corn borer; smut.

COTONEASTER: Scales; fire blight.

CRABAPPLE: Tent caterpillar; cankerworms; scab; fire blight.

CRAPEMYRTLE: Aphids; powdery mildew.

CUCUMBER: Spotted cucumber beetle; striped cucumber beetle; wilt; mosaic.

DAHLIA: European corn borer; leafhoppers; tarnished plant bug; Japanese beetle; stunt.

DELPHINIUM: Cyclamen mite; delphinium aphid; crown rot.

DOGWOOD: Borer; leaf spot; crown canker.

ELM: Elm leaf beetle; cankerworms; scales; Dutch elm disease.

EUONYMUS: Scales; aphids; crown gall.

GARDENIA: Whitefly; mealybugs; sooty mold.

GLADIOLUS: Thrips; yellows; scab.

GRAPE: Grape phylloxera (an aphid); grape berry moth; leafhoppers; Japanese beetle; rose chafer; black rot.

HAWTHORN: Lace bug; aphids; tent caterpillar; leaf blight; fire blight; cedar-apple and related rusts.

HEMLOCK: Mites; scales; bagworm; strawberry root weevil; caterpillars.

HIBISCUS ROSA-SINENSIS: Aphids; scales; thrips; nematodes.

HOLLY: Leaf miner; mites; scales.

IRIS: Iris borer; aphids; soft rot; crown rot.

IVY: Mites; aphids; scales.

JUNIPER: Scale; mites; bagworm; cedar-apple rust.

LAWNS: Brown patch; fading out; dollar spot; helminthosporium leafspot; snow mold.

LILAC: Borer; scales; powdery mildew.

LILY: Aphids; botrytis; virus diseases.

MAGNOLIA: Scales; mushroom root rot.

MAPLE: Sugar-maple borer; aphids; anthracnose; verticillium wilt.

MOUNTAIN LAUREL: Lace bug; leaf spot.

NARCISSUS: Bulb nematode; botrytis; mosaic.

OAK: Cankerworms; gypsy moth; leaf miners; scales; white oak borer; oak wilt.

OLEANDER: Aphids; scales; oleander caterpillar.

PALMS: Black vine weevil; mites; scales; mealybugs (indoors).

PEACH: Oriental fruit moth; peach tree borer; plum curculio; brown rot; scab; leaf curl.

PEONY: Thrips; rose chafer; botrytis; bud blast.

PHLOX: Mites; powdery mildew.

PINE: Sawflies; webworm; scales; aphids; white-pine weevil; white-pine blister rust.

PITTOSPORUM: Aphids; scales; mealybug; mushroom root rot.

PRIVET: Thrips; mites; scales; whitefly; sooty mold.

PYRACANTHA: Lace bug; fire blight; scab.

RASPBERRY: Sawflies; mosaic; botrytis; anthracnose; cane blight.

RHODODENDRON: Lace bug; borer; black vine weevil.

ROSE: Japanese beetle; aphids; mites; thrips; leafhopper; black spot; powdery mildew.

SPIREA: Aphids.

SPRUCE: Aphids; mites; bagworm; spruce budworm; canker.

SQUASH: Squash borer; squash bug; striped cucumber beetle; wilt; mosaic.

STRAWBERRY: Strawberry root weevil; spittlebugs; tarnished plant bug; leaf spot; botrytis; nematodes.

TOMATO: Cutworm; tomato hornworm; early blight; anthracnose; fusarium; mosaic; blossom-end rot.

TULIP: Aphids; botrytis; mosaic.

YEW: Mealybug; bud mite; strawberry root weevil.

ZINNIA: Japanese beetle; powdery mildew.

11

Cleaning Up the Garden

WITHOUT DOUBT, the most tedious operation in gardening is cleaning up. And nothing I can say will make it less so. Yet it is essential.

For one thing, a tidy garden like a tidy house is far more attractive than a messy one. More important—a clean garden is a healthy one. Our greatest plant doctors maintain that the one best thing the home gardener can do to control many serious insect pests and plant diseases is to clean up the debris in which they thrive. At the same time, keeping the garden clean discourages mosquitoes, flies, rats and other pests bothersome to man, and it helps to protect valuable plants from being damaged by the action of the elements.

¶ *What to clean up.* The type of debris that needs to be removed to keep a garden attractive is obvious. You should be equally aware of the kind that needs to be removed to keep a garden healthy. This includes the following:

Diseased leaves. These should be raked up and burned as soon as you find them. Otherwise the spores or bacteria may be transmitted from them to other plants.

Insect-infested plants. Corn borers, for instance, live and multiply in cut or broken corn stalks.

Weeds. Especially those that are about to set seed.

Grass clippings. Short clippings do not have to be removed from lawns, but long ones should be; otherwise they may act as small blankets that kill the grass underneath.

Broken branches. Diseases often enter trees through breaks in the bark, so cut off broken limbs cleanly and paint the wound if it is over 1 in. in diameter.

Leaves and twigs on the roof. Quite apart from causing leaks, they may cascade down in a soggy or frozen mass that weights down and breaks the plants on which they land.

Dead flowers. If these are not picked off, they start setting seed; and while this does not affect the health of the plant, it interferes with the production of more flowers.

¶ *Good cleanup practices.* The following suggestions will help to simplify the cleanup job and/or produce a healthier, more attractive yard and garden:

¶ *Don't be too neat.* Keeping a garden neat as a pin sometimes has unhappy results. Examples: (1) The leaves that collect around the bases of shrubs are an excellent mulch which turns into valuable humus; if you do not allow them to accumulate, both shrubs and soil may suffer. (2) If you keep soil that does not support plant growth raked too clean, water and wind may cause serious erosion. (3) If your hedges and vines are overly tidy, birds that would like to set up house in their protective cover are driven away.

In other words, a certain amount of mess may be a good thing. And it probably is not so objectionable to look at as you think.

¶ *Don't throw out all the trash that will make good humus.* Admittedly, you may not have space for *all* the leaves, grass clippings, etc., that accumulate over a year. But surely you can find space to pile some of them. You will be amazed how quickly a mountain of leaves turns into a thin layer of leafmold.

¶ *Don't mix dissimilar kinds of debris either when you collect it or when you make a rubbish heap of it.* In short, keep stones separate from branches, branches separate from leaves, leaves separate from weeds, and so forth. Jumbling them all together makes them hard to handle and, when you get around to it, hard to dispose of. In addition, whatever potential humus value some of the debris has is negated by the coarse or weedy stuff mixed with it.

¶ *Shake the soil out of the roots of plants you pull up.* Soil doesn't burn in a bonfire. It interferes with the decomposition of plants piled on a compost heap. And it is probably needed to fill the hole it came out of anyway.

¶ *Toss the trash you collect directly into a cart or basket; try not to make piles that must be picked up later.* All I am suggesting here is that you take two cleanup steps at once. Many people give themselves extra work—especially when cleaning borders—by tossing the trash on the ground and going back later to rake it up and put it in the trash basket. A more sensible practice—and much easier—is to toss the trash straight into the basket.

¶ *Pile the trash where it is to be disposed of.* This recommendation is really the same as the above except that I am here talking about the final disposition of trash.

¶ *When stacking tree limbs and the like, lay them up in parallel rows.* If you pile them every which way, they make a bigger pile that doesn't burn well and that is harder to handle if (heaven forbid) you have to move it.

¶ *Build fires where they will do the least harm.* Obvious, you say. But often ignored, say I. A hot fire not only burns out the grass and soil on which it is built but also does serious damage to surrounding and overhanging trees, even though the flames come nowhere near them.

12

Protecting Plants Against the Weather

THE PROBLEMS OF PROTECTING PLANTS against the many things that can harm them are discussed here and there throughout this book. For how to protect against drought, see Chapters 7 and 8. For how to protect against drowning, see Chapter 2. For how to protect against insects and other pests, see Chapter 10. And the subjects of how to protect against such things as transplanting shock, crowding, salt damage and being blown down by the wind, are covered in several chapters on how to raise different kinds of plants.

This immediate chapter deals with the broad subject of protecting outdoor plants against a variety of hazards which may be rather loosely lumped under the word "weather." And the first bit of advice I must give is a repetition of what was said at the start of Chapter 5: Plant only those species which are known to live happily in your part of the world. To do otherwise is to compound greatly the job of protecting the plants in your garden. And even so you may wind up with a shambles of dead plants.

¶ *Frost* must be ranked as one of the worst enemies of plants. Autumn frosts do little harm because plants start dying down or going into dormancy at this time anyway; however, I must admit that premature frost that lays low a garden that is still yielding a wealth of bloom and fruit is aggravating beyond words. But a spring frost, or a frost that hits the subtropics in winter, *may* be almost catastrophic.

I emphasize the "may" in the preceding sentence because not all frosts are ruthless murderers. Many—usually those that hit early in the fall and late in the spring—damage only the tenderest plants, such as tomatoes, cucumbers, nasturtiums, morning glories and carnations. These are called white frosts, or hoar frosts. But the killing, or black frosts that come later in the fall and earlier in the spring leave little greenery standing.

What can be done to prevent or at least to minimize the damage of a killing frost?

Avoid planting tender plants at the foot of a slope or in a hollow, where frost settles first. Plants on high land are the last to be nipped, because the cold air drains away from them.

If you enclose part of your garden with walls, either keep the walls under 30 in. in height or build louvered or latticed walls. Both measures are designed to encourage the flow of air through your garden and thus to keep it from being a frost trap.

Plant early-flowering fruit trees on a north slope or in another place where they are shielded to some extent from the late winter sun. If the trees are exposed to the full blast of the sun at this season, they may flower early—only to be killed by a late frost.

Broadleaf evergreens should also be shielded from the late winter sun in order to keep the sap from running too soon. If it should freeze, it might expand and burst the bark.

In warm climates, place tender plants where the winter sun will not reach them the first thing in the morning. This gives them a chance to warm up slowly if there has been a frost the preceding night; thus they are better able to shake off the effects of the low temperatures.

When plants are going dormant in the fall, try not to burn outdoor lights near them, because the lights prolong the days and thus retard dormancy. As a result, when there is a sharp frost, the plants (or branches) near the light may be injured while others further away escape because they are more nearly dormant.

There are various ways to help plants survive a frost when you have warning that it is coming. One is to cover small plants with baskets, paper bags. newspapers, burlap, plastic film—almost any-thing that comes to hand. Another is to put some warmth into the garden by hanging a few heat lamps over favorite flowers or by building a charcoal or wood fire in a barbecue brazier with a reflec-tor hood.

Keeping the air moving with electric fans is another effective frost-stopping method. And a fourth—unlikely as it may sound—is to keep a sprinkler going all night when a spring frost threatens. The ice coating that builds up on the leaves and stems protects them from the colder-than-ice night air and allows them to thaw out gradually the next morning.

¶ *Frost in the ground.* Low soil temperature sometimes kill the roots of woody plants; but the alternate freezing and thawing of the soil in the fall or spring is usually more of a problem. It may break tender roots or tubers, or heave them right out of the ground. To guard against this (and also to keep soil temperatures from going dangerously low), apply an organic mulch. Ideally this should remain on the ground the year round. But if for some reason you do not use a mulch in summer, let the soil in which small, easily up-rooted plants are growing freeze and then cover it with a mulch. This will hold in the frost and tend to prevent the freezing-thawing roller coaster.

¶ *Winter damage.* Plants in warm climates are more susceptible to damage caused by freezes that last half a day or more than those in cold climates. In warm areas, you can often protect your most valuable specimens by erecting burlap tents over them (the fabric should be at least 3 in. away from the foliage). Other plants are best protected simply by mounding straw, pine needles or peat up around the lower part of the stems. This permits new growth to spring from the base in case the top is killed.

Heat and air movement may also be used—either one alone or the two together—to pull warm-climate gardens through a freeze. You can use any of the methods discussed previously or the orchardists' smudge pots. Or if you have a large garden, you might lay in a sup-ply of inexpensive petroleum-coke bricks called Tree-Heet. When placed under the canopy of a tree and lighted, two of these will raise the temperature 2° to 2.5°F. for about four hours. Three or four will raise it even more. Yet there is no flame and very little smoke.

One of the most important things you can—and should—do to help shrubs, trees and vines (especially evergreen species of all three) come through the winter is to water them deeply and copiously just before the ground freezes in the fall. Then they will have a source of moisture to draw on even though precipitation is light and the ground freezes hard to a depth of several feet. (Even in dormancy, plants give off moisture through transpiration; and if they cannot replenish themselves through their roots, they dry up and die.)

Another step that should be taken to keep evergreens from being dried out by wind or scorched by the sun is to erect a screen of burlap on the windward or sunny side or even around the entire plant (the fabric should not touch the foliage). Small plants may be encircled with wire mesh which is filled loosely with leaves or hay.

An alternative method that is being used more and more to protect plants against wind and sun (both of which cause loss of moisture) is to spray the foliage—especially on the undersides—with an anti-transpirant, a liquid plastic that forms a thin coating. The first application is made about the time the soil freezes; a second is recommended when the ground begins to thaw in the spring. (The plastic coating sloughs off when new growth starts.)

To prevent heavy snow or ice from crushing evergreen shrubs, such as boxwood, and dense deciduous shrubs, such as *Euonymus alatus*, stretch burlap or snow fencing over them on a sturdy frame. Tie the topmost branches of upright evergreens, such as arborvitae, together. Plants growing under the eaves of buildings are particularly vulnerable to damage by snow and ice sliding off steep roofs and may need to be covered with a slanting roof of plywood. Small plants growing close to driveways should also be covered on top—and perhaps on the driveway side as well—to keep them from being flattened by snow piled up by plows and snowblowers. (If you live in the North, you will often hear it said that a snow cover is good because it insulates plants from deep freeze and puts moisture into the ground. This is true if the cover is composed of fallen or wind-blown snow, which is usually fairly light. But plowed and shoveled snow is dense and heavy and often turns into even weightier ice.)

Old, outstretched tree limbs may break under snow and ice unless supported as shown or with notched 2 x 4's. Fruit trees heavy with fruit often need the same sort of support.

Make a habit of knocking wet snow off large evergreens and—especially—leafed-out deciduous plants during bad storms. To keep outstretched branches of old or brittle trees from breaking under a snow load, support them on 2 x 4's. You should also prop 2 x 4's against the trunks of weak-stemmed plants such as gray birches (but it is better not to use such plants at all if you live in snow country).

Put tall, dark-colored stakes beside all small plants that might be injured by sledders and others cavorting across snowy countryside. Stakes are also needed along driveways to keep the plows off the lawns and away from small plants.

If you live in an area with heavy winter rains and set out plants that are normally covered by snow in winter (alpines, for instance), place conifer boughs above them so they will not be beaten down by the rain.

¶ *Wind*. The twisted cypresses that grow on the coast at Monterey, California, demonstrate the effect that strong winds can have on plants even in a benign climate. Of course if you like the rugged, ragged look of gnarled, weather-beaten trees, that is one thing. But few other kinds of plants are improved by being windblown (this is especially true of flowers), so you should erect a permanent barrier between them and the wind. This can be a hedge, or a windbreak of larger trees; or in areas such as Monterey, where the wind blows out of a gorgeous view, it is fairly common practice to build windshields of clear glass or plastic.

¶ *Stagnant air* has less effect on plants than wind but is sometimes a reason why they do not do well. Why this is we don't really know. But we do know that the spores of fungus pests settle more easily on plants growing in an air pocket than on those growing in a breezy location.

In any case, good air circulation is a garden essential. So avoid setting plants in corners where the air is unusually still. A few plants, such as delphinium, even resent being planted close to a straight wall that shuts off air movement on just one side.

¶ *Bright sun*. Innumerable plants grow best in shade—usually partial shade. But many plants that need sun in northern climates or when grown indoors cannot withstand long exposure to the intense sunlight of the South and Far West when grown outdoors.

Undoubtedly the easiest and least expensive way to protect both kinds of plants is to plant them under a tree, vine or shrub with a high, spreading canopy, or on the east or north side of a wall, fence, hedge or the like. A second solution—but applicable only to small plants and those in containers—is to erect an overhead shield that reduces the amount of sunlight reaching the plants but does not obliterate it completely. To screen plants on a sunny terrace, for instance, you might construct a "roof" of wires to support strips of canvas that are drawn across the terrace from about 10 A.M. to 3

Unusually handsome lath house provides the shade necessary for growing tuberous begonias and other semi-shade-loving plants in an otherwise sunswept location.

Since nothing would grow under this gutterless roof overhang, owners installed a gravel strip directly underneath. Shrubs are tucked back close to the house wall. Lawn around this Chicago home is kept very small to reduce mowing and other upkeep.

P.M. on bright summer days. Or you might build a permanent lath screen over the plants.

The latter kind of structure is found in many California gardens. Called a lath shelter, it may be designed strictly for the protection of plants; or it may cover an entire patio. In any case, the structure consists of a flat or sloping roof made of 2- or 3-in.-wide strips of wood (actual wood plaster laths are used only in crude structures) laid parallel and spaced the width of the strips apart. The strips run north and south (never east and west) so that they cast a constantly changing pattern of half-sun-half-shadow on the plants below. If additional protection is needed, lath walls may also be built.

¶ *Reflected light.* The effect of light reflected off a light-colored wall or paving is often overlooked. But it should not be. Plants set close to a white wall in full sun may be badly burned. And even though a shade-loving plant is growing in the shade, if it is near a wall that reflects a lot of light, it may be as badly retarded as if it were exposed directly to the sun. Moral: Maybe you should build outdoor walls and terraces of darker-colored material. (An additional advantage of dark paving is that the heat it absorbs during the day may help a little to protect nearby plants from frost at night. On the other hand, a terrace paved in dark material can be uncomfortable to sit on on a sunny day.)

¶ *Thunderstorms* do damage in the garden by battering small plants, eroding the soil and shattering mighty trees. Unfortunately, there is no practical way to prevent the first problem. The second, however, is readily stopped by slowing runoff with terraces, rocks and ground covers. As for the third problem, there is no way to predict which trees will be struck by lightning in the next storm; but it occasionally happens that one tree stands out like the Empire State Building, and is struck time and time again. If you have such a tree, you should consider protecting it with lightning rods.

¶ *Heavy rain* plays havoc with plants growing close to the house. For one thing, if you have no gutters, the water falling from the roof eventually kills the small plants below. So if you value your garden, you should either put gutters on the house or move the plants out from under the roof edge and put a drip strip of gravel between them and the foundation wall.

But gutters can create problems, too. When they are clogged, rain water thunders right on over them onto the plants below. Even worse —in winter the roof edges become festooned with giant icicles which crush plants as easily as a landslide. Fortunately, the solution to both problems is easy and obvious. Clean leaves and twigs out of the gutters regularly, especially in the fall.

¶ *Hail.* Even if you live in an area of frequent hailstorms, there is next to nothing you can do to protect your entire garden—or even a large part of it—against them. However, you may well find it worthwhile to put a roof of 1/2-in. wire mesh over choice specimens until the storm has passed.

13

How to Make
and Maintain a Lawn

A GOOD LAWN IS THE PRODUCT of hard work. But a poor lawn is hard work, too. So you really have little choice. If you are going to have a lawn at all, you might as well try to make it the best possible.

¶ *Designing the lawn.* The amount of maintenance that a lawn requires depends not only on the climate, soil, quality of grass, etc., but also on the way the lawn is laid out originally. It is very important to plan it with care. A number of things can be done to make maintenance easier.

(1) Round the corners. This permits continuous mowing: you don't have to stop and turn the mower at sharp corners.

(2) Don't plant trees in the lawn. If you can't bring yourself to do this, at least do not plant grass under trees; circle them instead with a ground cover, mulch or gravel.

(3) Make all paved areas flush with the lawn so that you can roll your mower easily from one surface to another. There is also less trimming.

(4) Build mowing strips between the lawn and all borders, tree pockets and walls. Mowing strips are continuous strips of brick, concrete, stone or wood, no less than 3-in. wide and set flush with the lawn. Their purpose is to support one wheel of the mower so that you can mow the edges of the lawn during normal mowing opera-

tions. Thus they eliminate hand trimming. They also prevent grass roots from creeping into surrounding borders.

(5) Provide a small paved area around lawn obstructions such as clothes poles, oil tank fill pipes, etc. This eliminates trimming.

(6) Provide grass or paved ramps between all lawn areas. They make it easy to roll the mower from one place to another.

(7) Depress gravel areas below the lawn and provide a curbing of steel, redwood, etc., between them. This helps to keep gravel out of the grass.

(8) Avoid planting grass where it will be difficult or dangerous to mow. Use ground covers instead. Substitute walls for banks.

(9) Avoid building a lawn athwart a heavily traveled path. If this is impossible, pave the path.

¶ *Preparing the soil.* Soil preparation for grass differs in one respect from that for other kinds of plants. You should not turn the topsoil under and bring the subsoil to the surface unless you find it necessary to plant cover crops prior to planting the grass (see Chapter 3).

If you don't need to improve your soil with cover crops, the proper procedure to follow in preparing for a lawn is this: If the grade needs to be changed, strip off the topsoil to a depth of between 4 to 6 in. and pile it to one side; then bring the subsoil to the proper grade. Be sure it slopes away from the house (thus assuring that the water will drain away from the foundations). Eliminate hollows in which water will stand. Now mix phosphate fertilizer lightly into the subsoil. Mix in lime if needed. Then spread the topsoil evenly over the subsoil.

For a good lawn you should have at least 4 in. of topsoil, and preferably more. If the soil is not good, mix in 2 to 4 cu. yd. of humus or sand or a combination of the two per 1000 sq. ft. of lawn area. At the same time, if the soil is very acid, add still more lime according to Table I on page 30. (If you add lime to the topsoil, you should now wait at least one week before proceeding with the rest of your work. If lime is not used, no waiting time is required.)

Your next step is to mix fertilizer into the topsoil. You can use any complete inorganic fertilizer such as those listed in Table V (page 165). Apply it at the rate shown in the table.

This southern Florida lawn is made of Ormond Bermudagrass. It must be kept short and watered sparingly to prevent fungus disease. In the spring it is renovated by cutting it close to the root tops and then cutting it vertically with rotating knives. Concrete mowing strip minimizes necessity for edging the lawn by hand, also keeps gravel from path out of the grass.

TABLE V
Fertilizer Application Rates for Lawns

Type of fertilizer	Pounds applied per 1000 sq. ft. if the soil is:		
	Unusually fertile	Average fertility	Infertile
5-10-5	20	40	60
4-12-4	25	50	75
5-10-10	20	40	60
10-10-10	10	20	30
8-8-8	13	25	38
10-6-4	10	20	30
8-6-4	13	25	38
4-8-4	25	50	75
6-12-4	17	34	50
16-8-8	6	13	19
18-6-9	6	11	17

The alternative, if you want to kill the weed seeds in the soil, is to apply 50 lb. of superphosphate, 20 lb. of muriate of potash and 60 lb. of calcium cyanamid to each 1000 sq. ft. of soil. The calcium cyanamid acts not only as a herbicide but also as a source of nitrogen. In addition, it helps to decompose whatever vegetable matter is in the soil. When it is used, you must keep the soil damp for six weeks. Do not plant grass seed during this period.

¶ *Seeding.* Most of the lawn grasses used in the northern half of the U.S. are grown from seed, and by far the best time to sow the seed is in late summer and early fall. Spring sowing is permissible but does not produce a first-class lawn because of the hot sun and the weed competition.

Most people use a grass-seed mixture containing two, three or sometimes even more types of grass. Such mixtures help to prevent widespread damage of lawns by disease since the different grasses have varying degrees of resistance to turf diseases. Some people, however, prefer a single type of grass since it gives a more uniform appearance. I suggest that you use whatever is recommended by a good local garden supply store, landscape architect or other local authority. The rate of application is usually printed on the seed package, or you can apply at the rate shown in Table VI.

TABLE VI
Rate of Applying Grass Seed
(Source: USDA)

Grass—seeded types	Pounds of seed per 1000 sq. ft
Bahia grass	2 - 3
Bermuda grass	2 - 3
Buffalo grass (treated)	½ - 1
Canada bluegrass	2 - 3
Carpet grass	3 - 4
Centipede grass	2 - 3
Chewings fescue	3 - 5
Colonial bent grass (Highland, Astoria)	1 - 2
Creeping bent glass (Seaside)	1 - 2
Japanese lawn grass (hulled)	1 - 2
Kentucky bluegrass	2 - 3
Merion Kentucky bluegrass	1 - 2
Red fescue	3 - 5
Redtop	1 - 2
Rough bluegrass	3 - 5
Rye grass (domestic and perennial)	4 - 6
Tall fescue (Alta, Ky. 31)	4 - 6
Velvet bent grass	1 - 2
Mixture for sunny areas: 75% bluegrass, 25% red fescue	2 - 4
Mixture for shady areas: 25% bluegrass, 75% red fescue	2 - 4

Grass—vegetative types	Amount of material per 1000 sq. ft.
Bermuda grass	10 sq. ft. of sod or 1 bu. of stolons
Buffalo grass	25-50 sq. ft. of sod
Carpet grass	8-10 sq. ft. of sod
Centipede grass	8-10 sq. ft. of sod
Creeping bent grass	80-100 sq. ft. of sod or 10 bu. of stolons
Velvet bent grass	80-100 sq. ft. of sod or 10 bu. of stolons
Zoysia	30 sq. ft. of sod when plugging; 6 sq. ft. of sod when sprigging

Minnesota lawn is made of bluegrass and fescue. Because the climate and soil seem to be especially favorable for grass, the lawn thrives with little attention under the tall trees. Neat, low hedge is of ninebark (Physocarpus), *an extremely hardy deciduous shrub.*

Before seeding a new lawn, rake the soil surface thoroughly with a steel rake. Remove stones and trash. If sowing by hand, mix the seed with a little sand or fine topsoil. This will help you to spread it more evenly. Then divide it into two equal parts and sow one part in one direction and the second part at right angles to this.

If you sow the seed with a spreader, take care not to overlap the strips so much that you produce an uneven stand of grass. Whether sowing is done with a spreader or by hand, the best way to make certain that you apply enough seed is to divide the lawn into 1000-sq. ft. sections (or smaller) and to apply to each section the weighed-out quantity of seed called for on the package.

After sowing, cover the seed lightly by raking with the back of a rake. Even if some of the seeds are not buried, they will come up; but be warned that they will also make excellent fodder for birds. Roll the soil very *lightly* with a water-filled steel garden roller from a tool-rental outlet. Then dampen the surface thoroughly with a gentle spray, and keep it moist—but not soaking wet—until the grass is well established.

To help keep the soil moist, to protect it from beating rains and to keep the seeds from washing away, you can cover the seeded area with a light scattering of weed-free hay or chopped straw. This will not interfere with the growth of the grass and need not be removed.

On slopes, to protect against erosion, cover the seeded soil with cheesecloth or commercial mulching cloth. This will rot away after the grass comes up through it.

Southern grasses which are grown from seed are handled in the same way. They are best planted in the spring, however.

¶ *Vegetative planting.* A number of grasses either do not come true from seeds or do not produce enough seeds for sowing. These must be planted by plug (or spot) sodding, strip sodding, sprigging or stolonizing. In warm climates, where most grasses of this type are grown, planting is done in late spring or early summer; but bent grass, which is grown in the North as well as the South, is planted in the fall.

Rake the soil well and remove all foreign matter. In plug sodding, the small pieces of sod (plugs) are planted by trowel in straight rows. The plugs are usually set 12 in. apart each way; but for faster coverage, the spacing may be reduced to 8 in.

In strip sodding, the sod is cut into strips 2 to 4 in. wide. These are laid end to end in rows 12 in. apart.

Sprigging is the most economical way to start a lawn by vegetative means. The sprigs are tiny pieces of rooted grass torn out of sods. They are best planted in straight rows 8 in. apart in both directions. (In the case of slow-spreading zoysia, however, the spacing should be 4 to 6 in. apart.)

Stolonizing is recommended only for very large lawns. Sods are shredded into small pieces which are spread by mechanical equipment. They are then embedded in the soil by disking, or by covering with additional topsoil and rolling.

Whatever planting method you use, the grass plants must be watered soon after they are in the ground, and they should be kept moist thereafter until they are established. To hasten the spread of the plants, fertilize them lightly every two to four weeks during the first growing season with nitrogenous fertilizer or a balanced fertilizer rich in nitrogen.

¶ *Sodding.* This is the most expensive way to establish a lawn but by far the quickest and easiest. It can be done at any time during the growing season. Soil preparation is the same as for seeding or vegetative planting, but there is no need for pretreatment of the soil with a herbicide because the thick covering of grass chokes out most weeds that try to push up through. After final raking of the soil, roll it lightly.

The sods should be 3/4 in. thick—definitely not more than 1 in. thick. Place them as close together as possible, tamp lightly, brush or rake a little topsoil into the joints, and keep watered until the grass takes hold.

¶ *To renovate an old lawn.* If a lawn is more or less uniformly poor—filled with weeds and bare patches—it is easier to tear up the whole thing and start fresh than to make repairs. However, if a lawn is poor only in spots or if the grass is simply a little thin, renovation is recommended.

Lawn renovation on a small scale can be done at any time during the growing season; but on a large scale, it should be done in early fall in the North and in late spring in the South. Use the same grass that is already growing in the lawn; otherwise you will create a patchwork quilt. If you live in the North and cannot identify the old grass, reseed with a grass-seed mixture: the new grass will blend in better with the old than a single type of grass.

To improve a lawn that has a uniform but thin stand of grass, cut the grass close and then run over it with a gasoline-powered lawn renovator. This removes embedded leaves and grass clippings (thatch) and slices vertically into the surface soil, thus increasing its porosity. Then apply grass seed at the rate specified in Table VI (page 166). Apply fertilizer at the rate called for in the second column of Table V (page 165). Water well.

To repair small bare or weedy patches in a lawn, pull out the unwanted vegetation and break up the soil to a depth of several inches by slicing into it with any sharp instrument. Then sprinkle on some seeds and tamp lightly. For faster results, dig up the small grass plants that have sprouted in flower beds, the driveway and other places and plant these in the bare spots.

If bare or weedy patches are of considerable size, spade the soil to a depth of 6 in. or more and pulverize well. Then apply fertilizer, lime and/or herbicide as necessary. Reseed. Cover with brush or hay to keep off dogs and children.

¶ *Routine maintenance. Spring care.* No matter where you live, the job of getting a lawn off to a good start in late winter or spring is the same: (1) Rake it vigorously to remove dead grass, clippings, leaves, etc. If the thatch is very thick, use an engine-driven lawn renovator. (2) Sow grass seed in thin spots. (3) If the soil is a heavy clay, go over the entire lawn with a gasoline-driven aerator. On porous soil, aeration is called for only when the soil has been compacted by heavy traffic. (4) Tamp down hummocky spots but do not pound any harder than necessary. By the same token, if you roll the lawn, use a light roller not a heavy one. Too much rolling or tamping often makes the soil too dense to support good grass.

¶ *Fertilizing.* The total amount of fertilizer applied annually to northern grasses should at least equal and can exceed the figures in the third column of Table V (that is, if you are using a 5-10-5 fertilizer, you should apply 60 lb. per 1000 sq. ft. during the course of the year). Approximately one-third of the total amount of fertilizer should be applied in early spring. The remainder should be applied all at once in early autumn or, better, half on about September 1 and the remaining half on about October 1. Use fast-acting fertilizer in the fall. In the spring, you can use either fast-acting or slow-acting fertilizer, but the latter is preferable.

The fertilizer requirements of warm-climate grasses vary. Bermuda grass should be given at least twice the amount of fertilizer shown in the third column of Table V. Five or six equal feedings should be made from early spring to late fall.

Magnificent lawn in San Francisco Bay area was planted with a mixture of perennial rye, creeping red fescue and Kentucky bluegrass. Lawn is fed in early spring, summer and late fall with a slow-acting, high-nitrogen fertilizer. It is cut very short in winter to discourage fungi, and is left rather long in summer, when there is little rain.

St. Augustine grass and zoysia should be given about twice the amount of fertilizer shown in the second column of Table V. Make three or four applications during the growing season.

Other warm-climate grasses, such as carpet grass, need only two or three feedings. The total of these should equal the figures in the third column of Table V.

¶ *Liming.* On acid soils make light applications of lime every second or third year. If the soil contains a great deal of clay, every other application should be a heavy one.

Although it does not make a great deal of difference when you lime a lawn, late fall or winter application is recommended. Do not apply nitrogen fertilizer for at least a week after that.

¶ *Watering.* How often your lawn should be watered and how much water it should be given depend on the rainfall, rate of evaporation of soil moisture, type of soil, etc. (see Chapter 7). The only accurate way to keep track of your lawn's water needs is to bury tensiometers at several points. Lacking these, your best bet is simply to make sure that the lawn receives 1 in. of water per week throughout the growing season (in warm, dry climates, where the evaporation rate is high, you will probably need more than 1 in. of water). If all or part of this water is applied by hose, apply it all at once, but slowly, not in a series of light springlings.

¶ *Mowing.* Keep your mower sharp; a dull blade bruises or tears the grass leaves.

There is considerable debate about whether grass clippings should be removed from the lawn after each cutting; and at this writing, the majority of turf experts seem to think they should be on the theory that, while the clippings form a splendid mulch, they may also encourage insect and disease attack. However, there is no very conclusive evidence that clippings less than 3/4 in. long do any harm. So the argument is pretty academic. From the standpoint of the weary gardener, this much can be said for certain: If you do not remove the clippings, you may have to mow the lawn a couple of times a week during the periods when the grass is growing in excess of 3/4 in. per week. By removing the clippings, therefore, you can

Hawaiian lawn is made of Tifton Bermudagrass. If kept short, fertilized every two months and watered frequently, it grows well in both sun and fairly deep shade. Because the soil here is naturally very shallow and underlain with volcanic rock, planting holes for the trees had to be blasted out and then filled with imported soil.

reduce frequency of mowing somewhat because you can let the grass grow longer between mowings. On the other hand, the actual job of removing grass clippings is a chore, even when you use the most efficient grass catchers; pushing a mower through tall grass is more difficult than going through shorter grass and produces a less even cut; and some physiological damage is done to grass when its height is sharply reduced. Conclusion: I personally am opposed to grass-clipping removal except when the clippings are very long (which, of course, they never should be).

Mowing should be started in the spring as soon as grass makes growth and it should be continued into the late fall, or until growth stops. Going into the winter with a thick mat of grass is an invitation to disease problems.

Northern lawn grass should be mowed to a height of 1 1/2 to 2 in. (bent grass, however, can be cut as close as 1/2 in.). If cut closer than this, especially in hot weather, grass may be burned out and lose its ability to overshadow weeds. Newly established grass should not be cut for the first time until it is at least 1 1/2 in. tall.

Bermuda grasses should be mowed to a height of 1/2 in. plus or minus 1/8 in. Other warm-climate grasses are mowed to a height of 1 in. New grass should not be cut for the first time until it is 75% taller than these figures.

There is no ideal mowing technique. Each gardener must go at the job in the way that best suits his lawn and himself. As noted earlier, however, you do save work if you mow, in effect, in continuous circles starting at the outer rim and working toward the center. If you use a rotary mower, the clippings should be thrown outward so that you do not mow over them and add to the work your mower must do.

An important point to be noted about using a power mower—especially a rotary—is that this is an exceedingly dangerous machine that has caused many fatal accidents. Here are rules suggested by the Outdoor Power Equipment Institute for using mowers:

¶ *Before mowing*
(1) Read owner's manual and know controls thoroughly before you start. Learn how to stop your machine quickly.

(2) Fill gas tank before starting. Filling a hot tank or a running engine can mean an explosion. Don't smoke while you fill the tank.

(3) Clear area of children and pets. They make good targets for flying debris tossed from your mower's discharge chute.

(4) Clean lawn of foreign objects that can be picked up and thrown by the blades.

¶ *While mowing*

(1) Keep feet clear of mower's blades at all times. A rotary's blade traveling at speeds of up to 2500 r.p.m. can do incalculable harm.

(2) Stay away from mower's discharge side. Foreign objects picked up by the mower's blades are hurled out at bullet speed.

(3) Push, do not pull the mower. You might pull it over your feet.

(4) Stop engine before pushing mower from one surface to another. It might pick up and hurl a stone.

(5) Stop engine whenever you leave the mower, even for a moment. A running mower can present a strong temptation for some playful youngster.

(6) Do not unclog while it is running. This is the most common cause of mowing accidents.

(7) Mow steep slopes sideways. Mowing up and down, you can be dragged under the mower or the mower can come down on top of you.

(8) Do not allow children to operate mower. Some states have laws prohibiting persons under 18 from using a power lawn mower.

(9) Stop engine and disconnect spark plug wire before storing or working on mower. A mower's blade is like an airplane propeller—one turn and it may start up.

¶ *If you are using a riding mower* (in addition to the rules above)

(1) Do not carry passengers. This is one of the most common causes of riding mower mishaps.

(2) Watch for holes and hidden hazards.

(3) Look behind before backing.
(4) Watch traffic near roadways. Try to keep your mower off roads. If you must use public thoroughfares, exercise extreme caution.
(5) Don't wear loose-fitting clothing. It can get caught in the machine's exposed moving parts.

¶ *Weeding.* The best way to control crabgrass in an existing lawn is to apply a pre-emergence herbicide such as Dacthal before the end of April. (Inasmuch as most of these chemicals also kill the seed of good grass, you usually must wait several months before sowing grass seed.) If crabgrass appears despite this treatment, treat it as soon as you discover it with a post-emergence herbicide (see Chapter 10).

Broadleaf weeds are readily eradicated by dusting or spraying when they appear with 2, 4-D or Silvex. These chemicals should be used only when you can be sure of a 12-hour dry spell. Do not mow the grass for about four days after application is made. Many weeds will disappear within several weeks after they are first treated. Some may need a second treatment (see Chapter 10).

If a lawn that needs renovation in the fall is widely infested with miscellaneous weeds, a quick way to solve the problem is to spray the entire lawn with cacodylic acid. This knocks down all plant life, including grass, but it has no residual effect to speak of in the soil; consequently, you can reseed the treated areas within two days (see Chapter 10).

¶ *Other problems.* For how to cope with moss, insects, fungi, moles, worms, etc., in lawns, see Chapter 10.

¶ *To improve the level of an existing lawn.* Rolling to level the lawn is not the answer. It does more harm than good.

To eliminate a high spot, carefully remove the sod from the area. Dig out the excess soil and bring what remains to the proper grade. Then replace the sods, tamp lightly and fill the joints with a little topsoil.

To eliminate a low spot, spread screened topsoil in the depression to a depth not greater than 1/2 in. This will not kill the grass you have covered (provided the tops are showing). If additional fill is necessary, repeat the process after the grass re-established itself.

¶ *The shade problem.* Grass rarely grows in deep shade, and most grasses have trouble even in fairly light shade—especially if the roots of the shade-making plants are close to the surface. However, some varieties are more tolerant of shade than others. The best of the northern grasses are red fescue followed by Chewings fescue. The best of the southern grasses are St. Augustine (for the deep South) and a form of zoysia, called Manila grass, for the mid-South.

Even with these grasses, special care is necessary. This should include:

(1) Fertilize heavily in the spring to give the grass a head start on the tree above it, and fertilize frequently, though lightly, through the growing season. In addition, to keep the tree roots from competing too vigorously for the grass food, fertilize them through holes punched deep in the soil (see Chapter 4).

(2) Thin out overhanging tree foliage as much as possible. Remove low branches especially.

(3) Cut out shallow tree roots as much as possible. They compete for fertilizer. Their loss will not damage the tree.

(4) Lime the soil if it becomes too acid.

¶ *Winter protection.* Snow mold and other fungus diseases often attack lawns in winter. The best way to guard against them is to cut the grass short in the late fall. Avoid late fall applications of nitrogen fertilizer, which stimulate growth at a time it is not wanted. For maximum protection, apply a turf fungicide such as Dyrene to the lawn after the first killing frost. Make a second application in mid-winter if there is no snow on the ground.

14

How to Raise Annuals, Perennials and Biennials

Here are most of the flowers we all know and love.

In 1966, after crisscrossing the country to photograph magnificent gardens from Boston to Haena, Hawaii, and from Seattle to Palm Beach, I wound up in the Berkshire Mountains of Massachusetts to look at just one more garden. It was a very simple place over-all, but in one corner was a half-acre garden of annuals, perennials and biennials. Nothing I had seen in this vast country was prettier, more varied, more exciting, more colorful.

Anyone who thinks we can live happily with fewer of these flowers (and there are plenty of minimum-maintenance gardening advocates who do) is slightly daft.

Annuals bloom the first year they are planted and then die. Biennials generally bloom the second year after they are planted and then die. Perennials generally bloom the second year after they are planted and live on for many years. Despite these differences, all are raised in much the same way.

¶ *Laying out a flower bed.* A flower bed can be any shape and length you choose; but if you want to get at the flowers in back without stepping all over those in front, you must limit its width. Beds that are accessible from only one side should not be more than 30 in. wide; those accessible from both sides should not be more than 60 in. wide.

Generally, you will do best to place the tallest flowers in back; the medium heights in the middle; and the smallest in front. But don't hesitate to place clumps of middle-size varieties here and there in both background and the foreground.

Arrange flowers of the same variety in roughly semicircular or oval clumps of five to seven plants. Use the same flowers in several places in the bed. The clumps should run lengthwise of the bed and should overlap some of the clumps in front and some of those in back (in other words, the clumps are arranged like a stack of eggs, not like a neatly tiered stack of bricks). For variation, some clumps can be laid out as long, ribbon-like drifts containing a dozen or more plants. Compact clumps of three or four tall plants can be used for accents.

To assure the best possible arrangement of a flower bed, measure it accurately and draw a plan to scale on a piece of graph paper. Then sketch in the flower clumps.

The space to allow between individual plants is one of the hardest things for beginning gardeners to figure out. Table VII (page 187) gives the spacing that is generally recommended for the various popular annuals, perennials and biennials. But I recommend that you allow less, especially for the plants requiring the most space. Some of the flowers may not develop quite as well as they should; but in overall, the bed will appear tighter, less spotty and with much more color.

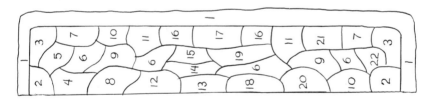

A flower bed is usually laid out in overlapping clumps, with the tallest varieties toward the back of the bed. This is a plan for a pink, white and blue annual border: 1. White sweet alyssum. 2. Blue arctotis. 3. Blue bedding petunia. 4. Pink zinnia. 5. Rose phlox. 6. White nicotiana. 7. Pale yellow nasturtium. 8. Yellow marigold. 9. Blue lupine. 10. Rose petunia. 11. Red celosia. 12. Pink cleome. 13. Rose-pink lavatera. 14. Maroon zinnia. 15. White zinnia. 16. Blue Chinese forget-me-not. 17. White petunia. 18. Pink cleome. 19. Pink phlox. 20. Yellow marigold. 21. Rose petunia. 22. Salmon-pink phlox.

One other thing to remember in laying out a flower bed is that perennials and biennials usually bloom for only a month or two—some species in the spring, some in summer, and some in fall. Therefore, if you want your flower bed to look more or less evenly full of color all the time, you should spot the spring bloomers, summer bloomers and fall bloomers throughout the bed. And you should also mix annuals—which bloom for most of the summer—in amongst them.

¶ *Seedings.* Annuals and biennials are usually raised from seeds. Perennials can also be raised from seeds but are brought to blooming stage faster if you start with divisions or, in a couple of instances, with stem cuttings.

The time and place for sowing the seeds of annuals are indicated in Table VII. Some annual seeds are sown directly where the plants are to grow as soon as the soil can be worked in the spring. These are technically known as hardy annuals, because they can withstand considerable cold and frost. Other annuals are called half-hardy (able to withstand a little cold, but not much) or tender (unable to withstand any cold). These are either seeded outdoors after all frost danger is past, or started under glass eight weeks before the last frost and then moved outdoors. The second course is the better because it assures a longer period of bloom.

Perennials and biennials are usually seeded outdoors in a nursery bed any time after the last frost through the end of June. Occasionally July and August sowing is recommended; but this is an English practice which is applicable only to warm U.S. climates.

(A very few perennials and biennials develop so rapidly that they will make some bloom the first year. These are often handled as tender annuals: started indoors, or in a cold frame, before the last frost.)

For the technique of raising plants from seeds, see Chapter 5.

¶ *Planting seedlings.* Plants that are seeded indoors in sand, vermiculite or sphagnum moss should be transplanted into soil in a larger flat (or in separate small pots or plant bands) when they get their second set of leaves, or first true leaves. (Seedlings growing in soil indoors or out may also be moved at this stage, but generally are not.)

Lift the seedlings gently from the flat in which they started life with a dull knife. Separate the plants. (Use tweezers to do this if the seedlings are too small to handle with your fingers.) Then with your knife make slits about 1 in. apart in the soil in the new flat and drop the roots of a single seedling into each slit. Firm the soil, and water thoroughly, using a fine spray, with a starter solution made by dissolving a concentrated plant food in water according to the manufacturer's directions. Keep the flat out of the direct sun for a day or two until the seedlings have recovered from the shock of being moved. Then move them into the sunlight until they are ready to be transplanted outdoors.

¶ *Hardening off.* If small plants that are grown from seeds under sheltered conditions are moved directly into the garden, the abrupt change in temperature and sunlight is likely to set them back and perhaps even kill them. To live outdoors, they need to become acclimated or—in gardening parlance—hardened off.

To harden off plants that have been growing indoors, all you have to do is move them outdoors for a longer and longer time each day for about a week before they are transplanted. Or if you have a cold frame, you can move the plants directly from the house into the frame for several weeks. In either case, increase exposure to the sun gradually for the first couple of days.

To harden off plants that have been started in a cold frame (or hotbed) or moved into a cold frame from indoors, gradually increase the amount of outside air you admit to the frame (see Chapter 6).

¶ *Transplanting small plants.* The technique is the same whether you are handling plants that have been growing indoors or in a cold frame, or those that are already in the garden. Annuals are transplanted in the spring when frost danger is past. New perennials and biennials are transplanted in late August or early September, or early the next spring when they are one year old.

If possible, the transplanting should be done on a cloudy day or in the late afternoon. This helps to prevent wilting.

Several hours before moving the plants, water them enough to

This rose and perennial garden is designed primarily to provide cutting flow-ers. Garden is laid out in long, straight, narrow beds, and plants are mainly in rows. Nevertheless, the flowers are so luxuriant that the garden is very pretty.

How to plant a seedling. As it is firmed in place, a small saucer is pressed into the soil around it with your fingers. This holds water and/or starter solution (liquid fertilizer).

make the soil stick to their roots. (If the soil is too wet, however, it is difficult to handle.)

Spade the soil in which the plants are to be set to a depth of 12 in. and pulverize it well. Add peat and sand as necessary. Then with a trowel scoop out holes for the plants.

Dig the plants from their flats with as much soil around the roots as possible. Set them in their permanent planting holes at the same level they were growing previously. Spread out the roots *if* the soil around them has dropped off; otherwise, leave them alone. Then fill the holes with soil and firm it well, leaving a small saucer-shaped depression around each plant. Fill the depression with a starter solution.

¶ *Growing requirements.* With some exceptions (see Table VII), annuals, perennials and biennials will take as much sun as you can give them. Their soil requirements vary, but most are well satisfied if you provide a reasonably light, deeply drained, neutral soil containing a fair amount of humus.

Water should be applied slowly and directly to the soil whenever the surface looks dry. Spray the foliage (in the morning) only if the plants get covered with dust or soot.

Keep the soil cultivated, weeded and, if possible, mulched. Fertilize annuals and less-than-year-old perennials and biennials two weeks after they are planted outside and at monthly intervals twice thereafter. Established perennials and second-year biennials should be fertilized as soon as growth starts in the spring and at four- to six-week intervals until they bloom.

In cold climates, tuck a light mulch of salt hay or evergreen boughs around (but not over) perennials and biennials after the ground is frozen.

¶ *Labeling.* Labels tell you where you have planted and what you have planted. Use them for all individual plants or groups of similar plants. Small, flat wooden labels—preferably white-painted—are excellent for newly seeded plants. Long-lasting, T-shaped plastic labels are recommended for established perennials because they last longer than wood and you don't have to stoop or twist sideways to read them.

¶ *Staking* is necessary to prevent some flowers from sprawling, to stiffen others against the wind, and to protect heavy flower spikes.

The best way to support sprawling or spreading species, such as platycodon, gypsophila and peonies, is to place tall collars of green wire mesh around them before they start to grow, or to set five or six 12- to 18-in. steel stakes around them and then to loop green twine from stake to stake.

Tall, upright species, such as cosmos, and those with large flower spikes such as delphiniums and hollyhocks, can be supported by single sturdy stakes of green bamboo or wood. Tie the plant stems to the stakes at 12-in. intervals with green twine or Twist-'ems. The loops should be loose around the stems and tight around the stakes. Patented metal stakes with a flat loop at the top may be used instead of ordinary wood or bamboo stakes but are more expensive and less sturdy.

¶ *Dividing established perennials.* If perennials are well grown, they usually need to be divided every second year. Chrysanthemums, however, should be divided every year. But peonies, Oriental poppies and bleeding heart resent being disturbed and should not be divided until they begin to put out smaller flowers or otherwise show they are losing vitality.

The technique for making divisions is described in Chapter 5. Replant the divisions in the way that you handle young plants (see above).

¶ *Disbudding* is one of the simplest but most important practices in flower growing. It is a form of pruning that involves nipping off buds with your fingernails in order to promote bushier growth and/ or bigger flowers.

For instance, in order to make little marigolds, zinnias, petunias and other annuals develop side branches, you should remove the terminal buds that first develop. (This practice is also called pinching back.)

Similarly, to make peonies and dahlias and other perennials develop blooms of maximum size, you should preserve the terminal buds but nip off the side buds. If a plant sends up an inordinate number of stems, you should also remove some of the weaker ones while they are small in order to stimulate stronger growth and better bloom.

To make seedlings and other spindling plants bush out, nip off one or more of the topmost buds with your fingernails. This is called pinching or disbudding.

¶ *Growth regulating.* Another way to make flowers bushier is to treat them with a growth regulator called B-Nine developed by Uni-Royal, Inc. This not only produces more compact plants with shorter stems but also promotes better flowering and leaves of darker green. In addition, treated plants are more resistant to drought and smog. And of course you do not have to disbud them in the way described just above.

TABLE VII
Annuals, Perennials and Biennials

This list is a practical guide to the propagation, location and spacing of favorite flowers and ornamental grasses.

The key to the abbreviations in the list is as follows:

A — annual
P — perennial
B — biennial
P as A — perennial grown as an annual
B as A — biennial grown as an annual
I — raise from seed started indoors about eight weeks before last frost. (Many of these plants can also be seeded outdoors where they are to grow after the last frost; but this greatly shortens the period of bloom.)
OALF — sow seed outdoors where plants are to grow after last frost
OWSW — sow seed outdoors where plants are to grow when soil is workable
* — usually propagated by vegetative means—in most cases, by division but in several cases by stem cuttings
S — grow in sun
Sh — grow in partial shade

The figures in the column headed "Space required (inches)" should not be taken too literally. Most plants in the average garden can be set somewhat closer together if you wish. Plants with a listing of "Spr." are spreading types that will often cover considerable ground if not pruned and divided regularly. When two figures separated by a hyphen are given it means simply that different varieties require different spacing. Plants marked "V" are vines.

	Type of plant	When & where to seed	Exposure	Space required (in.)
Acanthus mollis	P	OALF	Sh	24
Ageratum	A	I	S or Sh	6-9
Ajuga	P	OALF	S or Sh	Spr.
Alternanthera	P	*	Sh	Spr.

	Type of plant	When & where to seed	Exposure	Space required (in.)
Alyssum	P	OALF	S	12
Amaranthus	A	OALF	S	15
Anemone	P	❋	Sh	15
Arabis	P	OALF	S	9
Arctotis	A	I	S	9
Argemone	A	OALF	S	12
Armeria	P	OALF	S	8
Artemisia	P	❋	S	18-24
Aruncus	P	❋	Sh	24
Aster (*Callistephus chinensis*)	A	I	S	12
Aster	P	OALF	S	9-30
Astilbe	P	❋	S	12-18
Aubrietia	P	OALF	S	Spr.
Baby's breath (*Gypsophila*)	A & P	OALF	S or Sh	6
Balloon flower (*Platycodon*)	P	❋	S	12
Balsam (*Impatiens balsamina*)	A	I	S	9
Baneberry (*Actaea*)	P	❋	Sh	12
Beebalm (*Monarda*)	P	❋	S	12
Begonia	P as A	I	Sh	6
Begonia	P	❋	Sh	6-24
Bells of Ireland (*Molucella laevis*)	A	I	S	9
Bergenia semperflorens	P	❋	Sh	8
Bird of paradise (*Strelitzia*)	P	❋	S	24
Bitter root (*Lewisia rediviva*)	P	❋	S	4
Bleeding heart (*Dicentra spectabilis*)	P	❋	Sh	24
Bloodroot (*Sanguinaria canadensis*)	P	❋	Sh	6
Blue lace flower (*Trachymene coerulea*)	A	I	S	9
Boltonia	P	❋	S	12-36
Briza	A	OALF	S	9
Browallia	A	I	S	9
Butterfly weed (*Asclepias tuberosa*)	P	OALF	S	12
Calathea	P	❋	Sh	6-24
Calendula	A	I	S	12-15
California poppy (*Eschscholtzia californica*)	A	OWSW	S	9
Calliopsis	A	I	S	18
Campanula	A	I	S or Sh	6-12
Campanula	P & B	OALF	S or Sh	9-36
Candytuft (*Iberis*)	A	OWSW	S	6-10
Candytuft (*Iberis sempervirens*)	P	OALF	S	12
Castor oil plant (*Ricinus communis*)	A	I	S	48
Catananche	P	❋	S	12
Cat tail (*Typha latifolia*)	P	❋	S	Spr.

	Type of plant	When & where to seed	Exposure	Space required (in.)
Cerastium	P	OALF	S	Spr.
Chinese lantern (*Physalis alkekengii*)	P as A	l	S	15
Chrysanthemum	P	*	S	12-18
Clarkia	A	OWSW	Sh	9
Clintonia borealis	P	*	Sh	12
Cockscomb (*Celosia*)	A	I	S	9-18
Coleus	P as A	I	S or Sh	9-12
Collinsia bicolor	A	OWSW	Sh	6
Columbine (*Aquilegia*)	P	OALF	S or Sh	9-15
Coneflower (*Echinacea*)	P	*	S or Sh	24
Coreopsis	P	OALF	S	18
Cornflower (*Centaurea*)	A	OWSW	S	12
Cornflower (*Centaurea*)	P	OALF	S	12-18
Cosmos	A	I	S or Sh	30
Costus	P	*	Sh	36
Cup and saucer vine (*Cobaea scandens*)	P	I	S	V
Dahlia	A[1]	I	S	9-12
Datura	A	I	S	18
Daylily (*Hemerocallis*)	P	*	S	24
Delphinium	P	OALF	S	9-18
Dianthus	A	I	S	6
Dianthus	P & B	OALF	S	6-12
Dimorphotheca	A	I	S	9
Dodecatheon	P	*	S or Sh	6-10
Draba	P	*	S	6-10
Dusty Miller (*Centaurea gymnocarpa* or *Senecio cineraria*)	P as A	I	S	15
Edelweiss (*Leontopodeum*)	P	I	S	6-8
Egyptian paper plant (*Cyperus papyrus*)	P	*	S	18
Emilia	A	OALF	S	9
English daisy (*Bellis perennis*)	P	OALF	Sh	6
Epimedium	P	*	Sh	9
Erinus	P	*	S	4
Eulalia (*Miscanthus sinensis*)	P	*	S	12
Eupatorium	P	*	S or Sh	12-24
False dragonhead (*Physostegia virginiana*)	P	*	S or Sh	18
Feverfew (*Chrysanthemum parthenium*)	P	OALF	S	12

---

[1] Dahlias are normally propagated year after year by division of the tubers; but miniature dahlias especially make excellent annuals.

	Type of plant	When & where to seed	Exposure	Space required (in.)
Filipendula	P	✿	S or Sh	12-18
Fireweed (*Epilobium augustifolium*)	P	✿	S	15
Flax (*Linum grandiflorum*)	A	OWSW	S	9
Flax (*Linum perenne*)	P	OALF	S	9-12
Fleabane (*Erigeron*)	P	✿	S	12
Forget-me-not (*Myosotis*)	B as A	OWSW	S or Sh	6
Forget-me-not (*Myosotis*)	P	OALF	S or Sh	12
Four o'Clock (*Mirabilis*)	P as A	OWSW	S	12
Foxglove (*Digitalis purpurea*)	B	OALF	S or Sh	12-18
Foxtail lily (*Eremurus*)	P	✿	S	15
Francoa ramosa	P	✿	S or Sh	15
Gaillardia	A	I	S	9
Gaillardia	P	OALF	S	12
Galax aphylla	P	✿	Sh	12
Gas plant (*Dictamnus*)	P	2	S	24
Geranium (*Pelargonium*)	P	✿	S	9-12
Gerbera	P	OALF	S or Sh	12
Geum	P	OALF	S or Sh	9-12
Gilia	A	OWSW	S	9-12
Globe amaranth (*Gomphrena*)	A	OALF	S	12
Globularia	P	OALF	Sh	9
Glory flower (*Eccremocarpus scaber*)	P	OALF	S or Sh	V
Godetia	A	OALF	Sh	9-12
Gourds (name applied to several genera)	A	OALF	S	V
Heart seed (*Cardiospermum halicacabum*)	P as A	OALF	S	V
Helenium	P	✿	S	12-18
Helianthemum	P	✿	S	12-15
Heliconia	P	✿	S or Sh	24-48
Heliopsis	P	✿	S	36
Heliotrope (*Heliotropium*)	P as A	✿	Sh	12
Helipterum	A	OALF	S	6
Helleborus	P	✿	3	12
Hepatica	P	✿	Sh	9
Heuchera	P	OALF	S or Sh	9
Hibiscus moscheutos	P	✿	S	36
Hollyhock (*Althea rosea*)	B	OALF	S	12-18
Honesty (*Lunaria*)	B as A	I	Sh	12
Hosta	P	✿	Sh	12-24

---

2 Seed is sown outdoors in fall; germinates following spring. Seedlings are transplanted a year later.

3 Needs shade in summer; sun in winter.

	Type of plant	When & where to seed	Exposure	Space required (in.)
Hyacinth bean (*Dolichos lablab*)	P as A	OALF	S	V
Inula	P	*	S	12-24
Japanese hop (*Humulus japonicus*)	A	OALF	S	V
Job's tears (*Coix lacryma-jobii*)	A	OALF	S	12
Kochia	A	I	S	12-18
Lamb's tears (*Stachys lanata*)	P	*	S	6
Larkspur (*Delphinium*)	A	OWSW	S	9
Leopard plant (*Ligularia tussilaginea aureo-maculata*)	P	*	Sh	12-15
Leopard's bane (*Doronicum*)	P	*	S or Sh	9-12
Liatris	P	*	S or Sh	12
Lily-of-the-valley (*Convallaria*)	P	*	Sh	3
Limonium	A & P	OALF	S	15
Linaria	A	I	S	3-12
Linaria	P	*	S	6-9
Lizard's tail (*Saururus cernuus*)	P	*	Sh	12-15
Lobelia	A	I	Sh	6-9
Lobelia	P	OALF	Sh	9
Loosestrife (name applied to several genera)	P	*	S or Sh	24-36
Lupine (*Lupinus*)	P & A	OALF	S or Sh	12-24
Lychnis	A, B & P	I	S	9-12
Macleaya	P	*	S	48
Marigold (*Tagetes*)	A	I	S	6-18
Marsh marigold (*Caltha palustris*)	P	*	Sh	9-12
Maurandia	P as A	I	S or Sh	V
Mayapple (*Podophyllum peltatum*)	P	*	Sh	9
Meadow rue (*Thalictrum*)	P	*	S	12-24
Mertensia	P	OWSW	Sh	9
Mexican tulip poppy (*Hunnemannia fumariaefolia*)	P	4	S	9
Micromeria	P	*	Sh	Spr.
Mignonette (*Reseda*)	A	OALF	Sh	12
Momordica	A	OALF	S	V
Monkshood (*Aconitum*)	P	OALF	Sh	6-12
Moonflower (*Calonyction aculeatum*)	P as A	I	S	V
Moonseed (*Menispermum canadense*)	P	OALF	S or Sh	V
Morning glory (*Ipomoea purpurea*)	A	I	S	V
Mullein (*Verbascum*)	B	OALF	S	12-24
Musk mallow (*Malva moschata*)	P	*	S	9
Nasturtium (*Tropaeolum*)	A	OALF	S	6-12
Nemesia	A	I	S	9

4 Sow seeds outdoors two weeks before last frost.

	Type of plant	When & where to seed	Exposure	Space required (in.)
Nemophila menziesii	A	OWSW	S or Sh	8-12
Nepeta	P	OALF	S or Sh	6-12
New Zealand flax (*Phormium tenax*)	P	✿	S	Spr.
Nicotiana	A	I	S	12
Nierembergia	P as A	I	Sh	15-20
Nigella	A	OWSW	S	9
Oconee bells (*Shortia galacifolia*)	P	✿	Sh	8
Oenothera	P & B	OALF	S	8
Pampas grass (*Cortaderia selloana*)	P	✿	S	Spr.
Pansy (*Viola*)	B	OALF	S	6-9
Patience (*Impatiens*)	A	I	Sh	9
Penstemon	P	OALF	S or Sh	12
Peony (*Paeonia*)	P	✿	S	24
Petunia	A	I	S	6-12
Phlox	P	✿	S	9-12
Phlox	A	I	S	6-9
Pickerel weed (*Pontederia cordata*)	P	✿	Sh	12-15
Pitcher plant (*Sarracenia*)	P	✿	Sh	12-15
Polemonium	P	✿	S or Sh	9
Poppy (*Papaver*)	P	✿	S	6-12
Poppy (*Papaver*)	A	OWSW	S	9-12
Poppy mallow (*Callirhoe*)	P	✿	S	12
Portulaca	A	OWSW	S	6
Potentilla	P	✿	S	9-12
Primrose (*Primula*)	P	✿	Sh	6-12
Pulmonaria	P	OWSW	Sh	9
Pyrethrum (*Chrysanthemum coccineum*)	P	✿	S	12
Quamoclit	A	I	S	V
Red hot poker (*Kniphofia uvaria*)	P	OALF	S	12-18
Rehmannia elata	P	✿	S or Sh	18
Romneya coulteri	P	✿	S	18-24
Rudbeckia	P as A	I	S	12-18
St. Johnswort (*Hypericum*)	P	✿	Sh	15-18
Salpiglossis	A	I	S or Sh	9
Salvia	A & P	I	S	9-18
Santolina	P	✿	S	6-9
Sanvitalia procumbens	A	OWSW	S	9
Saxifrage (*Saxifraga*)	P	✿	Sh	Spr.
Scabiosa	A	I	S or Sh	12
Scabiosa	P	OALF	S or Sh	9-12
Scarlet runner bean (*Phaseolus coccineus*)	P as A	OALF	S	V

	Type of plant	When & where to seed	Exposure	Space required (in.)
Schizanthus	A	I	S or Sh	9-18
Sea holly (*Eryngium*)	P	*	S	12
Shasta daisy (*Chrysanthemum maximum*)	P	OALF	S or Sh	12
Sidalcea	P	I	S	12
Silene	A	OWSW	S	6
Silene	P	*	S	6-15
Snakeroot (*Cimicifuga*)	P	*	Sh	24-36
Snapdragon	P as A	I	S or Sh	9
Solomon's Seal (*Polygonatum*)	P	*	Sh	9
Spathiphyllum	P	*	Sh	9
Spider flower (*Cleome*)	A	OWSW	S	24
Spiderwort (*Tradescantia*)	P	*	S or Sh	12-18
Star of Texas (*Xanthisma texanum*)	A	OWSW	S	9-12
Stock (*Matthiola incana*)	B as A	I	S	6-18
Stokesia	P	*	S	12
Stone cress (*Aethionema*)	P	OALF	S	6
Strawflower (*Helichrysum bracteatum*)	A	OALF	S	9
Sunflower (*Helianthus*)	A	OWSW	S	12-36
Sunflower (*Helianthus*)	P	*	S	24-36
Swan river daisy (*Brachycome iberidifolia*)	A	I	S	6
Sweet alyssum (*Lobularia maritima*)	A	I	S	5-10
Sweet flag (*Acorus calamus*)	P	*	S or Sh	12
Sweet pea (*Lathyrus odoratus*)	A	OWSW	S	6
Sweet rocket (*Hesperis matronalis*)	B	OALF	S or Sh	15
Sweet sultan (*Centaurea imperalis*)	A	OWSW	S	12
Sweet woodruff (*Asperula odorata*)	P	OALF	Sh	9
Tahoka daisy (*Machaeranthera tanacetifolia*)	A	OWSW	S	9
Teucrium chamaedrys	P	*	S	6
Thermopsis	P	*	S	8
Thunbergia	P as A	I	S	V
Tithonia	P as A	I	S	36
Torenia	A	I	Sh	6
Trillium	P	5	Sh	6-9
Trollius	P	*	Sh	12-18
Turtlehead (*Chelone*)	P	*	Sh	9
Unicorn plant (*Proboscidea jussieui*)	P as A	I	S	48
Valeriana	P	OALF	S	12
Venidium	A	I	S	12

---

5 Sow seeds immediately after they are harvested in spring.

	Type of plant	When & where to seed	Exposure	Space required (in.)
Venus flytrap (*Dionaea muscipula*)	P	*	Sh	9
Verbena	P as A	I	Sh	12
Veronica	P	*	S or Sh	6-9
Vinca rosea	P as A	I	S or Sh	9-12
Viola	P	*	Sh	6
Virginia stock (*Malcomia maritima*)	A	OWSW	S	4
Wallflower (*Cheiranthus cheiri*)	P	OALF	S	9-12
Water arm (*Calla palustris*)	P	6	S	6
Water lily (*Nymphaea*)	P	*	S	36
Wild ginger (*Asarum*)	P	*	Sh	Spr.
Winged everlasting (*Ammobium*)	A	OALF	S	12
Xeranthemum annuum	A	OALF	S	9
Yarrow (*Achillea*)	P	I	S	12
Yucca	P	*	S	24
Zauschneria	P	*	S	9
Zinnia	A	I	S	9-15

6 Remove seeds from berries when ripe and sow in soil under water.

15

How to Raise Bulbs

Bulbs are generally easy to raise, but they are troublesome to discuss en masse. The problem arises from the fact that the plants referred to as bulbs, or bulbous plants, are enormously varied.

For one thing, not all bulbs are in fact bulbs. Some are corms, some are rhizomes, some are tubers. There are technical differences between all of these. But for the sake of simplicity, I shall call them all bulbs although in the tables that follow, under the heading "Type," I use the letters B, C, R and T to classify each "bulb" properly.

Another problem in discussing bulbs is that some are left in the ground the year-round (this is the kind that people refer to when they say nothing is easier to grow than bulbs) while others must be planted and lifted every year. Furthermore, they bloom in winter, spring, summer and fall. And like other types of plants, they have varying characteristics and requirements.

But one general statement that can be made about them is that they constitute an uncommonly delightful group of plants.

¶ *Planting.* Bulbs differ in the depth and time of year they should be planted (these points are covered later), but are very much alike in the way they should be planted and where.

With some exceptions (most notably tuberous begonias and caladiums), they need plenty of sun while they are growing and flowering. Spring-flowering bulbs, however, can be planted in a spot that is shaded in summer, because by that time they are going into dormancy.

The soil, as a general rule, need be only of average quality, reasonably fertile, well drained and with a pH of about 6 to 7. If it is also rich in humus, that will make some plants such as alpinia, caladium and elephant ear very happy; and it will make none unhappy.

When bulbs are planted in a border, you should turn over the soil to a depth of 12 to 15 in. Pulverize well and mix in a goodly amount of humus and bonemeal. If the drainage is poor, put 2 to 3 in. of gravel or crushed rock in the bottom of the bed: few bulbs tolerate a soggy soil.

If the bulbs are to be planted close together, you can scoop out one large hole for the lot of them; otherwise dig individual holes. Use a trowel for this, not the round, stick-like tool called a dibble, because this makes a pointed hole that leaves an air pocket below the bulb. All bulbs should be firmly cushioned either in pulverized soil or in a thin bed of sand. A sand bed is particularly recommended if the soil is dense, because it helps to improve drainage.

The depth at which bulbs are planted is measured from the top, or nose, of the bulb to the soil surface. (In other words, a bulb that should be planted 4 in. deep has its top—not its bottom—4 in. below ground level.) Be sure, of course, to plant the topside, or growing point, up. Then fill in the planting hole with soil, firm well and apply enough water to dampen the soil down at least to the bottom of the bulb. Stick a wood or plastic label into the soil so that you will not mistakenly dig up the bulbs during dormancy.

When bulbs are naturalized in a lawn, field, woods, etc., they can be—and ideally they should be—planted in the same way. Good soil preparation, in short, pays even when you are putting in the less expensive bulbs that are sold for naturalizing purposes. Most gardeners, however, do not go to such pains, and I must confess that I don't either. My usual procedure is simply to dig a little hole to the proper depth, drop in a bulb without further soil preparation, cover with soil and move on to the next planting location. Another procedure—which is better if you are in a hurry to plant several hundred bulbs—is to drive the point of a pick into the ground; rock it

Daffodils are here naturalized on a lightly wooded hillside. The field grass that grows up around the bulbs shortly after they stop blooming cannot be cut until the daffodils' leaves begin to wither.

Some ground covers make a charming background for bulbs growing up through them. In this Tulsa garden, tulips and ajuga are combined. The beds are edged with holly that is kept clipped as a small hedge. Ivy is trained on wires on the surrounding brick wall.

back and forth to open up the hole and loosen the soil; drop in a bulb; and kick and stamp the soil back in place.

¶ *Watering and fertilizing.* Unlike other plants, bulbous plants can live off their own fat, so to speak, for a considerable period of time. This is most apparent when you "dry off" a bulb (prepare it for dormancy by withholding water and plant food). In many instances, the foliage remains green and plump for weeks whereas an annual or perennial would soon turn brown and limp.

But despite this unusual ability, bulbs should not be allowed to go without sustenance for very long while they are in active growth. If the ground is dry, water them regularly from the time they are due to start putting out growth until about two weeks after the flowers have died down. Thereafter you can taper off rather rapidly. Dormant bulbs do not need and should not have any more water than nature ordinarily provides.

Most spring bulbs should be fertilized only once a season, when new growth is starting. Summer bulbs can be given two doses— when they are planted or soon after they appear above ground, and again several weeks before they bloom. Use a balanced commercial fertilizer that has a fairly low nitrogen content.

TABLE VIII
Hardy Spring Bulbs

The key to this table as well as to Tables IX, X and XI is as follows:

Under *"Where grown"*

Anywhere	— This is a slight exaggeration in the interest of saving space. Plants so marked grow almost anywhere in the U.S.
Cold	— Northernmost states
Mild	— From about southern New England to the Mason-Dixon line
Warm	— From the Mason-Dixon line to northern Florida
Warmest	— Florida, southern Texas, southern California, Hawaii, etc.

Under *"Type"*
B — bulb
C — corm
R — rhizome
T — tuber

	Type	Where grown	When to plant	Planting depth (in.)	Sun or shade
Allium	B	Anywhere	Fall	3	S
Anemone	T	Mild, warm	Fall	2	S
Brodiaea	C	Mild, warm	Fall	3	S
Bulbocodium	B	Mild	Fall	3	S
Camassia	B	Anywhere	Fall	4	S
Claytonia	C	Anywhere	Fall	3	Sh
Crocus	B	Cold, mild	Fall	3	S
Daffodil (*Narcissus*)	B	Anywhere	Fall	6	S
Dogtooth Violet (*Erythronium*)	B	Mild	E. Fall	3	Sh
Fritillaria	B	Cold, mild	Fall	4	Sh
Glory of the Snow (*Chionodoxa*)	B	Cold, mild	Fall	3	S
Grape hyacinth (*Muscari*)	B	Anywhere	Fall	3	S
Hyacinth (*Hyacinthus*)	B	Anywhere	Fall	6	S
Iris	B	Anywhere	Fall	4	S
Ixiolirion	B	Mild	Fall	3	S
Mariposa Lily (*Galochortus*)	C	Western U.S.	Fall	2	Sh
Puschkinia	B	Mild	Fall	3	Sh
Scilla	B	Mild	Fall	3	S or Sh
Snowdrop (*Galanthus*)	B	Cold, mild	Fall	3	Sh
Snowflake (*Leucojum*)	B	Anywhere	Fall	3	Sh
Star of Bethlehem (*Ornithogalum*)	B	Mild, warm	Fall	3	S
Tulip (*Tulipa*)	B	Anywhere	Fall	9^1	S
Winter Aconite (*Eranthis*)	T	Cold, mild	E. Fall	2	Sh

[1] 5 in. for the small early bloomers.

All the bulbs listed above are classified as "spring bulbs" because they bloom in late winter or spring, and as "hardy bulbs" because they are left in the ground the year round. But it should be noted that bulbs that are hardy in one climate may not be hardy in others; and while some are hardy fairly far north, they do not necessarily do well in the South. So in selecting bulbs for your garden, you should note where the different kinds of bulbs grow. Those marked "anywhere" grow in almost every part of the country. Those marked "cold, mild" grow very well in the North, but not too well in the South. Those marked "mild" or "mild, warm" grow in the middle reaches of the country—more or less from southern New England to the Mason-Dixon Line and from the Mason-Dixon Line to northern Florida. Mariposa lilies grow well only from the Mountain States westward.

Regardless of where these hardy spring bloomers grow, all but two are planted in the fall—from early September until the ground freezes. (Dogtooth violet and winter aconites should be planted just as soon as they come on the market—usually about the end of August or early September.)

In cold climates, in the first year that you plant bulbs, it is advisable to cover the soil, after it freezes, with leaves, straw or conifer boughs. Thereafter, most bulbs do not need a mulch. Anemones, however, must be covered every winter, after the soil freezes, with a thick layer of leaves or straw. And in the Rockies, tulips also need to be mulched annually.

To protect crocus and tulip bulbs from hungry rodents, either avoid planting in locations where these pests abound or enclose the bulbs in cages made of 1/2- to 3/4-in. wire mesh. Rectangular cages like the one illustrated can be whipped together in short order. Other spring bulbs sometimes require similar protection, but generally do not.

A most important point to remember about hardy spring bulbs is that, after they flower, the foliage must be allowed to ripen untouched for several weeks. This gives the bulbs a chance to recoup the strength that they put into growing and blooming. You may cut off the flower stalks if you wish, but do not cut the leaves until they are so far gone that they can be pulled off with a slight tug. If you object to the unkempt foliage, however, you can fold it down and put a rubber band around it. (If bulbs are planted in a lawn or meadow, the need to preserve the leaves interferes with spring mowing operations. But you can compensate for this to some extent by mowing the grass late in the preceding fall; then it may not need mowing until the bulb foliage is nearly gone in the spring.)

Because daffodils and most of the so-called "minor" bulbs produce large numbers of small bulbs (bulblets), it is necessary to dig them up about every five years and divide them (see Chapter 5). The job should be done any time after the foliage has died down, although there is no reason why you cannot wait until fall—provided, of course, you can then find the bulbs. Failure to divide bulbs leads to their eventual disappearence through crowding out.

Hyacinths that are left in the ground for too many years tend to develop scrawny flowers and long stems rather than fat flower heads. They should therefore be replaced occasionally.

Wire cages to protect bulbs in the ground from rodents are easily made out of 1/2-in. wire mesh, as shown.

To grow tulips in warm areas you must either buy "pre-cooled" bulbs or store ordinary bulbs in the fresh-food compartment of your refrigerator for six weeks before planting. Plant them in a spot that is shaded in winter. Tulips in the Mountain States do not need to be pre-cooled but should be planted where they will be lightly shaded in the spring.

TABLE IX [1]
Miscellaneous Hardy Bulbs

	Type	Where grown	Bloom	When to plant	Planting depth (in.)	Sun or shade
Bletilla	B	Mild, warm	Sum.	L. Spr.	½	Sh
Colchicum	B	Cold, mild	Fall	L. Sum.	3	Sh
Crocus	B	Cold, mild	Fall	L. Sum.	3	S
Cyclamen	C	Mild, warm	Sum.	Fall	1	Sh
Iris	R	Anywhere	Spr.	E. Sum.	½	S
Lily (Lilium)	B	Anywhere	Sum., Fall	Fall	4	S
Lycoris	B	Mild	Fall	Spr.	4	S
Sternbergia lutea	B	Mild, warm	Sum.	E. Fall	5	Sh

[1] For an explanation of terms used in this table, see key to Table VIII (page 199).

These are hardy bulbs that are planted and bloom at different times of the year. Otherwise, they are like the hardy spring bulbs, and are handled in the same way. The most important of the group are the lilies and the rhizomatous iris.

Plant lily bulbs as soon as possible after they have been harvested: they suffer somewhat from being out of the ground. Set them in a spot with good air circulation. The soil should be slightly acid. If there are rodents in the garden, enclose the bulbs in wire-mesh cages (see illustration on page 202). Keep the soil mulched at all times with peat or some other slightly acid organic mulch. Fertilize established bulbs in early spring and again two months later. Keep the soil moist. Remove dead flowers, but allow the foliage to die down naturally in the late summer and fall. Divide clumps that become crowded in the fall.

Iris rhizomes should be divided every three or four years in July. Keep the plump, new sections of root and discard the old. Each new section should have a small fan of leaves which is trimmed to a height of 6 in. If the rhizomes are rotten and contain borers, soak them in a bichloride of mercury solution for 30 minutes. Then lay them flat in the planting hole with the leaves pointing up, and cover with a very thin layer of soil.

Water iris only when soil becomes quite dry (the Louisiana and Japanese iris, which are native to swamps, however, must be kept continually moist while they are making growth in spring and summer). Fertilize in early spring. Cultivate very shallowly. Do not cut

TABLE X[1]
Tender Summer Bulbs

	Type	Where grown	Planting depth (in.)	Sun or shade	Where to store
Acidanthera	C	Anywhere	4	S	Open
Agapanthus	T	Anywhere	1	S	In tub
Alstroemeria	T	Anywhere	4	Sh	Sand
Begonia	T	Cold, mild	½	Sh	Open
Caladium	T	Warm	1	Sh	Sand
Chlidanthus fragrans	B	Anywhere	3	S	Peat
Cooperia	B	Anywhere	2	S	Peat
Crocosmia aurea	C	Anywhere	4	S	Open
Dahlia	T	Anywhere	6	S	Peat
Elephant Ear (Colocasia esculenta)	T	Anywhere	½	Sh	Peat
Eucomis comosa	B	Anywhere	1	S	Peat
Galtonia candicans	B	Anywhere	3	S	Open
Gladiolus	C	Anywhere	6	S	Open
Gloriosa	T	Anywhere	4	S	Peat
Ixia	C	Anywhere	2	S	Open
Jacobian lily (Sprekelia formosissima)	B	Anywhere	3	S	Open
Lapeyrousia	C	Mild	3	S	Open
Oxalis	B	Anywhere	2	S or Sh	Open
Ranunculus	T	Anywhere	1	S	Sand
Spider lily (Hymenocallis)	B	Anywhere	3	S	Open
Tigridia	B	Anywhere	4	S	Open
Tritonia	B	Anywhere	4	Sh	Open
Tuberose (Polianthes tuberosa)	T	Anywhere	2	S	Peat
Watsonia	C	Warm	4	S	Open
Zephyr lily (Zephyranthes)	B	Anywhere	1	S or Sh	Peat

[1] For an explanation of terms used in this table, see key to Table VIII (page 199).

foliage except when dividing the rhizomes, but remove dead leaves and old flower stalks.

In most parts of the U.S., the summer-flowering bulbs listed above must be dug up in the fall and stored over winter; in sections where the temperature rarely drops below freezing, however, many of them can be left in the ground the years round.

The majority of summer bulbs are planted outdoors where they are to grow after all danger of frost is past. For earlier bloom, however, tuberous begonias and elephant ear are sometimes started indoors or in the cold frame in pots and then transplanted to the garden after the last frost. Agapanthus is also started indoors—but in a tub; and it does best if kept in the tub.

Fertilize the bulbs after the tops have appeared and again about three weeks before flowering. If you want to make an additional light application of fertilizer after flowering, it will help the bulb to increase its strength but is not really necessary.

Keep tuberous begonias well watered throughout the summer and mist the tops occasionally if your area does not have the fogs these plants dote on. Water dahlias sparingly until they start to bloom, then water thoroughly every week.

In the fall, when the foliage dies down naturally, dig up the bulbs, remove the tops if they are easy to tug off and let the bulbs dry in an airy place. (If the foliage does not die down but is killed back by frost, dig up the bulbs, cut off all but 6 in. of the tops and let the bulbs dry.) Then shake off the dirt. Do not disturb the small roots on the bulbs, but pick off any little bulbs you find. Then store the bulbs in a dry, cool (50° to 60° F.) place. As the list points out, some bulbs should be stored in boxes of dry sand or peat; others are simply spread in a single layer in open trays. Bulbs that have been growing in pots are best left in the pots.

Examine the stored bulbs occasionally during the winter to make sure they are in good condition. Throw out any that are rotten, mushy and full of holes. If bulbs stored in sand or peat look shriveled, dampen the storage medium very slightly. (Dahlia tubers are particularly inclined to shrivel if they are exposed too long to the sun when they are being dried off and/or if they lose too much moisture during storage.)

T A B L E   X I [1]
Bulbs for Warm Climates Only

	Type	Where grown	Bloom	When to plant	Planting depth (in.)	Sun or shade
Alocasia	R	Warmest	Spr.	Spr.	2	Sh
Alpinia	R	Warmest	Sum.	E. Spr.	2	Sh
Amaryllis (*Hippeastrum*)	B	Warmest	Spr.	Fall	⅛	S
Amazon Lily (*Eucharis grandiflora*)	B	Warmest	Win.	Spr.	⅛	Sh
Arum palestinum	T	Warm	Sum.	L. Spr.	1	Sh
Babiana	C	Warmest	Spr.	Fall	2	S
Blood lily (*Haemanthus*)	B	Warmest	Spr.	E. Spr.	⅛	Sh
Calla Lily (*Zantedeschia*)	T	Warm	Spr., Sum.	Fall	3	Sh
Crinum	B	Warm	Spr., Sum.	Fall	⅛	S
Freesia	C	Warmest	Spr.	Fall	2	S
Hedychium	R	Warmest	Sum.	Spr.	S	Sh
Hydrosme rivieri	T	Warmest	Spr.	E. Spr.	3	Sh
Kafir Lily (*Schizostylis coccinea*)	T	Warm	Fall	Spr.	3	S
Moraea	C	Warm	Sum.	Fall	4	S or Sh
Nerine	B	Warm	Fall	E. Fall	3	S
Scarborough Lily (*Vallota speciosa*)	B	Warm	Sum.	L. Spr.	⅛	Sh
Sparaxis	C	Warm	Spr.	Fall	2	S

[1] For an explanation of terms used in this table, see key to Table VIII (page 199).

These bulbs grow outdoors only in warm climates. They are left in the ground all year.

The initial planting should be made in accordance with column 4 in the table above. Subsequent division and replanting should take place at the same time of year.

Like many tropical plants, the bulbs are for the most part large and vigorous growers. Keep them well watered during their growth period, and fertilize twice—when they first start to make growth and again several weeks before they start to bloom.

Allow the foliage to die down before removing it.

16

How to Raise Trees, Shrubs and Vines

THESE ARE THE WOODY PLANTS—the most important and valuable of all that we grow. By and large, they are also the least troublesome and demanding of attention—provided that they are given a good start and provided also that they are grown under conditions that they tolerate.

¶ *Where to plant.* Tables XII (page 226), XIII (page 232) and XIV (page 237) will help you to decide where to plant trees, shrubs and vines, respectively, in your garden. But in general there are three points to consider:

(1) The exposure. With some exceptions, trees need sun. There are, however, a number of shrubs and vines that should be grown in partial shade (few do well in deep shade).

(2) The soil. Most woody plants are content in ordinary garden soil. But a number require a low pH, while a few require a high pH.

Probably the least desirable soil condition for these plants is a high water table. Not many will live for long if their roots are immersed in water.

(3) The spacing of the plants. Although almost all plants in a forest grow tall, straight and skinny, this is usually not their natural habit of growth. Given elbow room, they grow outward as well as upward. What's more, if they are given attention, they make growth very rapidly.

This should be remembered when you are setting out woody plants. If you place them too close together or too close to the house, they will not develop branches normally. Furthermore, since they will be forced to grow up rather than out, they may in time screen your windows and shade so much of your garden that you can grow little else.

PLANTING AND TRANSPLANTING

¶ *Timing.* Because several plants, such as magnolias, cannot always be moved safely in the fall and because almost no plants can be moved safely in the fall in very cold climates, the best rule for setting out woody plants is to do it in the spring. Deciduous types are planted any time after the ground thaws until the plants begin to develop leaves. Evergreens are planted from thawing-out time until the plants begin to make new growth.

Fall planting is permissible (though not always safe) for deciduous plants any time after the leaves start to turn color. Fall planting of evergreens can be done from about September 1 to a month before the ground freezes hard.

Summer planting is possible, but should be attempted only if there is an urgent reason. Balled-and-burlapped or canned specimens that are in vigorous shape are by far the safest to handle. If you are planting bare-root specimens, the tops must be completely saturated with a plastic antitranspirant spray to reduce the loss of moisture. Even then, the risk is very great. (Bare-root seedings less than 1 ft. tall, however, are rarely protected with an antitranspirant.)

If you are moving plants from the wild—regardless of whether it is spring, fall or summer—it is advisable to root-prune them a year or two before you actually dig them up and transplant them (see Chapter 9).

¶ *Heeling in.* When you buy woody plants by mail, you almost always receive bare-root specimens. If these arrive before you are ready to plant them, they should be removed from their wrappings and heeled in in a shady spot. Dig a rough, slanting hole large enough to hold the roots, set the plants in at an angle, and cover the roots with soil. Water well. Bare-root plants handled in this way can be held safely for several weeks, but don't press your luck too much.

Balled-and-burlapped or canned plants that arrive before you are able to plant them need only to be kept watered. Covering the rootball with leaves helps to hold in moisture.

¶ *Preparing the planting hole.* Inasmuch as trees, shrubs and vines are usually expected to fend pretty much for themselves (this is not right, however), it is essential to plant them with care. The hole you dig should be 8 to 12 in. deeper than the root system and also considerably wider. For plants with a rootball less than 12 in. in diameter, dig a hole 24 in. across; for those with a rootball up to 24 in. in diameter, dig a hole 42 in. across; and for those with larger rootballs, dig holes at least 24 in. wider than the balls.

Draw a rough outline of the hole on the ground and spread one or two large pieces of burlap, canvas or tar paper close by. The soil you dig up goes on these. Place the sods and topsoil in one pile; the subsoil in a second. Dig the sides of the hole straight up and down. When you have excavated to the correct depth (don't guess: measure the depth of the rootball or roots), put a 2- or 3-in. layer of stones in the bottom of the hole to improve drainage (this is unnecessary in sandy or gravelly soil). Then toss in the sods and on these —gradually—the topsoil. For every two shovelfuls of soil, add one shovelful of peat or other humus. Mix well.

When you have filled the hole to about the rootball depth, firm the soil well to make sure that you really are at rootball depth. (Peat makes soil fluffy, with the result that when you drop a heavy plant into the planting hole, the rootball may sink lower than its proper depth.) Then smooth the soil off roughly.

¶ *Planting.* The plant should be centered in the hole, of course. Evergreens are planted to the depth at which they formerly grew; that is, the top of the rootball should be level with the top of the planting hole. Deciduous plants can be set 1 in. deeper.

If you are planting a balled-and-burlapped specimen, leave on the burlap and twine until the plant is in the ground and the hole is almost filled; then simply loosen the covering from around the stem of the plant. It will rot quickly and will not interfere with root growth.

If a plant is in a can, you may be able to loosen it by knocking the sides of the can with your shovel. If this proves difficult, cut the sides of the can with tin snips.

Check plants for broken and splintered roots. Trim off any you find with pruning shears.

Now, if the plant is small, grasp the trunk or the strongest stem just above the roots and set the plant in the hole. Then turn it around until you have the best side facing in the right direction. If the plant is large, decide on the best side before putting the plant in the hole.

Handling a large plant with a several-hundred-pound rootball is heavy work and usually calls for the combined efforts of two or three strong men. First position the plant on the ground above the hole so that it is facing properly. To drop the plant into the hole, you may then inch it straight to the hole by pulling and twisting until,

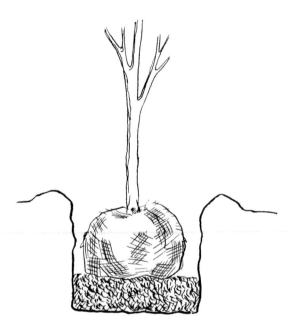

How to plant a balled-and-burlapped or canned tree, shrub or vine. Make sure soil in bottom of hole is well firmed, otherwise heavy rootball may sink too deep.

with one mighty heave, you are able to drop it into the hole. Or you may tip the plant forward to the ground, pull it toward the hole until the rootball rests on the edge, and then tip it up and backwards into the hole. When the plant is centered, if it proves to be too low or too high in the hole, you can make adjustments by tipping to one side and adding or removing soil; then tipping to the other side to add or remove soil.

Roots of bare-root plants should be spread out in the hole as naturally as possible. If a root projects beyond the sides of the hole, don't try to make it conform to the hole, but dig a trench beyond the hole to receive it.

Fill in around the roots or rootball with whatever top soil is left, then with the better subsoil, then (if it is needed) with the poorer subsoil. Mix peat with all three.

As you fill the hole, tamp down each new layer of soil. Use a stick to work it in around a bare-root specimen. When the filling is completed, build a dike of soil around the edge of the hole. This should be about 3 in. high for a small plant, up to 6 in. high for a large plant. Fill the saucer thus formed with water. Thereafter, for about the next two or three weeks, fill the saucer with water every three days.

Wrap trunks of trees that are planted in the fall with strips of burlap, tarpaper, etc., extending from the ground up to the first branches. These help to prevent damage by sunscald.

When planting a living Christmas tree, dig the hole before the ground freezes (frozen soil can, however, be thawed with boiling water). Do not keep the tree in the house any longer than necessary, and don't let it dry out.

If you label plants, emboss the names on thin metal or plastic tapes with a rotating tape-writer. Tack the tags to the trunks of large trees. Tie to a smaller plant with a copper wire inserted through the end of the tag; but don't loop the wire tightly around a branch lest it eventually strangle the branch.

¶ *Planting large trees.* It is worth noting that, according to some nurserymen, more and more well-heeled homeowners are today planting trees that have already attained much of their total growth.

There is, of course, nothing wrong with this. If you have plenty of money, why should you wait for a young tree to grow large enough to give you the shade and effect you want? But moving trees of this size is no job for the amateur. It calls for a nurseryman with plenty of large equipment. In his hands, trees of almost any size have perhaps a 75% chance, or better, of withstanding a move.

¶ *Initial pruning.* Balled-and-burlapped and canned plants generally do not require pruning when they are transplanted (although it never hurts to ask the nurseryman about this). What you do about bare-root plants, however, is a matter of choice. The old idea was that the tops of these should be cut back rather severely to compensate for the loss of roots when the plants were dug. Modern theory is that pruning is not necessary and, indeed, may retard the plants unnecessarily. My own experience in moving a considerable number of bare-root plants tends to support the latter idea.

In short, I recommend top pruning at transplanting time only if the plants are deciduous and if they were not previously root-pruned; and even then you should remove only those branches that you might consider as excess growth.

¶ *Staking.* There is no question that a good many trees are staked that do not need it. This is particularly true of specimens with large rootballs. Yet I doubt if there is anyone in the world who can say with certainty: This plant does not need staking. Wind, soil instability and accidents are simply too unpredictable.

To be on the safe side, stake every tree whip (very young, slender-trunked tree) no matter how tall, and every tree over 5 ft. tall that is in an open location.

For whips and other small trees, drive a stake 1 in. or more across well into the soil close to the trunk and tie the two together loosely but securely with strong twine.

Guy conifers over 5 ft. and deciduous trees over 10 ft. with three strong wires (baling wire is about the right weight) secured to stakes spaced equally around the trunk. At the point where the wires circle the trunk, slip each one through a short length of hose to protect the bark. The angle of the wires should be about 45°; and the wires should be so tight that the trunk cannot shake and thus loosen the roots.

Shrubs generally are not staked, probably because they have a low center of gravity and are not placed in such exposed situations as trees. Staking, however, may be advisable if a plant is moved with bare roots, if it has an unusually heavy top, or if it is planted in a heavy clay soil or a light sandy soil in a very windy location.

Vines need to be staked initially only if they have nothing else to grow on for a while.

Stakes and guy wires should be left in place for at least a year—and longer if a tree is very large or does not appear to have made very strong growth.

¶ *Mulching.* All woody plants are greatly benefited by application of a mulch at the time of planting. This should be maintained forever after. In addition to conserving moisture, the mulch helps to assure the continued strong growth of the plant by smothering the grass or weeds that would grow around it otherwise.

Seedling trees and similar small woody plants should be mulched at time of planting with white polyethylene film which helps to raise the soil temperature in the spring and thus promotes stronger root and top growth at this time of year. Larger plants can be mulched with any organic material.

REGULAR CARE OF WOODY PLANTS

¶ *Watering.* As I write this, trees, shrubs and vines in my area are dying like flies for lack of moisture. Some are small; but an amazing number are large and presumably in the prime of life. The widespread loss demonstrates a fact that many people are inclined to overlook: even mighty oaks need water. True, they often seem like camels, able to go for weeks without a drink. But don't count on it.

For how to water woody plants, see Chapter 7. Only one additional point needs to be made here:

If you take a long vacation during a dry summer, try to make arrangements with someone to water your garden. If you are unable to do this or are not sure how reliable your stand-in will be, you can protect valuable small shrubs by spraying them thoroughly before you leave home with a plastic antitranspirant. By reducing the amount of moisture that the plants give off through their leaves, this reduces the amount of water they need to take up from the soil.

¶ *Fertilizing.* Young trees, shrubs and vines need fertilizer to become established and to put on growth. Old plants need it to remain vigorous.

A balanced fertilizer with a high nitrogen content (12-6-4, 14-7-7 or 16-8-8) is recommended for most woody plants; but broadleaf evergreens respond better to a 10-8-8, 8-8-8 or 6-6-6, while fruit trees should be given a fertilizer recommended for your particular soil by your Agricultural Extension Service.

The best time to fertilize all woody plants is in the early spring. Some plants, such as roses and vigorous vines, may also be fed a second and even a third time up to about July 15. No fertilizer should be applied for some time after this date because it simply promotes growth which may not have time to ripen properly before cold weather sets in. However, feeding of deciduous trees is permissible after the leaves fall.

Balled-and-burlapped and canned plants can be fertilized when they are planted in the spring (but not in the fall) since they have

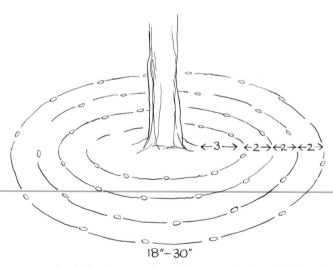

To feed a tree, make holes in ground at 18- to 30-in. intervals in circles 2 ft. apart and distribute fertilizer evenly among them. Outer ring of holes should be about 2 ft. out beyond branch tips.

a root system that is functioning well enough to absorb the nutrients almost immediately. But bare-root plants do not have a functioning root system, so it is best to wait three or four weeks after they are planted before feeding them. In both cases, you should scatter the fertilizer on the soil and water it in. Do not mix it with the soil in the planting hole since it may burn small roots.

Established shrubs and vines are also usually fed by scratching the fertilizer into the soil over the entire root system and then watering well. However, very large plants may be fed in the manner described below for trees. A once-a-year application is all that most of these plants need.

Established trees should be fertilized annually if they are young and growing strongly or if they are old and growing slowly or if—age does not matter—they are exposed to diseases or serious insect attacks. Otherwise, every-second-year feeding is enough.

Since the majority of a tree's feeding roots are some distance below the surface of the soil, the only way to get fertilizer down to them quickly and efficiently is to drop it into holes 18 to 24 in. deep made with a crowbar or power-driven earth auger. The holes should be 18 to 30 in. apart, and should be fairly evenly distributed around the tree in a wide ring. The inside edge of the ring should be about 3 ft. from the tree trunk (closer in the case of small trees); the outer edge should be about 2 ft. beyond the ends of the branches.

Give trees 3 to 5 lb. of fertilizer for each inch of trunk diameter at breast height (that is, a tree with a 10-in. trunk should get from 30 to 50 lb. of fertilizer). The more vigorous the tree, the less fertilizer it needs. Distribute the fertilizer equally between the holes. In dropping it in, take care not to leave any on grass surrounding the holes. Then fill the holes with topsoil or a mixture of peat and sand.

PRUNING AND TRAINING

For basic information about pruning and training, see Chapter 9. For when to prune different kinds of woody plants, see Tables XII (page 226), XIII (page 232) and XIV (page 237).

¶ *Trees.* Leave major pruning in the tops of trees to professionals. The work is dangerous.

When two branches rub together, remove the smaller or less desirable of the two before the other is badly wounded.

Eliminate Y-shaped crotches by removing the smaller or less desirable of the two branches. An alternative is to cut the weaker branch somewhat. This stimulates the growth of the stronger branch and strengthens the crotch.

If a young tree is crooked, bend it forcibly in the opposite direction and then tie it securely to a straight stake.

To save a young tree which has died back at the top, cut out the dead wood and give the tree a dose of fertilizer. After the tree has grown for a season, cut off all but the most vigorous branch; bend this upward and tie to a stake. It will develop as the trunk of the tree.

When the leader (tip of the trunk) of a conifer is broken or dies, follow more or less the same procedure: tie one of the topmost laterals to an upright stick which is tied to the top of the trunk.

If a conifer has two leaders, remove one of them.

To retard the growth of pines, cut the candles (new growths) in half as they start to grow in the spring. Other conifers are held in check by nipping off the growth buds or young shoots at the ends of branches.

To avoid killing branches of conifers, always cut them above green growth. If you cut below the last needles, the branches will die.

To improve the density of conifers, such as those which might be used as Christmas trees, shear them with hedge clippers when new buds are just forming. Shearing should start when trees are 2 to 3 ft. tall. Some that are growing very rapidly or in unshapely fashion need to be sheared annually thereafter; others can be sheared every other year. The process consists of cutting the leader back to 10 to 12 in. from the upper whorl of branches (cut on a sharp angle to lessen the possibility of developing a double leader). Cut the laterals of the whorl about 2 in. shorter than the leader. Then trim back the next lower branches, and the next, until you reach the ground.

If a conifer loses its leader, one of its branches will usually in time grow up to form a new leader; but you can hasten this process by developing one of the branches as the leader by splinting it with a stick of wood.

Ideally, a sheared tree should have a 60% taper; that is, it should be half again as tall as the base is wide.

¶ *Shrubs.* When thinning out a shrub that sends up stems from the crown, follow the practice of removing only 20% to 25% of the stems each year. This maintains balanced growth whereas removal of too many stems at one time stimulates too much new growth. Of course only the old and weak stems should be taken out.

If it is necessary to renew an old plant, such as a lilac, by cutting it back close to the ground, it is better to remove a third of the plant each year for three successive years than to cut it back all at once. Not only does the plant look better, but growth seems to be better.

Keep an eye out for suckers that develop below the graft on grafted plants and remove them promptly. They have no ornamental value and also interfere with the growth of desirable stems.

When pruning a grafted plant, avoid cutting back the top too much lest you encourage the growth of suckers.

¶ *Vines.* Even though it means that you must get out your pruning shears several times during the summer and that you may lose some bloom the next year, thin vines frequently to keep them looking and growing well. A vine that is too dense is prey for insects and diseases. It may also cause damage to the wall or support on which it is growing.

Avoid training vines in the direction of nearby trees: they have a disconcerting habit of leaping across to a tree and taking off up it like a scared monkey.

To prevent a vine from making a rat's nest of itself, keep the stems growing in more or less straight lines. Cut out at least some of those that crisscross.

¶ *Major tree repairs.* Cavities in trees are caused by decay which sets in when the bark is broken. If you do nothing about them, the decay is likely to spread deeper until the tree dies or collapses.

Large cavities in trunks should be filled only by professionals; but you can take care of small ones. The first step is to cut out the decayed wood completely. Use a sharp knife and chisel and perhaps a brace and bit. Do not open the mouth of the hole any more than

One reason for keeping strong, large twining vines off trees is that they may in time kill the trees by girdling. Look what happened to this ash when bittersweet was allowed to grow up it.

is necessary. Leave the cavity lining as smooth as possible. Then disinfect it with denatured alcohol; and when the wood has dried, apply a coat of shellac and then tree paint.

If it is possible to shape the cavity so that water will not stand in it, do so. But if this necessitates unnecessary enlargement of the cavity or the drilling of a hole into the bottom of the cavity, it is better to leave well enough alone. You can keep water out of such a hole by tacking above it a piece of metal that will act as a roof.

A branch or trunk that is partially split can often be mended (if you give it firm support during the process) by driving screws or bolts through the break.

To prevent two large limbs from splitting at a fork, drill holes through both and insert a long steel bolt of 1/2 in. or larger diameter. (For very large limbs use two or three bolts.) The bolt should first be coated with asphaltum or tree paint. Countersink the head and the nut below the cambium so that the wood will grow over them. If the bolt projects beyond the nut, it should be cut off.

Large trees that have been permanently bent over by heavy snow can usually be straightened with a block and tackle and then bolted or guyed to a larger upright tree, a building or a rock. Insert the bolt through the tree and put a large washer under the head so that the strain does not pull the bolt deep into the wood. Never simply loop a cable or chain around a tree trunk or branch that needs supporting because it will in time girdle the trunk and kill it.

If bark is partly ripped from a tree by lightning or some other accident, nail it back in place as soon as possible.

When a tree is blown over in a violent storm, it can often be saved by prompt action. Trim the broken roots and cover them with wet burlap. Enlarge the hole in the ground enough to accommodate the roots comfortably. Then winch the tree upright and anchor it with three or four guys wires as you would a newly planted tree. Pack soil firmly around the roots and form a saucer to hold water. Water well and regularly, and if it is not too late in the year, give the tree fertilizer.

¶ *If you lower the grade* around a tree you want to save and it is not possible to replant the tree, measure at least halfway from the

To prevent one of the large oaks overhanging this house from splitting in two, the two trunks were tied together with a steel rod and, higher up, a steel cable.

trunk to the tips of the branches and draw a circle around the tree. Then dig a trench on the outside of the circle to the depth you intend to lower the grade. Cut off the roots in the trench. Build a retaining wall of brick or concrete block around the tree. Replace the soil as necessary inside the retainer. Then lower the grade outside the retainer.

¶ *To raise the grade around a tree.* Although some trees can survive even if you put a foot of light soil over the roots, the majority will not. Soil pushed against the trunk of a tree causes rot; and roots that are shut off from their normal supply of air and water die.

If you must raise the grade around a tree, therefore, you should first spread a 6- to 12-in. layer of coarse, crushed stone over the roots from the trunk out to the ends of the branches. Cover this with a thin layer of smaller stones to keep the soil from sifting down and clogging the coarse rock.

The second step is to protect the tree trunk. The easiest way to do this is to encircle it with coarse crushed rock to the level of the new

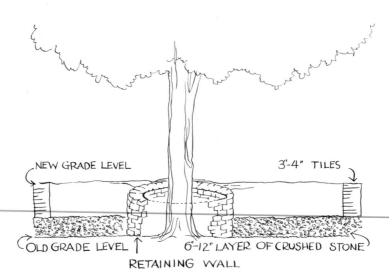

One way to raise the level of soil around a tree: Cover the entire root area with a layer of small rocks. Build a circular wall around the tree out of concrete block, stones, etc. This well can be left open or filled with smaller rock. Install drain tiles to carry air and water to the roots.

grade. The circle should be about 3 ft. in diameter. The alternative is to build a circular retaining wall about 3 ft. across around the trunk. The top of the well thus created can be covered with a grating to keep out coarse debris, animals and children, or you can fill the well with coarse rocks.

The final step—not always essential but advisable, especially if the tree is large and the roots are covered with a considerable thickness of soil—is to sink into the fill vertical tiles or pipes around the perimeter of the foliage. The purpose of these is to carry air and water from the surface down into the gravel over the root area.

If you pave around a plant, you will do no harm—and may even do some good—if you use brick, stones or other paving blocks laid loose on a thin layer of gravel and sand. This permits water and air to reach the roots; and you can easily lift out the paving blocks when fertilizing the plant. Solid paving, such as blacktop or concrete, should be avoided. But if you must use it, do not pave within a foot—preferably 2 ft.—of the trunk. And do not pave over more than 50% of the root area. To do otherwise is to assure the plant's almost certain death. In laying solid paving material, if it is necessary to level the ground in the root area, try to make the change by raising the grade with sand or gravel. If you lower the grade, you may cut into the roots.

¶ *Salt damage.* One of the increasingly serious killers of trees planted next to northern highways is the salt used to melt snow and ice. There is no way to prevent this problem, but it can be minimized in several ways.

(1) If you are developing a new garden, do not plant species with low-hung branches near the highway. A friend of mine lost a whole row of hemlocks to the salt water that was splashed up on the branches.

(2) Slope the soil away from trees so that the salt water runs off rapidly.

(3) If a particularly handsome tree is growing in a spot where the melt water collects, ask your street department about the possibility of changing the street grade. Enlist the support of your town tree warden or park commissioner if you get into an argument. You

may not win your way, but if you make enough fuss, you have a good chance.

(4) If you have a fine conifer with low-hanging branches, erect a stout barrier of plywood or polyethylene film on the street side of it.

(5) Help your street department to keep drains in front of your property open after snowstorms. The faster the melt water can run off, the less the damage that will occur.

(6) Hose down your trees with fresh water when they have been splashed with salt water. Flood the ground on which salt water has stood with fresh water.

SPECIAL REQUIREMENTS OF SPECIAL PLANTS

¶ *Roses.* Hybrid teas, floribundas, grandifloras and miniatures—the most popular types of roses—require especially good drainage, and should therefore be planted in holes that have 2 to 4 in. of coarse gravel or crushed rock in the bottom.

In the North, plant the bushes so that the graft is level with the soil surface; in the South, it should be 1 in. below. Give each plant about a cupful of a balanced rose food, such as 8-8-8.

Established roses should be given a good handful of fertilizer in early spring, again about May 15 and once again no later than July 15. To control insects and diseases, spray or dust the plants at seven to ten-day intervals (and always after rains) from the time they leaf out until growth stops in the fall. Use a special rose spray plus Phaltan.

Keep dead and weak wood and suckers pruned out, and cut back the roses in early spring to green wood. It is not necessary to prune in the fall unless the canes are very long; in that case, they should be shortened somewhat so that they are not tossed about and damaged by winter winds. To protect plants against low winter temperatures, mound soil up around them in the fall. In the coldest climates, the mounds should be about 12 in. high; in milder areas, 6 in. is enough. Further south no mounding is necessary.

Climbers should be pruned *after* they flower in the spring by removing old canes at the base. Tie the stems to the trellis or whatever support you are growing the plants on. In the extreme North,

Roses grow in just about every part of the United States. This lovely sunken rose garden is in the Berkshire Mountains in western Massachusetts, where winters are frigid and the frost-free growing season may not be more than three months long.

plants should be protected in winter by wrapping in burlap and straw.

Tree roses are handled like hybrid teas, but in cold climates they should be wrapped in burlap, straw, building paper, etc., in winter. In the northernmost states, they should be bent to the ground and covered with soil.

¶ *Azaleas and rhododendrons.* Mix large amounts of peat into each planting hole. The soil must be acid; if necessary, mix in powdered sulfur (see Chapter 5). Set the plants at the same level they grew before, never any lower. Because the roots are very shallow, do not cultivate around established plants. Maintain a mulch of oak leaves or pine needles. Fertilize every spring with cottonseed meal or balanced acid fertilizer—about 1/2 cupful to a 12-in. plant; more to larger plants. Pick off all flowers after they die.

¶ *Camellias* should be grown in well-drained, acid, very humusy soil in a partially shaded location that has good air drainage and is protected from cold winds. Water the soil to a depth of 18 in. whenever it dries out, and spray the tops of plants with water daily in summer. Fertilize plants up to 4 ft. tall with 2 to 3 tbs. of a 6-6-6 or 8-8-8 fertilizer before growth starts in the spring, again after new growth starts to harden, again in midsummer and once again in early winter. Increase amount for taller plants. Keep mulched with oak leaves or pine needles. Trim out branches occasionally to let light into the plants; but avoid hard or frequent pruning except to remove branches infected by die-back. Spray with dimethoate after the first spring growth hardens and about four weeks later to control scale insects and mites.

TABLE XII
Trees

The key to this table as well as to Tables XIII, XIV, XV, XVI, XIX, XX and XXII is as follows:

Under "Where grown"

Anywhere	— This is a slight exaggeration in the interest of saving space. Plants so marked grow *almost* anywhere in the U.S.

Cold   — Northernmost states

Mild   — From about southern New England to the
                               Mason-Dixon line

Warm   — From the Mason-Dixon Line to northern
                               Florida

Warmest   — Florida, southern Texas, southern California,
                               Hawaii, etc.

Eastern ½ and Western ½ — From the Plains States east or west

Under "Exposure"

    S — sun.   Sh — shade (really partial shade)

Under "When to prune"

    Win. — Winter

    Spr. — Spring

    Sum. — Summer

    EW — Early winter

    ES   — Early spring

    LF   — Late fall

    AF   — After flowering

    AFr — After fruit

    Any. — Any time

Plants marked with an asterisk * require acid soil. Those marked with two asterisks ** require an alkaline soil.

	Where grown	Height (ft.)	Deciduous, evergreen	Exposure	When to prune
Acacia	Warmest	60	D	S	AF
Acanthopanax	Warm	90	D	S or Sh	Win.
Ailanthus	Mild	60	D	S or Sh	Win.
Alder (*Alnus*)	Cold, mild	70	D	S	Win.
Anacahuita (*Cordia boissieri*)	Warmest	15	E	S	Win.
Aralia	Warm, mild	45	D	S	ES
Arborvitae (*Thuja*)	Cold, mild	60	E	S	Spr.
Araucaria	Warmest	100	E	S	Win.
Arbutus	Warm	80	E	S	AF
Ash (*Fraxinus*)	Cold, mild, warm	80	D	S	Win.
Australian silk oak (*Grevillea robusta*)	Warmest	150	E	S	AF

	Where grown	Height (ft.)	Deciduous, evergreen	Exposure	When to prune
Bald cypress (*Taxodium distichum*	Mild, warm	120	D	S	Win.
Bauhinia	Warmest	25	E	S	AF
Beech (*Fagus*)	Eastern ½	100	D	S	Win.
Birch (*Betula*)	Cold, mild	90	D	S	Win.
Brachychiton acerifolium	Warmest	60	E	S	AF
Brisbane box (*Tristania conferta*)	Warmest	100	E	S	AF
Buckthorn (*Rhamnus*)	Mild, warm	40	D and E	S or Sh	Win.
Buttonwood (*Platanus occidentalis*)	Eastern ½	100	D	S	Win.
California laurel (*Umbellularia californica*)	Far West	85	E	Sh	Win.
Carob (*Ceratonia siliqua*)	Warmest	50	E	S	Win.
Cassia	Warmest	30	D and E	S	AF
Casuarina	Warmest	60	E	S	Win.
Catalpa	Eastern ½	50	D	S	Win.
Cedar (*Cedrus*)	Mild, warm	150	E	S	Spr.
Cephalotaxus	Mild, warm	30	E	Sh	Spr.
Chinaberry (*Melia azedarach*)	Warm	50	D	S	AF
Chinese chestnut (*Castanea mollissima*)	Mild, warm	90	D	S	Win.
Chinese wingnut (*Pterocarya stenoptera*)	Mild, warm	60	D	S	Win.
Chinquapin (*Castanea pumila*)	Mild, warm	20	D	S	Win.
Cork tree (*Phellodendron*)	Cold, mild, warm	50	D	S	Win.
Crinodendron dependens	Mild, warm	25	E	S	Win.
Cryptomeria	Warm	150	E	S	Spr.
Cunninghamia lanceolata	Warm	75	E	Sh	Spr.
Cypress (*Cupressus*)	Warm	90	E	S	Spr.
Dawn redwood (*Metasequoia glyptostroboides*)	Far West	150	D	S	Spr.
Dogwood (*Cornus*)	Mild, warm	90	D	S	Win.
Dombeya	Warmest	30	E	S or Sh	AF
Douglas fir (*Pseudotsuga taxifolia*)	Northwest	220	E	S	Spr.
Dove tree (*Davidia involucrata*)	Mild, warm	50	D	S	AF
Elm (*Ulmus*)	Cold, mild	140	D	S	Win.
Erythrina	Warmest	45	E	S	AF
Eucalyptus	California	200	E	S	Win.

	Where grown	Height (ft.)	Deciduous, evergreen	Expo- sure	When to prune
Evodia	Mild	25	D	S	Win.
False cypress (*Chamaecyparis*)	Cold, mild, warm	175	E	S	Spr.
Fiddle-leaf fig (*Ficus lyrata*)	Warmest	10	E	Sh	Win.
Fir (*Abies*)	Cold, mild	300	E	S	Spr.
Firmiana simplex	Warmest	40	D	S	AFr
Flowering apricot (*Prunus*)	Far West	30	D	S	AF
Flowering cherry (*Prunus*)	Mild, warm	25	D	S	AF
Flowering crab (*Malus*)	Mild, warm	25	D	S	AF
Flowering peach (*Prunus*)	Mild, warm	25	D	S	AF
Flowering plum (*Prunus*)	All but coldest	25	D	S	AF
Franklinia	Mild, warm	30	D	S or Sh	Win.
Fringe tree (*Chionanthus*)	Mild, warm	25	D	S	AF
Ginkgo	Mild, warm	120	D	S	Win.
Goldenchain tree (*Laburnum*)	Mild, warm	30	D	S or Sh	AF
Golden chinquapin (*Castanopsis chrysophylla*)	Far West	100	E	S	Win.
Golden larch (*Pseudolarix amabilis*)	Mild	100	D	S	Win.
Goldenrain tree (*Koelreuteria paniculata*)	Mild, warm	25	D	S	Win.
Guatemala holly (*Olmediellia betscheleriana*)	Warmest	25	E	S or Sh	Win.
Hackberry (*Celtis*)	Eastern ½	100	D	S	Win.
Halesia	Mild, warm	90	D	Sh	Win.
Hawthorn (*Crataegus*)	East, South	30	D	S or Sh	AF
Hemlock (*Tsuga*)	Northeast, Northwest	100	E	S	Spr.
Hickory (*Carya*)	Eastern ½	130	D	S	Win.
Holly (*Ilex*)	Cold, mild, warm	60	E and D	S	ES
Honey locust (*Gleditsia*)	Anywhere	90	D	S	Win.
Hop hornbeam (*Ostrya virginiana*)	Eastern ½	40	D	S	Win.
Hornbeam (*Carpinus*)	Mild	50	D	S or Sh	Win.
Horse chestnut (*Aesculus*)	Mild, warm	100	D	S	Win.
Incense cedar (*Libocedrus decurrens*)	Far West	100	E	Sh	Spr.
Jacaranda	Warmest	40	D	S	AF

	Where grown	Height (ft.)	Deciduous, evergreen	Exposure	When to prune
Japanese pagoda tree (*Sophora japonica*)	Mild, warm	60	D	S	Win.
Japanese raisin tree (*Hovenia dulcis*)	Mild	30	D	S	Win.
Jujube (*Zizyphus*)	Warmest	30	D or E	S	Win.
Juniper (*Juniperus*)	Anywhere	60	E	S	Spr.
Kafir plum (*Harpephyllum caffrum*)	Warmest	35	E	S	AFr
Katsura Tree (*Cercidiphyllum japonicum*)	Mild	60	D	S	Win.
Kentucky coffee tree (*Gymnocladus dioica*)	Eastern ½	90	D	S	Win.
Larch (*Larix*)	Northeast, Northwest	100	D	S	Win.
Laurel cherry (*Prunus caroliniana*)	Warmest	25	E	S	AF
Leptospermum	Far West	30	E	S	AF
Leucadendron argenteum	Warmest	30	E	S	Win.
Linden (*Tilia*)	Mild	110	D	S	Win.
Locust (*Robinia*)	East	80	D	S	Win.
London plane tree (*Platanus acerifolia*)	Mild	120	D	S	Win.
Maackia amurensis	Cold, mild, warm	40	D	S	Win.
Magnolia	All but coldest	120	E and D	S or Sh	AF
Maple (*Acer*)	Anywhere	120	D	S	Win.
Mayten tree (*Maytenus boaria*)	Warm	40	E	S	Win.
Mountain ash (*Sorbus*)	Mild	60	D	S	Win.
Oak (*Quercus*)	Anywhere	100	D	S	Win.
Osage orange (*Maclura pomifera*)	Mild, warm	60	D	S	Win.
Oxydendrum arboreum	Mild, warm	60	D	S	Win.
Palms	Warmest	100	E	S	Win.
Paper mulberry (*Broussonetia papyrifera*)	Mild	50	D	S	Win.
Parkinsonia	Warmest	25	D	S	Win.
Paulownia tomentosa	Mild, warm	50	D	S	AF
Pepper tree (*Schinus*)	Warmest	40	E	S	Win.
Pine (*Pinus*)	Anywhere	180	E	S	Spr.
Plumeria	Warmest	35	D	S	AF
Plum yew (*Cephalotaxus*)	Mild	30	E	S	Spr.
Podocarpus	Warmest	60	E	S	Win.
Poplar (*Populus*)	Anywhere	80	D	S	Win.

	Where grown	Height (ft.)	Deciduous, evergreen	Exposure	When to prune
Pterostyrax hispida	Mild, warm	45	D	S	AF
Redbud (*Cercis*)	Mild, warm	30	D	S	AF
Royal poinciana (*Delonix regia*)	Warmest	40	D	S	Win.
Russian olive (*Elaeagnus angustifolia*)	All but coldest	20	D	S	Win.
Sassafras	East	60	D	S or Sh	Win.
Sea grape (*Coccolobis uvifera*)	Warmest	20	E	S	Win.
Sequoia	Far West	340	E	S	Spr.
Shadblow (*Amelanchier*)	Mild	45	D	S	AF
Silk tree (*Albizzia julibrissin*)	Warm	40	D	S	AF
Smoke tree (*Cotinus*)	Mild	25	D	S	Win.
Spathodea campanulata	Warmest	40	E	S	AF
Spruce (*Picea*)	Cold, mild	180	E	S	Spr.
Stenocarpus sinuatus	Warmest	25	E	S	AF
Styrax japonica	All but coldest	30	D	S	Win.
Sumac (*Rhus*)	Anywhere	30	D	S	Win.
Sweet bay (*Laurus nobilis*)	Warmest	30	E	S	L. Spr.
Sweet gum (*Liquidambar tinctoria*)	Cold, mild, warm	110	D	S	Win.
Sweetleaf (*Symplocos tinctoria*)	Warm	25	E	S or Sh	Win.
Sweet olive (*Osmanthus fragrans*) *	Warmest	25	E	Sh	AF
Tamarisk (*Tamarix*)	Mild, warm	30	E	S	AF
Tanoak (*Lithocarpus densiflora*)	Far West	90	E	S	Win.
Torreya	Warm	75	E	S	Win.
Tulip tree (*Liriodendron tulipifera*)	Eastern ½	80	D	S	Win.
Tupelo (*Nyssa*)	Mild, warm	80	D	S	Win.
Umbrella pine (*Sciadopitys verticillata*)	Mild, warm	100	E	S	Win.
Walnut (*Juglans*)	Anywhere	110	D	S	Win.
Willow (*Salix*)	Anywhere	60	D	S	Win.
Yellow wood (*Cladrastis lutea*)	Mild	60	D	S	Fall
Yew (*Taxus*)	Cold, mild, warm	60	E	S	Spr.
Zanthoxylum	East, South	50	D	S	Win.
Zelkova	Mild	80	D	S	Win.

TABLE XIII[1]
Shrubs

	Where grown	Height (ft.)	Deciduous, evergreen	Expo- sure	When to prune
Abelia	Warm, mild	5	E or D	S	Win.
Acalypha	Warmest	10	E	S	Spr.
Allamanda	Warmest	6	E	S	AF
Amorpha	Warm, mild	15	D	S	ES
Aralia	Warm, mild	25	D	S	ES
Ardisia crispa	Warmest	5	E	Sh	ES
Aspidistra	Warmest	3	E	Sh	ES
Aucuba japonica	Warm	10	E	Sh	Win.
Azalea°	All but coldest	15	E and D	S or Sh	AF
Baccharis	East, Far West	10	E and D	S	Win.
Barberry (*Berberis*)	All but coldest	8	E and D	S or Sh	Win.
Beach plum (*Prunus maritima*	Northeast	6	D	S	Win.
Beauty bush (*Kolkwitzia amabilis*)	Mild	6	D	S	AF
Bladder nut (*Staphylea*)	Cold	15	D	Sh	AFr
Blood leaf (*Iresine herbstii*)	Warmest	6	E	S	Any.
Blueberry (*Vaccinium*)°	Cold,mild, warm	15	D	S	ES
Blue sage (*Eranthemum nervosum*)	Warmest	5	E	Sh	AF
Blue spirea (*Caryopteris incana*)	Warm	5	D	S	Fall
Box (*Buxus*)	Mild	25	E	S or Sh	Sum.
Breath of heaven (*Diosma ericoides*)	Warmest	4		S	AF
Broom (*Cytisus*)	Mild, warm	10	D and E	S	AF
Bruckenthalia spiculifolia	Mild, warm	1	E	S	ES
Brunfelsia°	Warmest	5	E	S or Sh	Sum.
Buddleia	Mild, warm	10	D	S	ES
Button bush (*Cephalanthus occidentalis*)	Mild, warm	20	D	S or Sh	Win.
Calliandra°	Warmest	12	E	S	Sum.
Callicarpa	Warm	10	D	Sh	Fall

[1] For an explanation of terms used in this table, see key to Table XII (page 226).

	Where grown	Height (ft.)	Deciduous, evergreen	Expo-sure	When to prune
Callistemon	Warmest	30	E	S	Fall
Calycanthus	Warm	12	D	S or Sh	Win.
Camellia°	Warm	30	E	Sh	AF
Carpenteria californica	California	7	E	S	Win.
Ceanothus	Far West	35	E and D	S	AF
Ceratostigma	Mild, warm	4		S or Sh	AF
Cestrum	Warmest	12	E	Sh	AF
Chamaelaucium	Warmest	12	E	S	AF
Chinese hat plant (*Holm-skioldia sanguinea*)	Warmest	10	E	S or Sh	AF
Chinese hibiscus (*Hibis-cus rosa-sinensis*)	Warmest	20		S	AF
Chokeberry (*Aronia*)	Eastern ½	8	D	S or Sh	Win.
Chorizema varium	Warmest	2	E	S or Sh	AF
Clethra alnifolia	Warm	9	D	S or Sh	Win.
Cleyera (*Eurya*)°	Warm	10	E	Sh	AF
Cocculus laurifolius	Warm	25	E	Sh	Fall
Colutea	Mild, warm	4	D	S	Win.
Coral plant (*Russelia equisetiformis*)	Warmest	4	E	S or Sh	AF
Correa	Far West	2½	E	Sh	AF
Corylopsis	Mild, warm	6	D	S	AF
Cotoneaster	Mild, warm	12	D and E	S	Win.
Crape jasmine (*Ervatamia coronaria*)	Warmest	6	E	S	Win.
Crape myrtle (*Lagerstroemia*)	Warm	20	D	S	Win.
Crossandra infundibuli-formis	Warmest	3	E	S	EW
Croton (*Codiaeum*)	Warmest	6	E	Sh	Win.
Crowberry (*Empetrum nigrum*)	Cold	1	E	S	Win.
Cyrilla racemiflora	Warm	20	E and D	Sh	AF
Daboecia cantabrica°	Mild, warm	18	E	S	ES
Daphne	Mild, warm	5	E and D	S or Sh	AF
Daphniphyllum macro-podum	Warm	25	E	S or Sh	Win.
Desert willow (*Chilopsis linearis*)	Warm	20	D	S	Win.
Deutzia	All but coldest	8	D	S or Sh	AF
Dipelta floribunda	Mild, warm	15	D	S	AF
Dracaena	Warmest	15	E	Sh	Win.
Duranta repens	Warmest	15	E	S	AFr

	Where grown	*Height (ft.)*	*Deciduous, evergreen*	*Exposure*	*When to prune*
Elaeagnus	All but coldest	18	D	S	Win.
Elsholtzia stauntonii	Mild, warm	4	D	S	ES
Enkianthus	Mild	15	D	S	Win.
Escallonia	Far West	25	E	S or Sh	AF
Euonymus	Mild, warm	20	D and E	S or Sh	Win.
Fatsia japonica	Warm	15	E	Sh	Win.
Flowering almond (*Prunus*)	Mild, warm	10	D	S	Win.
Flowering currant (*Ribes*)	Warm	12	E and D	S	AF
Flowering maple (*Abutilon*)	Warmest	10	E	Sh	Fall
Flowering quince (*Chaenomeles*)	Mild, warm	10	D	S or Sh	AF
Forsythia	Mild	12	D	S	AF
Fothergilla	Mild, warm	10	D	S	AF
Fremontia	Far West	15	E	S	AF
Fuchsia	Warm	20	E	S or Sh	ES
Furze (*Ulex*)	Warm	3	D	S	Win.
*Gardenia jasminoides**	Warm	6	E	S	AF
Garrya	Far West	8	E	S or Sh	AFr
Genista	Mild, warm	20	D and E	S	AF
Gunnera	Warmest	6	E	Sh	Win.
Hakea	Far West	30	E	S	AFr
Heath (*Erica*)*	Mild, warm	18	E	S	ES
Heather (*Calluna vulgaris*)*	Mild	3	E	S	ES
Hebe	Far West	6	E	S	AF
Holly (*Ilex*)	Mild, warm	25	E and D	S	ES
Holodiscus discolor	Western ½	20	D	S or Sh	AF
Honeysuckle (*Lonicera*)	Anywhere	15	D and E	S or Sh	ES
Huckleberry (*Gaylussacia*)*	Eastern ½	6	D and E	S or Sh	ES
Hydrangea	Anywhere	15	D	S or Sh	AF
Itea ilicifolia	California	10	E	Sh	AF
Ixora	Warmest	6	E	Sh	AF
Jacobinia carnea	Warmest	4	E	Sh	AF
Jasmine (*Jasminum*)	Warm	20	E and D	S	Win.
Jatropha	Warmest	10	E and D	S or Sh	ES
Jerusalem sage (*Phlomis fruticosa*)	Mild, warm	4	D	S	Spr.
Juniper (*Juniperus*)	Anywhere	15	E	S	ES
Kerria japonica	Mild, warm	8	D	S or Sh	AF

	Where grown	Height (ft.)	Deciduous, evergreen	Exposure	When to prune
Lantana	Warmest	4	E and D	S	ES
Leatherleaf (*Chamae-daphne calyculata*)	Mild, warm	5	E	S	AF
Lemon verbena (*Lippia citriodora*)	Warmest	10	E	S	Fall
Lespedeza	Mild, warm	9	D	S	ES
*Leucophyllum texanum***	Warmest	12	E	S	Win.
*Leucothoe**	Mild, warm	12	E	Sh	AF
Lilac (*Syringa*)	Cold, mild	30	D	S	AF
Loropetalum chinense	Warm	10	E	Sh	AF
Malpighia	Warmest	10	E	S	AFr
Malvaviscus	Warmest	10	E	S or Sh	Any.
Manzanita (*Arcto-staphylos*)	Far West	20	E	S or Sh	AFr
Mexican orange (*Choisya ternata*)	Warm	8	E	S or Sh	AF
Mimulus	Far West	5	E	S	AF
Mockorange (*Phila-delphus*)	Cold, mild, warm	12	D	S	AF
Mountain heath (*Phyllodoce*)	Mild	1	E	Sh	Win.
Mountain laurel (*Kalmia*)*	Mild	10	E	S or Sh	Win.
Myrica	Cold, mild	8	D and E	S	Win.
Myrsine africana	Far West	3	E	S or Sh	Win.
Myrtle (*Myrtis communis*)	Warmest	10	E	S	Win.
Nandina domestica	Warmest	8	E	S	Win.
Natal plus (*Carissa grandiflora*)	Warmest	15	E	S	Win.
Neillia	Cold, mild	6	D	S	AF
Ninebark (*Physocarpus*)	Cold, mild	8	D	S	AF
Oleander (*Nerium oleander*)	Warmest	25	E	S	AF
Orange jasmine (*Muraya exotica*)	Warmest	10	E	Sh	AF
Oregon grape holly (*Mahonia aquifolium*)	Mild	10	E	Sh	AFr
Oxera pulchella	Far West	10	E	S	AF
Pachistima	Mild	4	E	Sh	AF
Pernettya mucronata	Warm	3	E	S	Win.
Phillyrea	Warm	8	E	S	Win.
Photinia	Mild, warm	30	D and E	S	Win.
Pieris japonica	Mild	8	E	Sh	AF

	Where grown	Height (ft.)	Deciduous, evergreen	Exposure	When to prune
Pineapple guava (*Feijoa sellowiana*)	Warmest	12	E	S	AFr
Pittosporum tobira	Warmest	10	E	S or Sh	Win.
Plumbago	Warmest	8	E	S	ES
Poinciana	Warmest	10	D	S	Spr.
Privet (*ligustrum*)	All but coldest	20	D and E	S	ES
				S	AF
Pussy willow (*Salix discolor*)	Anywhere	18	D	S	AF
Pyracantha	All but coldest	20	E	S or Sh	Win.
Raphiolepis	Warmest	10	E	S	AF
Rhododendron*	Mild	30	D and E	Sh	AF
Rhodotypus	Mild, warm	6	D	S	AF
Rondeletia	Warmest	15	E	Sh	AF
Rose (*Rosa*)	Anywhere	10	D	S	ES and AF
Rose of Sharon (*Hibiscus syriacus*)	All but coldest	15	D	S	Win.
Sanchezia nobilis	Warmest	5	E	Sh	Win.
Sand myrtle (*Leiophyllum*)	Mild, warm	1½	E	S or Sh	AF
Sarcococca*	Mild, warm	5	E	S or Sh	AF
Sea buckthorn (*Hippophae rhamnoides*)	Anywhere	25	D	S or Sh	Sum.
Shepherdia	Cold, mild	18	D	S	Win.
Skimmia	Mild, warm	5	E	Sh	Win.
Sorbaria	Mild	18	D	Sh	ES
Spartium junceum	Warmest	8	D	S	AF
Spicebush (*Benzoin*)	East	15	D	Sh	AF
Spirea (*Spiraea*)	Anywhere	6	D	S	AF
Stephanandra	Mild, warm	8	D	S	Win.
Stewartia	Warm	15	D	S or Sh	Win.
Stranvaesia	Northwest	20	E	Sh	AF
Symphoricarpos	Anywhere	7	D	S or Sh	Win.
Ternstroemia*	Mild, warm	8	E	S or Sh	AF
Tetrapanax papyriferum	Warmest	7	E	S or Sh	Spr.
Tibouchina	Warmest	20	E	Sh	Win.
Velvet plant (*Gynura aurantiaca*)	Warmest	4	E	Sh	Win.
Viburnum	Anywhere	30	D	S or Sh	Win. and AF
Vitex	Warm	12	D	S	ES

	Where grown	Height (ft.)	Deciduous, evergreen	Exposure	When to prune
Weigela	All but coldest	10	D	S	AF
Wintersweet (*Chimonanthus praecox*)	Warm	10	D	S	AF
Witch hazel (*Hamamelis*)	Mild, warm	25	D	Sh	AF
Xylosma senticosa	Warm	6	E	S	ES
Yellow elder (*Stenolobium stans*)	Warmest	15	D	S	AF
Yellow oleander (*Thevetia nereifolia*)	Warmest	8	E	S	AF
Yellow root (*Zanthorhiza simplicissima*)	East	20	D	Sh	Win.
Yew (*Taxus*)	Cold, mild, warm	15	E	S or Sh	Spr.

TABLE XIV[1]
Vines

	Where grown	Height (ft.)	Deciduous, evergreen	Exposure	When to prune
Actinidia	Warm	30	D	S or Sh	ES
Akebia quinata	Warm, mild	20	E	S	Spr.
Allamanda	Warmest	30	E	S	AF
Ampelopsis	Anywhere	30	D	S or Sh	ES
Asparagus fern (*A. plumosus*)	Warmest	6	E	Sh	Any.
Beaumontia grandiflora	Warmest	30	E	S	AF
Bignonia capreolata	Warm	40	E	S or Sh	Spr.
Bittersweet (*Celastrus*)	Anywhere	25	D	S or Sh	ES
Boston ivy (*Parthenocissus tricuspidata*)	All but coldest	35	D	S or Sh	ES
Bougainvillea	Warmest	20	E	S	AF
Brazilian nightshade (*Solanum seaforthianum*)	Warmest	25	E	S	AF
Calico flower (*Aristolochia elegans*)	Warmest	20	E	Sh	AF
Cape honeysuckle (*Tecomaria capensis*)	Warmest	12	E	S	AF

[1] For an explanation of terms used in this table, see key to Table XII (page 226).

	Where grown	Height (ft.)	Deciduous, evergreen	Expo-sure	When to prune
Carolina jasmine (*Gel-semium sempervirens*)	Warm	20	E	S or Sh	AF
Catsclaw creeper (*Dox-antha unquis-catii*)	Warm	40	E	S	AF
Chayote (*Sechium edule*)	Warm	50	D	S	Fall
Cistus	Warm	8	D	S	Win.
Clematis**	Anywhere	20	D or E	S	Win.
Clereodendron	Warmest	15	E	S or Sh	Win.
Climbing hydrangea (*H. petiolaris*)	All but coldest	50	D	S or Sh	ES
Climbing ylang-ylang (*Artabotrys odora-tissimus*)	Warmest	10	E	S or Sh	AF
Cobaea scandens	Warm	25	D	S	Fall
Congea tomentosa	Warmest	40	E	S	AF
Coral vine (*Antigonon leptopus*)	Warmest	40	D	S	Fall
Creeping fig (*Ficus pumila*)	Warmest	50	E	Sh	Fall
Derris scandens	Warmest	35	E	S or Sh	Win.
Dutchman's pipe *Aristolochia durior*)	Anywhere	30	D	S or Sh	ES
Euonymus radicans	Mild	30	E	S or Sh	ES
Evergreen grape (*Cissus capensis*)	Warmest	50	D	Sh	AFr
Firecracker vine (*Manettia*)	Warmest	6	E	S	ES
Flame vine (*Pyrostegia ignea*)	Warmest	35	E	S	AF
German ivy (*Senecio mikanioides*)	Warm	10	D	Sh	AF
Glory grape (*Vitis coignetiae*)	All but coldest	65	D	S	Spr.
Glory vine (*Clytostoma callistegioides*)	Warmest	30	E	S	AF
Grape ivy (*Cissus rhombifolia*)	Warmest	20	E	Sh	Win.
Hibbertia volubilis	Warmest	30	E	Sh	ES
Honeysuckle (*Lonicera*)	Anywhere	30	D or E	S or Sh	ES
Ivy (*Hedera*)	Anywhere	90	E	Sh	ES
Kadsura japonica	Southeast	10	E	S	ES
Kangaroo vine (*Cissus antarctica*)	Warmest	10	E	Sh	Spr.

	Where grown	Height (ft.)	Deciduous, evergreen	Exposure	When to prune
Lycium	All but coldest	8	D	S or Sh	Spr.
Madagascar jasmine (Stephanotis floribunda)	Warmest	15	E	Sh	ES
Mandevilla suaveolens	Warm	15	D	S or Sh	AF
Magnolia vine (Schisandra propinqua)	Southeast	20	D	Sh	Spr.
Monstera	Warmest	20	E	Sh	AF or AFr
Pandorea	Warmest	30	E	S or Sh	ES
Passiflora	Warmest	35	E	S	LF
Paullinia thalictrifolia	Warmest	10	E	Sh	Win.
Phaedranthus buccinatorius	Warmest	70	E	S	ES
Queen's wreath (Petrea volubilis)	Warmest	20	E	S or Sh	AF
Rubber vine (Cryptostegia grandiflora)	Warmest	10	E	S	Win.
Silk vine (Periploca)	Mild, warm	40	D	S	ES
Silver lace vine (Polygonum aubertii)	All but coldest	25	D	S	ES
Solandra	Warmest	30	E	S	AF
Star jasmine (Trachelospermum jasminoides)	Warm	20	E	Sh	Fall
Stauntonia hexaphylla	Warm	40	E	Sh	ES
Stigmaphyllon ciliatum	Warmest	12	E	Sh	ES
Supplejack (Berchemia scandens)	Warm	20	D	S	Spr.
Thunbergia	Warm	50	D	S	ES
Tradescantia	Warmest	3	E	Sh	AF
Trumpet creeper (Campsis)	All but coldest	30	D	S	ES
Virginia creeper (Parthenocissus quinquefolia)	All but coldest	40	D	S	ES
Wax plant (Hoya carnosa)	Warmest	10	E	Sh	ES
Wisteria	All but coldest	60	D	S	AF

17

How to Raise Hedges

A WELL-KEPT HEDGE CAN BE one of the most striking features in a garden. It may also serve the practical purpose of breaking the wind, providing privacy and, to a limited extent, filtering noises from the street or neighboring homes. On the other hand, if a hedge is not given attention, almost nothing in the garden looks so bad.

¶ *Planting.* Since hedge plants are woody plants (although there is no reason why Southwesterners should not use cacti or succulents), they should be planted at the same time and in the same general way as the plants discussed in Chapter 16. The plants may be set in a trench or in individual holes. In either case, be sure they are spaced evenly, in a straight line and standing upright.

Spacing of the plants depends on the species and the ultimate desired size of the hedge. The recommended minimum spacing for different plants is given in Table XV (page 245). You should also give some thought to the space on either side of the hedge. If it is too close to a tree, it may not only be too heavily shaded but it may also lose out in the competition for moisture. And if it is placed hard against a wall, its root system is even more restricted than it would be normally.

¶ *Pruning and trimming.* During a hedge's early years the main aim of pruning is to force bushy growth at the base. This is accomplished by cutting back the tops of the plants and thus encouraging the outward growth of the side branches.

Evergreens are pruned rather lightly; you need do nothing more than nip off young succulent top growth as it starts to develop. But privet and other deciduous shrubs (and to a lesser extent, deciduous trees) are pruned severely. The recommended practice is to cut the tops back about a third at planting time. Then let the branches grow about 12 in. and cut them back 6 in. Repeat this process a second and perhaps a third time until the plants have thickened out.

Once a hedge, whether evergreen or deciduous, has begun to develop the proper shape, pruning becomes a job of trimming. You may have to do this several times a year or only once in the spring. The simplest practice—provided your hedge does not have important blooms—is to clip the hedge in the spring. Then, after it leafs out and starts to grow, spray it with maleic hydrazide. This will prevent all further growth except for a few stray shoots that the spray does not happen to strike.

Whether you trim a hedge to a smooth, formal shape or to a more natural informal shape is a matter of choice; but in either case it is important not to cut the hedge so that it is wider at the top than at the bottom (hedges under about 5 ft. should actually be narrower at the top than at the bottom). If it is wider, the bottom branches will not receive enough light and will gradually grow ratty and perhaps die.

Another important point to remember when growing a hedge that is to exceed a height of 4 1/2 ft. is that it should not be more than 5 ft. wide. The reason is this: It is not difficult to trim the top of a wide hedge if it is low enough for you to stand on the ground while wielding your shears. But if you have to climb a ladder to trim a hedge, it is extremely difficult and even risky to remove the center branches from the top of a hedge that is wider than twice the length of your arms.

A second reason for restricting the width of hedges—and here I include low evergreen hedges—is that the side branches are shorter and the central stems more vigorous (because they receive more

If it is not clipped too much, boxwood develops into a large, dense evergreen hedge in warm and mild climates. Here it is used to screen one of the yard's least attractive areas—the garage turn-around and parking area—from the street. The homeowner keeps it trimmed in the rounded shape natural to the plant.

Because this hemlock hedge is trimmed narrower at the top than at the bottom, the sun reaches all the branches (except those behind the fence). Strong, uniform growth is the result.

This huge formal garden gains much of its beauty from carefully trimmed
hedges and tall yews. Hedges are luxuriant from ground up because they are
sheared so that sun reaches bottom branches as well as top.

light); consequently, they are able to stand up under heavy snow loads better.

¶ *Other care.* Because hedge plants are crowded close together and because the loss of just one plant or even part of a plant can spoil the entire effect, you should give them somewhat more attention than free-standing shrubs and trees. But this really means nothing more than seeing that the hedge has a good supply of moisture at all times; that it is fertilized every spring; and that it is sprayed with the appropriate chemical at the first sign of insect infection or disease. You should also keep an eye out for seedling trees, shrubs and vines that try to establish themselves in the middle of a hedge, for once they get a foothold, they are almost impossible to eradicate without eradicating part of the hedge.

TABLE XV
Selected Hedge Plants

	Where grown[1]	Deciduous, evergreen	Minimum trimmed height (in.)	Space plants (in.)
Abelia grandiflora	Warm, mild	D	60	36
Arborvitae (*Thuja occidentalis*)	Cold, mild	E	96	24-36
Barberry (*Berberis thunbergii*)	Cold, mild	D	36	18-24
Barberry (*B. thunbergii minor*)	Cold, mild	D	15	9-12
Box (*Buxus sempervirens suffruticosa*)	Mild	E	18	6-18
Cotoneaster divaricata	Mild, warm	D	36	24-30
Euonymus alatus compactus	Cold, mild	D	48	36
Hemlock (*Tsuga canadensis*)	Northeast, Northwest	E	120	36-48
Holly (*Ilex crenata convexa*)	Cold, mild, warm	E	24	12-24
Malpighia coccigera	Warmest	E	24	18-24
Osage orange (*Maclura pomifera*)	Mild, warm	D	96	12-24
Pittosporum tobira	Warmest	E	72	48

[1] For an explanation of terms used in this column, see key to Table XII (page 226).

	Where grown[1]	Deciduous, evergreen	Minimum trimmed height (in.)	Space plants (in.)
Podocarpus macrophylla makii	Warmest	E	96	30-42
Privet (*Ligustrum amurense*)	Anywhere	D	48	12-24
Privet (L. *ovalifolium*)	Mild, warm	D	36	9-15
Privet (L. *japonicum*)	Mild, warm	E	48	12-24
Pyracantha coccinea	All but coldest	E	48	24-36
Rose (*Rosa*)	Anywhere	D	24	18-24
Russian olive (*Elaeagnus angustifolia*)	All but coldest	D	120	48-60
Sarcocca hookeriana humilis	Mild, warm	E	18	15-18
Sweet bay (*Laurus nobilis*)	Warmest	E	72	42-54
Yew (*Taxus baccata*)	Mild, warm	E	120	36-60
Yew (*T. cuspidata*)	Cold, mild, warm	E	48	24-42

18

How to Raise Fruit

ANYBODY CAN GROW THE DECIDUOUS tree fruits listed below and get some fruit from them; but to grow them so that they produce consistently large, sound and delicious fruits is another story. They need a *lot* of attention, particularly in the spraying and pruning departments.

TABLE XVI
The Deciduous Tree Fruits

	Where grown[1]	*Height (ft.)*	*Space plants (ft.)*
Apple	Anywhere	50	40
Apricot	Anywhere	25	20
Cherry	Mild, cool	50	20-30
Crabapple	All but coldest and warmest	25	20
Fig	Mild, warm	30	15-20
Mulberry	Cold, mild	60	40
Nectarine	California	25	20
Pawpaw	Eastern U.S.	35	25
Peach	Anywhere	25	20
Pear	Anywhere	40	20-25
Persimmon	Warm	50	20
Plum	Anywhere	30	20-25
Quince	Eastern U.S.	20	20

[1] For an explanation of terms used in this column, see key to Table XII (page 226).

¶ *Tree selection.* Do you want standard-size or dwarfed varieties? The former produce most fruit and put on the largest show of color in the spring. They are also handsome trees that bring beauty and shade to the yard. The main advantage of the dwarfed trees—aside from the strange fascination that all undersized things have for most of us—is that they make it possible to grow some normal-sized fruit even in a very small garden. They are also easier to prune and spray, and start bearing at an earlier age.

Whether you plant large or dwarfed trees, start with one-year-old plants. They are the most economical. Older specimens of dwarfed trees can be used, however, if you prefer letting the nurseryman do the early training of the trees. Such trees will also give fruit at an earlier date. (However, almost any well-grown fruit tree should be in good production at five years of age.)

Since a great many varieties of fruits will not set fruit with their own pollen, it is often necessary to plant two compatible varieties. In buying deciduous fruit trees, therefore, remember to ask the nursery whether the varieties you have selected are self-fruitful or self-unfruitful. In the case of mulberries, you should be sure to get both male and female plants.

Your Agricultural Extension Service is probably the best source of advice about the varieties that will grow best in your area.

¶ *Planting.* Plant the trees in full sun and, if possible, in a location where they will not be damaged by spring frosts that strike after they blossom. Farmers, for instance, plant fruit trees on hillsides, never in valleys where frost settles first. In the case of very early blooming trees, such as apricots, farmers also try to plant the trees on the north side of a hill where they will receive a little less sun in late winter (this helps to delay blossoming and thus helps to protect against late frosts).

The soil should be well drained and fertile. In general, a sandy loam with a porous clay subsoil is best.

When digging a planting hole, make it large enough to allow the roots to be spread out; and add several spadefuls of humus. Do not mix in fertilizer.

Standard trees should be planted at the depth they previously grew or about 1 in. deeper. Dwarfed trees must be planted so that the graft joint is 1 or 2 in. *above* the surface. (Dwarfed trees owe their small size to the fact that they are grown on dwarfing root-stocks. If the scion—the upper part of the tree—is at ground level, it sometimes takes root and causes the tree to grow larger than it should.) Staking should not be necessary except to protect very small trees from being run down by bicycles, etc. But if you put in large trees, support them in the way discussed in Chapter 16.

Planting may be in spring or fall, except in very cold climates where spring planting is essential. The plants should not be in leaf.

During the first winter, to protect the bark of trees with good-size trunks against injury by the sun, wrap the trunks with burlap up to the bottom branch. This can be removed the following year. Loop wire mesh around the trunks to protect against rabbits and field mice, if these pests are present in sizable numbers.

¶ *Regular care.* During the growing season, do not allow the soil in which fruit trees are growing to dry out to a depth of more than 12 in.

To hold in moisture and also to encourage maximum tree growth and fruit production, keep the entire area under the branches covered at all times with an organic mulch. Note, however, that rodents may find this a good nesting place, so keep the mulch pulled away from the trunks or wrap the trunks loosely in wire mesh. The practice of planting ground covers under fruit trees is not recommended. To be sure, they eliminate a certain amount of yard maintenance because they conceal the fruits that fall from the trees; but they take moisture and nutrients away from the trees.

Trees planted in the fall should be fertilized for the first time the following spring. Spring-planted trees are fed three weeks after planting. Thereafter, all trees should be fertilized in early spring. Use a balanced fertilizer recommended by your Extension Service or, lacking such a recommendation, use one that is rich in nitrogen and potassium. Applications should be at the rate of about 1 lb. of fertilizer for each year of tree age up to a maximum of 10 lb. Scatter the fertilizer on the soil over the entire root area and water it in well.

If at any time you notice that the leaves are turning yellow in spots between the veins, send a soil sample to your Experiment Station. It may be that it is deficient in magnesium, an element especially important to fruit trees. This can be corrected by applying Dolomitic limestone to the soil, or you can spray the foliage three or four times at fortnightly intervals with 1 lb. of epsom salts in 8 gal. of water.

¶ *Insects and diseases.* All fruit trees except those mentioned separately below should be sprayed regularly to protect them against insects and diseases. Ask your Extension Service to tell you what schedule to follow and which sprays to use. Pest problems vary widely from one part of the country to the next. As a very, very general rule, however, you should apply a dormant-oil spray when the leaves of the blossom buds are 1/4 in. long. Then apply an all-purpose fruit spray (1) when the blossoms begin to show color, (2) when the last petals are falling and (3) every ten days thereafter until two weeks before the fruit is ready to harvest. (Ready-made, all-purpose sprays are on the market, or you can make your own with 1 tbs. malathion or 3 tbs. Sevin mixed with 1 1/2 tbs. captan in 1 gal. water.)

Figs should be sprayed with 4-4-50 Bordeaux Mixture as soon as the leaves are full size and monthly thereafter. This guards against rust.

Persimmons, mulberries and pawpaws need to be sprayed only when they are under attack by occasional pests. They do not have too many problems.

¶ *Pruning.* At time of planting, cut one-year-old bare-root trees to a height of about 3 ft. and remove all but a few main branches. But do not prune trees that are growing in cans.

After fruits have been growing in your garden for one summer, prune them annually in early spring. Do not remove any more wood than is necessary to maintain a strong, healthy, open tree. (Hard pruning encourages suckering.) The branches should not be so numerous that the lower branches or a high percentage of the fruits are hidden from the sun. The following points should be borne in mind:

(1) All branches less than 3 ft. above the ground should be removed.

(2) Main branches should take off from the trunk at an angle of 45° to 90°. If the angle is less than 45°, the crotch is weak and the branch should be removed.

(3) A well-pruned tree has a total of about five main scaffold branches. These should take off from the trunk in different directions and at somewhat different heights. If there are several at the same height, the tree may split.

(4) As a tree gets older and bears fruit, the branches bend down. If any actually point toward the ground, either remove them or cut them back to a side branch that is growing upward. Down-growing branches are weak and unproductive.

(5) Excess small branches that shade the heart of the tree should be cut out.

(6) Remove suckers and dead, diseased or weak branches whenever you find them.

(7) To renew old trees that have grown too large for efficient spraying and harvesting (a common problem with apples), remove up to three of the large center limbs. This will cause watersprouts to grow. When these are a year old, select a few small ones to bear fruit and cut out the rest. Allow the selected sprouts to develop without end pruning (which delays fruiting). At the same time, to encourage unproductive older branches to produce more and larger fruit, cut back the tips about 6 in.

Figs are best grown in the form of a bush with three to eight well-spaced stems up to a 4 in. in diameter rising from the ground. The stems should be cut back one-third to one-half their length in the spring after the last frost but before growth has started.

Prune persimmons, mulberries and pawpaws as necessary only to maintain shapely, healthy growth.

¶ *Thinning fruit.* Most fruit trees have a habit of dropping some of their fruit in the spring (this is called "June Drop," although it may occur several months earlier). This is nature's own way of keeping a tree from overproducing, and is not cause for alarm.

Sometimes, however, trees do not drop enough fruit to assure

An apple tree before and after pruning. Main aim in pruning tree is to elim-
inate diseased branches and those with weak crotches that may break under the

weight of the fruit. Thus you keep the trees open so that sun can penetrate.
(NEW YORK STATE AGRICULTURAL EXPERIMENT STATION)

that what remains will be of good size. In this instance, you can help matters by removing some of the less desirable fruits by hand. The earlier in the season that you do this, the better the results. Thin apples, quinces and pears to about 6 to 8 in. apart; peaches and nectarines to 4 to 6 in.; large plums to 2 to 4 in.

¶ *Winter protection.* Fruits that are properly selected for the area in which you live should be able to survive the winter without damage. Large, outstretched branches of old trees may, however, need to be supported on 2 x 4's to prevent heavy snowfalls from breaking them.

The one fruit that is occasionally grown in colder climates than it can normally withstand is the fig. The best way to protect it is to cut the branches back to the desired height as soon as the leaves fall in the autumn. Then pull all the stems and branches together in a loose bundle and tie them. Pack hay tightly between them and wrap a thick layer around them. Over-wrap in burlap, canvas or old blankets. Then cover the bundle with tar paper or heavy polyethylene film, making sure that rain cannot leak through the top seams. (Another way to grow figs in the North is to plant them in tubs which are brought into a cool basement or greenhouse for the winter. They do not need sunlight during this period.)

TABLE XVII
The Citrus Fruits (Evergreen)

	Height (ft.)	Space plants (ft.)
Calamondin	20	15
Grapefruit	25	30
Kumquat	15	15
Lemon	25	25
Lime	25	20
Limequat	25	15
Orange	25	25
Tangelo	25	20
Tangerine	25	20

¶ *Tree selection.* The citrus fruits, of course, grow only in our warmest climates; but even these climates are hit by frost. If you live in an area where frosts are fairly common, select citrus varieties which are likely to produce mature fruit before cold weather strikes. (Citrus fruits do not withstand low temperatures as easily as the trees that bear them.)

Buy one- or two-year-old trees that are balled-and-burlapped or in cans. The trees should have a caliper of 1/2 to 1 1/4 in. measured just above the graft.

¶ *Planting*. In the West, plant trees in March, April or May; elsewhere, plant them any time between mid-December and mid-February. The trees should be dormant.

Soil should be well drained, humusy and fertile. The trees must be grown in the full sun and well removed from septic fields. Do not plant them in a depression where frost may settle. If your garden is exposed to steady winds, you should erect a windbreak of some sort.

Plant the trees slightly higher than they formerly grew and water two or three times a week for the first fortnight. The soil saucer holding water should be 4 in. deep and at least 30 in. across.

To keep the trunks of the young trees from being sunburned, wrap them in heavy paper or paint them with whitewash.

¶ *Fertilizing*. Citrus trees require very heavy feeding throughout the growing year. They also require special formulas that may include various minor elements. In Florida, for example the Agricultural Extension Service recommends a fertilizer containing 6% nitrogen, 6% phosphorus, 6% potassium, 4% magnesium, 3/4% manganese and 1/4% copper. Ask your State Extension Service for its recommendation.

The first feeding is made four to six weeks after planting and is followed by additional feedings at six-week intervals until August 15. Apply 1/2 lb. of fertilizer per tree at the first feeding, and gradually increase this to 1 1/4 lb. at the last feeding. For second-year trees, work up gradually to 2 1/4 lb. per tree per feeding; and for third-year trees work up to 4 lb. per tree per feeding.

In the fourth year the feeding schedule should be reduced to three applications a year—in January-February, May-June and October-November. The amount of fertilizer applied at each feeding from that time until a tree attains ten years of age should be 2/3 lb. per year of age. In other words, a five-year-old tree is given 3 1/3 lb. of fertilizer three times a year. A ten-year-old tree should be given double this amount.

Trees between 11 and 30 years of age should get 1 lb. of fertilizer per year of age at each feeding. After 30, a total of 90 lb. of fertilizer per year is enough.

In addition to feeding citrus trees through their roots, it may be necessary to apply foliar sprays to bearing trees once or twice a year. Nutrients applied by this means include boron, zinc, molybdenum, copper and/or manganese.

The pH of the soil should be maintained at between 5.5 and 6.2.

¶ *Other regular care.* Keep the soil under the trees free of grass, weeds and other growth. Mulching is frowned on by some authorities, advocated by others. If you use an organic mulch, leave 1 ft. of clear space around the trunk. This helps to guard against fungus attacks.

Water trees heavily when the soil dries out to a depth of 12 in. Because citrus trees are evergreen and and therefore use much more water than deciduous fruits, and because the climates in which they grow are fairly uniform the year round, the need for water is fairly constant from month to month.

¶ *Frost protection.* Keeping the trees fed, well watered and free of insects and disease is essential. In November, mound clean earth up around the trunks of trees under five years of age. The bank should be 15 to 20 in. high. To protect against termites, mix chlordane dust into the banked soil. Remove the bank in the spring.

When frost does strike, keep petroleum bricks burning under the trees (see Chapter 12).

¶ *Pruning.* The best time to prune citrus trees is after harvest, but no damage is done by pruning at other times. Actually, however, little pruning is called for if you start with a shapely tree. Just remove branches that develop below the main scaffold branches while the tree is young. Thereafter, cut out dead and broken wood and suckers. Removing too much wood reduces leaf area which in turn reduces fruit production.

If trees are severely damaged by frost, restrain your desire to go at them with pruning shears. Wait until new growth has developed sufficiently for you to determine exactly how much dead wood needs to be removed.

¶ *Insects and diseases.* Follow the spray schedule recommended by your State Extension Service for your area. Citrus trees are prone to considerable damage by a number of small pests.

Another fairly common problem is fruit-splitting. But unfortunately, the cause of this is not known, and there is no sure preventive treatment other than good cultural practices.

This is an extremely diverse group, including a number of plants about which relatively little is known. They grow mainly in south-

TABLE XVIII
Tropical and Subtropical Fruits (Evergreen)

	Type of plant	Height (ft.)	Space plants (ft.)
Avocado	Tree	50	25-35
Banana	Tree	25	10-20
Barbados cherry	Shrub	10	8
Chayote	Vine	50	10
Chilean guava	Shrub	6	6
Date palm	Tree	60	30
Eugenia	Shrub or tree	20	10
Guava	Shrub	30	18-24
Jujube	Shrub or tree	30	20
Kafir plum	Tree	35	35
Loquat	Tree	20	15
Lychee	Tree	40	25-30
Mango	Tree	90	35-40
Monstera	Vine	20	15
Natal plum	Shrub	15	10
Olive[1]	Tree	25	30-40
Papaya	Tree	25	7-10
Passion fruit	Vine	8	12-15
Pineapple	Bromeliad	5	2
Pineapple guava	Shrub	12	15
Pomegranate	Shrub	20	15

[1] The olive is classified as a subtropical plant, but requires considerable cold to bear fruit. It grows as far north as Shasta County in California.

ern Florida, southern California and Hawaii. In general, they are grown pretty much like the citrus fruits but with less frequent and lighter feedings.

In the home garden, the two most popular fruits are the following:

¶ *Avocado.* Plant two different but compatible varieties. The soil should be of average to good quality and it must be very well drained, otherwise incurable avocado root rot may set in. The feeding schedule recommended by the Hawaii Agricultural Extension Service is as follows: 1/4 lb. of an 8-10-8 fertilizer at planting, 1/4 lb. four months later and 1/2 lb. four months after that. In the second year, apply a total of 2 lb. of fertilizer in two or three equal doses. Thereafter apply 1 lb. of fertilizer per inch of trunk diameter in each of two or three equal doses. When trees start to bear heavily, switch to a 10-5-20 fertilizer.

Water about once a week when the trees are making growth. The soil should be wet to a depth of 18 to 22 in., since most root activity is in this region. Diseases and insects are not a particularly serious problem. Unless a tree is growing into an awkward shape, try not to prune it until it is well filled out. Even then, you should prune as little as possible.

¶ *Mango.* Plant grafted varieties during the rainy season. The soil should be well drained and of good quality. A sunny location that is protected from strong winds is required. Newly planted trees should be watered once or twice a week if the rains are not adequate, but established trees can go long periods without water, especially during flowering and fruit setting.

Fertilize with a 10-10-10 formula. Follow the schedule for avocados during the first two years. In the third and fourth years make two or three 1 1/2-lb. applications. Thereafter, feed the trees two or three times a year at the rate of 2 to 4 lb. per feeding. Use more fertilizer in dry climates; less in wet climates.

When a tree is small, remove all branches less than 2 ft. above ground, and develop three or four well-spaced branches into scaffold branches. From then on, keep pruning to a minimum.

To control anthracnose, spray every week during the blossoming and fruiting season with Captan. Other pests are not serious as a rule.

TABLE XIX
The Small Fruits

	Where grown[1]	Type of plant	Height (ft.)	Space between rows (ft.)	Space between plants (ft.)
Blackberry	Anywhere	Bramble	6	6	3
Blueberry	Cold, mild, warm	Shrub	15	8-10	4-5
Boysenberry	Warm	Bramble	6	6	8
Currant	Cold, cool	Shrub	6	5	3-5
Dewberry	Warm	Bramble	6	6	3
Elderberry	Anywhere	Shrub	25	10-15	10
Gooseberry	Cool	Shrub	5	5	3-5
Grape	Anywhere exc. desert	Vine	50	7	7
Loganberry	Warm	Bramble	6	6	8
Raspberry	Mild, cool	Bramble	8	7	3
Strawberry	Anywhere	Perennial	−1	2	1
Youngberry	Warm	Bramble	6	6	3

[1] For an explanation of terms used in this column, see key to Table XII (page 226).

The small fruits grow pretty much all over the country, though some prefer a cool climate while others prefer warm. Most are brambles, like the raspberry. But the most popular are the strawberry, a perennial, and the grape, which is naturally a vine though often not allowed to develop in that way. Two of the shrubby types —the currant and gooseberry—have a bad reputation because they are an alternate host for the white pine blister rust. This means that they should not be planted anywhere that white pines grow.

¶ *Plant selection.* Always use healthy, disease-resistant stock. Grapes must have a well-developed root system. Blueberry plants should be two years old and about 12 to 18 in. high. Put in two different varieties of elderberries to ensure fruiting.

¶ *Soil and planting.* The small fruits need full sun and a soil that is well drained and of about medium consistency. When putting in plants, turn the soil to a depth of 1 ft. and add humus as necessary. The soil for blueberries should have a pH of 5 or less, and ideally it should be a 50-50 mixture of soil and peat. If you have a small raspberry patch, fumigate the soil with formaldehyde to help minimize disease problems.

Early spring planting is recommended except in the Deep South, where fall planting is preferable. Set the plants in rows according to the table above. For small plants, scoop out a hole with a trowel or shovel, spread the roots slightly and firm the soil around them. (If you are setting out a lot of plants, the fastest planting method is simply to thrust the trowel deep into the soil, pull it forward, drop in the plant behind it, and firm the soil.) For larger plants, such as blueberries, dig a hole as for any other shrub. If a blueberry (a handsome plant) is set in a grassy area for ornamental purposes, remove the grass around it in a 3 ft. circle (the planting hole may, however, be smaller). Grass interferes with the shrub's development.

Balled-and-burlapped and potted plants need not have their tops pruned at planting; but it is generally advisable to trim back the tops of bare-root plants about one-third to compensate for the loss of roots in transplanting. Grapes are reduced to one cane, which is then shortened to two buds.

Strawberries should be planted as deeply as possible, but the crowns must not be covered. All other plants go 1 in. deeper than they previously grew.

Water each plant thoroughly. Bare-root plants are also benefited by a cupful of starter solution.

¶ *Fertilizing.* If you do not apply a starter solution at planting, mix a small handful of balanced commercial fertilizer into the soil around each plant and water well. Use the type of fertilizer that is recommended by your Agricultural Extension Service.

Use the same fertilizer for established plants. Make a fairly heavy application in the early spring; and if the plants need it, make one or two additional light applications up to July 15. After this date, feed the plants only if you live in a warm climate where early frosts are not a problem.

¶ *Watering.* During the growing season the small fruits need the equivalent of about 1 in. of rainfall a week (in warm climates and if the soil is sandy, plants are likely to need more). Use a perforated hose or porous soaker laid close to the plant rows.

¶ *Mulching.* No matter what you do about mulching other parts of your garden, by all means use one here. Not only does a mulch conserve moisture but it virtually eliminates the need for cultivating and weeding—a difficult task because the roots of the small fruits lie close to the surface.

One mulch is about as good as another. But transparent polyethylene film is recommended—especially for strawberries—if you live in a climate that is not usually afflicted by late spring frosts (see Chapter 8).

¶ *Pruning.* Bramble fruits bear fruit on two-year-old canes. As soon as the fruit has been picked, cut these canes to the ground and burn them. Other pruning of the brambles is done in late winter, when excess canes should be removed and the remaining canes should be cut back 1 ft. (or even more in poor soil). If you save the new plants that some bramble fruits, notably black raspberries, produce by tip layering, cut the old canes rising from the roots to the ground. In summer, the tips of the new canes on black raspberries and blackberries should be pinched out so that side branches will be produced. Remove suckers between rows.

Although some varieties of bramble fruits produce canes that are stiff enough to stand upright, most should be trained to a support. For the home gardener, the simplest consists of two strong wires stretched between posts. The lowest wire is about 30 in. above the ground, the other between 48 and 60 in. Some gardeners use a telephone-pole arrangement with two wires about 18 in. apart on cross arms 30 and 48 in. above ground. Tie the canes along the wires at intervals. You can bundle several canes together without interfering with fruit production.

Currants and gooseberries are pruned in late fall or winter. Since these plants generally do not produce very much fruit on stems that are more than three years old, pruning should consist of a complete removal of all four-year-old stems. A productive plant should have about nine stems total, of which roughly one-third are a year old, another third are two years old and the remaining third are three years old. The one-year-old stems should be cut back a few inches at pruning time to encourage branching. If gooseberries produce too many lateral branches, some of these should be removed at the same time.

Grape pruning is controlled by the fact that fruit is borne only on year-old branches and that the best fruit clusters are produced by the third to about the tenth buds from the base of each branch. It follows that most grape vines (except muscadines) need to be pruned quite severely every year in the early spring or late winter.

The pruning system most commonly used is called the Kniffin system. It requires construction of a trellis with two strong wires stretched between posts at a height of 30 and 60 in. The first year after a vine is planted, the stems produced are trained straight up and tied to the wires. In the second year, cut out all but one stem and trim this back to the top wire. This will develop into the trunk. In the third year, remove all but four pencil-size branches—two at the top wire and two at the bottom—and four spurs (short branches) close to the branches. Cut the branches back to four buds and tie them to the wires on either side of the trunk. Leave the four spurs alone. In the fourth year, cut out the previous year's pencil-size branches and tie the new pencil-size branches which developed from the spurs to the wires. Trim these branches back to about eight buds. Save one newly formed spur near each branch and remove all other growth. In succeeding years, repeat the procedure of the fourth year.

Muscadine grapes are normally trained overhead on an arbor. Each vine has a main stem and, on top of the arbor, six to eight branches. Pruning consists of cutting back the small branches that develop from the main branches to two or three buds.

Blueberries should be pruned in early spring to remove dead wood and some of the stems that are over three years old. If a plant contains a great many plump, rounded fruit buds, part of these should also be removed; otherwise the fruit produced is likely to be smaller than it should be.

Pruning of elderberries in early spring consists of removing all but five or six one-year-old canes and one or two two-year-old canes. Cut off the tips of these canes if they have been winter-killed.

¶ *Pests.* The best way to assure against diseases and insects is to plant disease-resistant varieties; keep dead and spent wood cut out;

rogue out (pull up) plants that are not doing well; and keep the garden clean. For specific control of pests, see Chapter 10.

Birds may be more of a problem, especially if you grow blueberries. Some can be frightened off by various kinds of scarecrows and noisemakers. But if the birds give real trouble, the best protection is to cover the plants with cheesecloth when the fruit begins to ripen.

¶ *Strawberries.* Most of the above instructions apply to strawberries, but additional points should be noted.

Plant in early spring—as soon as the soil can be worked—in soil that has been fumigated to kill insects and weed seeds. Set out the little plants as soon as possible after they are delivered to you. If they are sealed in plastic bags, remove them so they do not become overheated. If any plants must be held for several hours, "heel them in" by covering the roots with soil. Just before planting, nip off old, dry leaves, leaving two or three young ones, and cut long roots to 4 in.

The two most popular methods for laying out and training strawberries in the home garden are known as the hill method and the matted-row method. There is no agreement as to which is the bet-

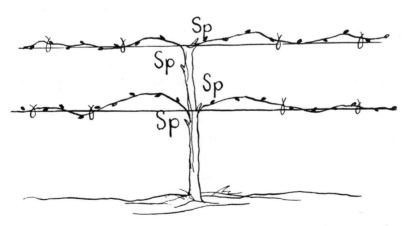

Kniffin system of pruning an established grape vine. Four long, pencil-size branches will bear fruit this year; four spurs (Sp) will develop into next year's bearing branches.

ter. In the hill method, plants are spaced 1 ft. apart in rows 2 ft. apart. Keep runners cut off as soon as they form. In the matted-row system, set plants 2 ft. apart in rows 3 to 4 ft. apart. Keep about six runners per plant (remove all others). Plant the little runner plants around the mother plant at a distance of 6 to 9 in.

Fertilize plants when they start developing runners and again in August. Use the fertilizer recommended by your Extension Service or a 5-10-5. In the hill system, use 1 tsp. per plant per feeding. In the matted-row system, scatter about 15 lb. of fertilizer per 1000 sq. ft.

During the first year, remove the blossoms on spring-bearing varieties until late June. On everbearing varieties, remove the blossoms until mid-July.

To control insects and diseases, the New York State College of Agriculture at Cornell recommends an all-purpose mixture composed of 2 tbs. malathion, 3 tbs. methoxychlor and 2 tbs. Captan per gallon of water. Apply this as soon as buds appear in the spring and just before bloom.

To control weeds and hold in moisture, keep plants mulched with organic material or polyethylene film. If the latter is used the initial feeding should be doubled and the August feeding omitted.

In the fall, after ground is frozen but before the temperature falls below 20°F., cover the plants and the rows between them with hay or salt hay to a depth of 2 to 3 in. Remove this from over the plants in the spring when new growth starts to turn yellow.

Everbearing varieties produce fruit in the fall of the first year and in the spring and fall of the second year. The plants should then be discarded.

Other varieties produce one crop—in the spring of the second year. If you use the hill method of culture, the plants should then be replaced (you can raise your own replacement plants by allowing one or two rows of plants to produce runner plants). If you use the matted-row method, rip out two-thirds of the plants immediately after the last fruit is harvested; apply fertilizer at the rate of 25 lb. per 1000 sq. ft., and keep the remaining plants mulched and watered.

TABLE XX
Nut Trees

	Where grown[1]	Deciduous, evergreen	Height (ft.)	Space trees (ft.)
Almond	Warm	D	20	30
Chestnut (Chinese)	Mild, warm	D	40	25
Coconut palm	Warmest	E	100	30
Filbert	Northwest	D	30	25
Hazelnut	Anywhere exc. coldest, warmest	D	15	10-12
Hickory	Eastern U.S.	D	130	60-90
Macadamia	Warmest	E	60	35
Pecan	South	D	120	60-90
Pistachio	Warmest	E	30	30
Walnut	Anywhere	D	150	60-90

[1] For an explanation of terms used in this column, see key to Table XII (page 226).

A strawberry plant in a matted row. The daughter plants are spaced around the parent plant. When they develop, they will form a mat 15 to 18 in. wide.

The nut trees, by and large, are handsome, sturdy trees that are often grown more for the beauty they bring to the garden than for their nuts. When this is the case, their culture is the same as that of other trees (see Chapter 16). But if you are interested in them mainly for the gustatory pleasures they produce, various additional cultural steps should be taken.

¶ *Tree selection.* Numerous varieties of the various nut trees have been developed by orchardists. For best results, ask your Extension Service which are recommended for your particular area. In the case of almonds, Chinese chestnuts, filberts and hazelnuts, you must plant specimens of at least two varieties in order to produce a crop. Similarly, you must plant both male and female trees to raise pistachio nuts.

In all cases, buy trees that have been budded or grafted. Those grown from seeds may not produce as well as you would like.

¶ *Soil.* If this is of average quality, the trees should do well enough. But if it is above average—well drained, moisture retentive, full of humus and rich—the trees will grow far better and yield more heavily.

¶ *Planting.* In very cold climates, plant the trees in a sunny location in early spring. In milder climates, plant in late fall or early spring. Unless you can lay hands on balled-and-burlapped or potted plants, start with bare-root plants that are about 5 ft. tall. Smaller plants may turn out to be runty trees; larger ones may come with mangled roots. A good root system is important to the growth of all young nut trees, but especially to the walnuts, pecans and hickories, which have long tap roots.

Trees of this size should not have to be pruned hard at planting time. Keep the main branches that will become the scaffold branches, and trim out all others.

If rabbits or other rodents are a problem, place a wire-mesh collar around the trunk of each tree.

¶ *Watering.* Nuts develop in three rather distinct stages. In the first stage, they grow in size. In the second stage, which starts about the time the shells have reached full size (and in some cases when the shells start to harden), the kernels fill the shells. In the third stage, which starts about a month later, in the fall, the nuts mature.

Ample moisture is extremely important to bearing trees during the first and second stages. If this is lacking, the nuts will not attain good size and/or fill out properly.

How much water does a bearing tree need? Like all similar questions, this is unanswerable. Each tree in every year is different. But you can tell when a nut tree needs water by regularly checking the condition of the soil during the spring and summer. When it dries out down to a depth of 12 to 18 in., haul out your hose.

In the years before a tree reaches bearing age, water need not be applied on quite such a formal basis; but at no time should foliage be allowed to show even incipient signs of wilting.

¶ *Fertilizing*. Along with ample water, ample nutrition is the key to maximum nut production. One way to make sure your trees are well cared for in this respect is to remove all grass, ground covers, weeds, etc., from under the canopies of the trees. Keep the exposed soil covered with an organic mulch.

Feed a new spring-planted tree for the first time at the time of planting; A fall-planted tree the following spring. From then on, feed all trees early every spring with 1/2 to 1 lb. of fertilizer per inch of trunk diameter. Use the formula recommended by your Extension Service or a 5-10-10. If the tree is mulched, simply scatter the plant food over the entire root system and water it in. If the trees are growing in a lawn without a mulch, apply the fertilzer in holes reaching down to the deep roots (see Chapter 16).

If for no other accountable reason the foliage of a nut tree shows mottling and begins to fall early, have the soil analyzed to determine whether there is a deficiency in trace elements such as iron, boron or zinc. Nut trees apparently need more of these elements than other trees.

¶ *Pruning* is done in the winter. When a tree is young, your main aim should be to develop a system of strong, well-distributed scaffold branches. For ease in harvesting, the lowest of these should be about breast height; the next, 12 to 18 in. above this and about one-third of the way around the trunk; the next, 12 to 18 in. above this and another one-third of the way around the trunk; and so on. If a tree tries to throw up more than one trunk (this is a failing of Chinese chestnut and Persian walnuts), remove the extras promptly.

¶ *Thinning nuts.* If you want to enjoy the largest nuts with the largest kernels, do not permit a tree to produce an abnormally large crop. Pick off the excess nuts as early in the season as you can. Preventing a tree from producing too many nuts also helps to assure that it will produce again the following year. It may not otherwise.

¶ *Diseases and insects.* Like fruit trees, nut trees have more than their share of troubles. But these are so diverse that it is impossible to give a general schedule of spraying. Besides, a full-grown nut tree is too large for the home gardener to spray himself.

But two general problems that you should watch out for are (1) wholesale defoliation by various types of caterpillars in the spring and (2) weevils that eat the nut kernels in late summer and fall.

Defoliation of all trees does harm; but a nut tree without leaves or without enough healthy leaves does not produce many good nuts. Dr. H. L. Crane of the USDA has made the flat statement that "under normal conditions the size of the crop and the degree to which the nuts are filled is directly related to the leaf area and the length of time it is carried by the tree." To prevent loss of foliage, spray in the spring with DDT or Sevin.

Weevils, as a rule, can be controlled on all nut trees by spraying with DDT about six weeks before the nuts ripen. Spray again two weeks and four weeks later.

19

How to Raise Vegetables

ONE OF THE MOST SATISFYING experiences in life is to eat vegetables you have grown yourself. This is reason enough for putting in a small vegetable garden. But there are others. Right-from-your-own-garden vegetables are more nutritious and tasty than purchased vegetables. They save a great deal of money. And they are immediately available when you get a sudden hankering for an ear of corn or a fresh salad. You can also have varieties which are generally not available in the market.

¶ *Garden size and layout.* There is no law that vegetables must be grown in a vegetable garden. If you want just a few vegetables of a few types—say, tomatoes, peppers and some lettuce—you can grow them in with your flowers or anywhere else you like. I had a friend who grew a couple of tomato plants beside his front door. They produced bountifully and were a marvelous conversation piece.

But if you want to grow vegetables on any scale, it is convenient to relegate them to their own patch of ground. How big a patch do you need? If you have a family of six, a 2500 sq. ft. garden should produce all the vegetables you can consume during the summer and leave a lot for freezing; and once planted, it should not demand more than an hour of work per day. If, on the other hand, you want nothing more than a salad garden, a 15 x 15 ft. plot will yield all the lettuce, tomatoes, herbs and cucumbers you can ask for.

The best rule for the beginning vegetable gardener is to start small and work up.

Vegetable gardens are usually rectangular, but any other shape that suits your lot will work just as well. If you are gardening on a hillside, run the rows across the hill rather than up and down. This makes best use of water and minimizes erosion. Whether you have paths through the garden is a matter of choice. You don't really need them—in a small garden at least—since the spaces between vegetable rows serve as paths.

All vegetables can be grown in rows; but cucumbers, fall and winter squash, melons and pumpkins are best grown in hills (a hill is a circle of seeds about 1 ft. across; the vines grow out from this in all directions). The recommended spaces to allow between rows and between plants in the row are given in Table XXI (page 275).

Some suggestions (they are nothing more) for the general location of vegetables in the garden follow.

(1) Grow asparagus and rhubarb—both perennials—together at one end of the garden where they will not interfere with the planting of the annual vegetables.

(2) Place tall vegetables next to medium-height vegetables, and these next to small vegetables; then none will be seriously shaded. Ideally, your rows should run east and west and the tallest vegetables should be on the north side of the garden.

(3) Plant quick crops such as radishes between slower crops such as lettuce. (This is called intercropping.) Because the quick crops will be out of the way by the time the slower ones begin to attain full size, you can space the slow crop rows normally, as if the quick crops never existed.

(4) Make a practice of rotating crops. Sometimes when the same vegetables are planted in the same spot year after year, the diseases and/or insects that attack them multiply excessively, or the vegetables create an unusual drain on the nutrients in the soil at that spot.

¶ *Selecting vegetable varieties.* Vegetables vary widely. Some grow best in cold weather (examples: peas and lettuce); some grow best in hot weather (examples: tomatoes and lima beans). Some are planted in the garden as soon as the soil can be worked; some, shortly

Small herb garden is laid out in a formal, stylized design known as a knot garden. Boxwood in the center is trimmed in the shape of a duck (this is known as topiary work). Lath house provides shade for potted plants.

before the last frost; some after the last frost. A few are best started indoors or in a cold frame or hotbed, and then moved outdoors. Some will yield a spring crop and a fall crop; others will yield a series of crops pretty well through the summer.

There is also considerable variation in the time it takes different varieties of the same vegetable to mature. For example, you can buy a variety of sweet corn that matures in about 65 days; another that matures in about 90 days; and there are many others that mature in about 70, 75, 80 or 85 days.

Feet

00	
1	Snap beans — Plant May 1. Harvest July 1.
2½	Tomatoes, staked. Plant May 15. Harvest July 25 to frost. Interplant with lettuce plants, onion sets, or radishes.
5	Early cabbage plants — Plant April 1. Harvest July 10. Follow with 2 rows late beets.
7½	Early carrots — Plant April 15. Harvest July 5. Follow with fall cabbage plants — Plant July 5 to 10.
10	Onion sets — Plant April 1. Harvest August 1. Follow with 2 rows fall spinach.
12½	Pepper plants — Plant May 15. Harvest July 25 to frost.
15	Swiss chard — ½ row. Plant April 1. Harvest June 15 to frost. Lettuce — ½ row. Plant August 1.
17½	Early beets — Plant April 1. Harvest June 10. Follow with 4 hills of vine squash. Plant June 20. Harvest before frost.
20	Early bush peas — Plant April 1. Harvest June 5. Follow with late snap beans — Plant June 5.
22½	6 hills summer squash — Plant May 1. Harvest July 5. Follow with fall carrots, turnips. Plant July 15. Store for winter. Or lima beans — Plant May 10. Harvest August 5 to frost.
25	

Plan for a small, 25 x 25 ft. garden suggested by the New Jersey Agricultural Extension Service. The dates are approximate even for New Jersey but give an idea of when to plant and when you should expect to be able to harvest. Some of the vegetables mentioned, such as carrots, beets, radishes, onions and lettuce, can be sown in rows closer together than those shown.

What does all this mean? Simply that, in planning a vegetable garden, you should try to work things out so that the garden is working for you most of the time. And in order to do this, you should find out from some old-time local gardener or your Agricultural Extension Service (1) the date when frost is usually out of the ground in your area, (2) the date of the last spring frost and (3) the date of the first fall frost.

For example, suppose frost is usually out of the ground April 1, the last spring frost is usually May 27 and the first fall frost is usually September 18. This schedule will permit you to start the season on April 1 by planting a row of Grand Rapids lettuce, which matures in 45 days. On June 1, in the same row, you can plant Bountiful string beans, which mature in 50 days. Then, on about August 15, the beans can be succeeded by Comet radishes, which mature in 25 days. This is called succession cropping.

You can also have a continuing series of crops of the same vegetable either by making a series of plantings at two-week intervals or by making a simultaneous planting of varieties that take different lengths of time to mature. For example, if you want to enjoy a long season of corn, you can make a first sowing of Marcross hybrid corn (which matures in 75 days) one week before the last frost; then make a second sowing a week after the last frost; and make a third and even a fourth sowing at fortnightly intervals thereafter. That will give you about eight to nine weeks of good corn eating. The alternative, if you prefer to get your planting done all at once, is to sow varieties, such as the following, a week before the last frost (or at some slightly later date): Early Sunglow, which matures in 63 days; Marcross; Golden Cross Bantam (85 days); and Stowell's Evergreen (95 days). This will give you six to seven weeks of corn eating.

¶ *Growing requirements.* All vegetables need full sun.

The soil should be not-too-heavy loam with sand and humus and good drainage. The pH should be between 6 and 7. Remove stones in areas where you plant root crops. If possible, spade or rotary-till the garden in the fall to give the frost a chance to work on the soil and improve its texture. A cover crop of rye grass may also be planted at this time and turned under in the spring (see Chapter 3).

Side-dress all vegetables with a balanced fertilizer such as 4-8-4 or 8-16-8, when you thin the seedlings. Give vegetables with large fruits (tomatoes, eggplants, squash and cucumbers) a second dose of food when they start setting fruits. Well-rotted manure is very beneficial to vegetables if available.

Water heavily in long dry spells. Tomatoes, cucumbers, squash, pumpkins and melons especially need water and respond enthusiastically when given a regular supply.

Cultivate between rows to keep out weeds. Better still, mulch the entire garden with hay, any other plentiful organic mulch or polyethylene film (see Chapter 8).

¶ *Planting.* Follow the seed-sowing directions given in Chapter 14. Vegetables that are started indoors or in a cold frame or hotbed are handled like annual flowers. Spacing for vegetables is given in Table XXI.

¶ *Staking* is necessary only for peas and pole beans; but tomatoes are usually staked and you may feel it advisable to stake other tall, heavily laden vegetables such as eggplants and peppers. It saves space besides keeping the fruits off the ground (though there is nothing wrong with this).

For peas use twiggy branches 2 or 3 ft. long or chicken wire. For pole beans, use rough 6 to 7 ft. wooden stakes about 1 in. square. Neither of these vegetables needs to be tied. Tomato stakes are about 4 to 5 ft. long and 1 in. across. Tie the plants at 9 to 12 in. intervals.

¶ *Blanching* is a method of either keeping or turning certain vegetables almost white. Late celery and asparagus may be blanched (it is not essential) by mounding soil up around the stalks so that only the tops show. Early celery is most easily blanched by placing two boards on either side of the row and hooking them together loosely just below the leaves.

¶ *Harvesting.* Many vegetables are at their best just before they reach full size. These include beans (especially lima beans), beets, cabbage, carrots, corn, peas, radishes and summer squash. Corn and peas should be picked at the last possible minute before you sit down to eat them.

Pumpkins and winter squash should be ripened on the vine; and it is best to allow tomatoes and melons to ripen in that way, too.

Lettuce, spinach and other leafy vegetables become tough when they start going to seed. Beet and turnip tops are most edible before the roots start to flesh out.

TABLE XXI
Vegetables

Key: I–raise from seed started indoors about eight weeks before last frost.
OALF–sow seed outdoors where plants are to grow after last frost.
OWSW–sow seed outdoors where plants are to grow when soil is workable.

	When & where to seed	Depth to plant seed (in.)	Space plants apart in row (in.)	Space rows apart (in.)
Asparagus	1	1	18-36	24-36
Beans, snap	OALF	1	3-4	18-24
Beans, lima	OALF	1	6-8	18-30
Beets	OWSW	½	2-4	18-24
Broccoli	I	¼	18-24	24-36
Brussels sprouts	I	¼	18-24	24-30
Cabbage	I	¼	18-30	24-36
Carrot	OWSW	½	1-3	18-24
Cauliflower	I	¼	18-24	24-36
Collards	OWSW	¼	4-8	18-24
Celery	I	⅛	12-18	24-36
Corn	OALF	1	8-12	24-36
Cucumber	OALF	1	3-6	36-60
Eggplant	I	½	18-24	24-36
Endive	OWSW	¼	8-12	18-24
Kale	OWSW	½	12-24	18-24
Kohlrabi	I	¼	6-8	18-24
Lettuce	OWSW	⅛	6-12	18-24
Muskmelon	OALF	1	36-48	72-96
Mustard	OWSW	¼	8-12	12-18
Okra	OALF	1	18-24	24-36
Onion	OWSW	½	2-3	15-30
Parsley	OWSW	¼	4-8	12-18
Parsnip	OWSW	¾	3-6	18-24
Peas	OWSW	1½-2	2-3	24-36

1 Start from roots which may be purchased.

	When & where to seed	Depth to plant seed (in.)	Space plants apart in row (in.)	Space rows apart (in.)
Pepper	I	¼	18-24	18-30
Pumpkin	OALF	1½	3-6	72-96
Radish	OWSW	½	1-2	12-18
Rhubarb	1	1	36-60	36-60
Rutabaga	2	½	6-8	18-24
Spinach	OWSW	½	3-4	12-18
Squash, summer	OALF	1	36-48	36-48
Squash, winter	OALF	1	48-72	72-96
Tomato	I	¼	36-48	36-48
Turnip	OWSW	½	3-4	15-24
Watermelon	OALF	1	72-96	72-96

2 Sow seeds where the plants are to grow 110 days before first fall frost.

20

How to Grow
Miscellaneous Plants

GROUND COVERS

GROUND COVERS ARE LOW-GROWING PLANTS that are used instead of grass to blanket a section of the garden. They are planted in areas where, for one reason or another, grass is hard to grow. They are planted in shrubbery borders to cover the bare soil and discourage weeds. And they are often planted under litterbug trees to conceal fallen fruits, nuts and leaves and thus make raking unnecessary.

Table XXII (page 284) describes a number of good ground cover plants. The kind you use depends on the effect you wish to achieve, the exposure, and the principal purpose of the ground cover. One point to bear in mind when selecting a ground cover to conceal tree litter is that, while all of them readily swallow up fruits and nuts, none—not even juniper—absorbs leaves quickly or effectively. And to make matters worse, all ground covers are extremely difficult to rake clean.

You should also remember that if a ground cover is planted in an area that is traversed by dogs, only the tougher, woody types, such as juniper, lantana, trailing roses and cotoneasters, should be used. Others will be beaten down in a distinct, unerasable path.

Inasmuch as ground covers fall into several plant categories, I cannot give a single set of directions for growing them. For how to grow perennial varieties, follow the general directions for all peren-

277

nials in Chapter 14. For how to grow woody varieties, see Chapter 16. And for how to grow ice plant, see the section below about cacti and succulents.

The following special points, however, apply to all ground covers:

(1) Once it is established, a thick, healthy ground cover smothers almost all weeds that try to come up through it. But until it is established, weeds are usually a major nuisance. You can keep them from becoming so, however, by fumigating the soil in which the ground cover is to be planted (see Chapter 10).

(2) Ground covers compete vigorously for water and nutrients with the trees, shrubs or vines under which they may be planted. For this reason, you should avoid planting a ground cover around trees, etc., until these are well established and able to fend for themselves. Thereafter, you should increase the amount of water and fertilizer given the trees (or ground cover) about 50% or more.

FERNS

Although most ferns grow in partial shade, some also grow in full sun. Plant both kinds in the spring in ordinary garden soil that is well drained and rich in humus (if you transplant ferns from a woodland, bring along some of the soil in which they were growing). Take care not to cover the crowns of the plants with soil. Allow about 1 ft. space between ferns that grow a foot high; 2 ft. between those than grow to 3 ft.; 3 ft. between those that grow to 5 ft. Good air circulation is important.

Water the plants well until they are established. After that, water deeply in dry spells. If it does not upset your esthetic sense, leave the old fronds on the ground where they collapse: they are a good mulch.

Fertilizing is usually unnecessary.

If ferns become crowded (though I have never noticed that this bothers them greatly), dig them up in early spring or fall and divide them carefully. But avoid handling them in summer or walking through them, because the fronds are easily broken.

Do not be alarmed by small specks which appear on the undersides of the fronds. If they are arranged in neat lines or clusters,

Periwinkle is a fairly unusual ground cover because it grows almost as well in sun as in shade. It is just tall enough to conceal unsightly foundation walls, as here; but unless a roof has gutters, it is soon beaten down by rain dripping from the eaves.

This velvety, hummocky grass is a type of ground cover often grown in the far West in sunny locations. It is named Zoysia tenuifolia. Though it has fair resistance to traffic, it soon wears out if dogs and people beat a path across it.

Most ferns—but not all—grow in shade. Here they are used to good effect to fill in the open space under a Southern California hillside house.

they are the spore cases from which a new generation of plants will be produced.

CACTI AND SUCCULENTS

Some cacti are tropical, tree-perching plants that can only be grown indoors in most parts of the U.S. The cacti considered here are the desert types that thrive outdoors (as well as in) in many parts of the West.

Cacti are able to survive drought by storing water inside. Succulents are related plants that are able to survive drought simply because they do not need a great deal of moisture. They, too, are largely desert plants; but some species grow in wet, cold climates.

Cacti and succulents are grown outdoors in the same way.

Plant them in the spring in a spot which gets all-day sun and in which late spring frosts will not settle. The ideal soil consists of equal parts of loam, humus and sand, and should be 12 in. deep. Under this there should be a 6-in. layer of mixed small and coarse gravel to assure perfect drainage.

At planting time the soil should be dry. Set the plants at the depth they previously grew, and firm the soil around the roots. Stake upright plants to keep them from toppling. Do not water for three days; then dampen the soil slightly. For the next two months keep the soil on the dry side. Thereafter, in spring and summer, when the plants are making growth and flowering, they should be watered deeply whenever the soil dries out on top. In fall and winter no water need be applied unless you live in a totally arid region.

Fertilize cacti and succulents with a little balanced commercial plant food or bone meal every spring. Pull out weeds from around the plants but otherwise leave the soil uncultivated. If a plant is injured, cut out the damaged area with a sterile knife and dust the wound with sulfur. Spray for insect pests as with other plants.

WATER LILIES

Allow about 10 sq. ft. of water surface per plant.

Plant hardy water lilies shortly before the last killing frost;

tropical species in late spring when the water has reached a temperature of 68°F. or more.

Both types should be planted in containers 15 to 18 in. across and 10 in. deep. Fill these with any good soil to which you have added dried manure at the rate of one part manure to ten parts soil. Roots of the tuberosa and odorata type of water lilies are planted horizontally and 1 in. deep. Marliac roots should be upright, and the crown should be just above the soil. Take care not to injure the growing points of the plants, which should extend above the soil surface. Cover the soil with pebbles if there are fish in your pool. This helps to prevent roiling of the water by the fish.

Before setting the plant boxes in the pool, fill the pool to the desired depth and allow the water to warm up for a couple of days. Place the boxes on bricks so that the soil surface at the start is no more than 2 in. below the water level. This permits the sun to reach the growing points. Later, when growth starts, drop the boxes to the bottom. Hardy water lilies generally should have about 1 ft. of water over them; the tropicals need only 8 in.

During the first summer, the only thing you have to do for most water lilies is to maintain the water level. Do not let the pool become overcrowded with foliage. Stick a plant tablet or two in the soil in which tropical varieties are planted. The hardy lilies can be fertilized in the same way but require it only if they seem to be somewhat sluggish.

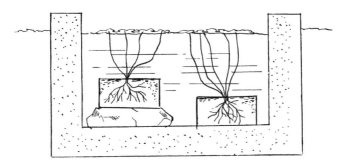

How to plant water lilies. Tubs can be raised or lowered as necessary to provide proper water depth over the roots.

When autumn comes, cut out the excess stems and foliage. If the boxes are below the usual frost line for your area (ask an old-time gardener), you can leave the plants in the water. They do not need protection. But if the boxes are above the frost line, you should either cover the pool with boards and mounds of straw and leaves, or you should take up the roots and store them in moist sand indoors. The tropical lilies must always be stored indoors in this way, but even so they are very difficult to carry over.

Hardy lilies that are left in the pool over winter should be repotted in fresh soil every second or third year. Divide the roots at that time. New manure is required every year.

TABLE XXII
Selected Ground Cover Plants

	Type	Where grown[1]	Height (in.)	Expo- sure	Deciduous, evergreen
Ajuga reptans	Peren.	All but coldest	10	S or Sh	E
Bearberry (*Arctostaphylos uva-ursii*)	Shrub	Cold, mild	6	Sh	E
Candytuft (*Iberis sempervirens*)	Peren.	Anywhere	6	S	E
Ceanothus grisens horizontalis	Shrub	California		S or Sh	E
Ceratostigma plum- baginoides	Peren.	Mild, warm	9	Sh	
Cotoneaster horizontalis	Shrub	Mild, warm	24	S or Sh	D
Dichondra carolinensis	Peren.	Warmest	3	S or Sh	E
Euonymus radicans	Vine	Mild, warm	12	Sh	E
Iceplant (*Mesembryanthe- mum crystallinum*)	Succu.	Warmest	8	S	E
Ivy (*Hedera*)	Vine	All but coldest	10	S or Sh	E
Juniperus horizontalis	Shrub	Anywhere	10	S	E
Juniperus horizontalis douglasii	Shrub	Anywhere	10	S	E
Lantana	Vine	Warmest	3	S	E
Lily turf (*Ophiopogon japonicus*)	Peren.	Warm	12	S or Sh	E

[1] For an explanation of terms used in this column, see key to Table XII (page 226).

	Type	Where grown[1]	Height (in.)	Exposure	Deciduous, evergreen
Lily of the valley (*Convallaria*)	Peren.	Mild, warm	8	Sh	
Liriope	Peren.	Warm	18	Sh	E
Pachistima canbyi	Shrub	Mild, warm	12	S or Sh	E
Pachysandra terminalis	Peren.	Cold, mild, warm	8	S or Sh	E
Periwinkle (*Vinca minor*)	Peren.	Anywhere	24	Sh	E
Rose (*Rosa Max Graf*)	Shrub	Anywhere	24	S	D
Rose (*Rosa Wichuraiana*)	Shrub	Anywhere	18	S	D
Sedum acre	Succu.	Mild, warm	4	S or Sh	E
St. Johnswort (*Hypericum moserianum*)	Shrub	Mild, warm	24	S or Sh	D
Wandering Jew (*Zebrina pendula*)	Vine	Warmest	6	S or Sh	E

21

How to Raise Plants in Containers

THERE ARE ANY NUMBER OF REASONS for the upsurge in popularity of container, or pot, gardening. It is an ideal way to pretty up a terrace, patio, porch or poolside. It permits you to change your "planting" plan or outdoor color scheme at a moment's notice. It involves little physical labor. And the containers themselves can add considerable interest and beauty to the area in which they are used.

¶ *Container types.* Anything that holds soil can be used for container gardening: painted tin cans, concrete blocks, hollow building tiles, copper and iron kettles, giant seashells, short lengths of bamboo, barrels, wicker baskets, hollow logs, etc. But containers generally fall into one of five categories:

(1) Flower pots range from 1 3/4 to 14 in. in diameter. So-called standard pots—the kind most often used—are as deep as they are wide. There are also three-quarter pots (three-quarters of the standard depth); pans (half of the standard depth); and saucers, which are very shallow and usually used only under pots to keep them from dripping water all over the place.

Most pots are made of unglazed red clay and have a drainage hole in the bottom. Nothing is better for holding plants. The pots are cheap. And because the clay is fairly porous, the soil can breathe to a certain extent. Such pots are also quite good-looking when clean —but it takes a lot of elbow grease to keep them clean.

Plastic pots with drainage holes are easier to clean but not so good-looking. They are also much lighter than the clay pots and less breakable. But they do not admit air to the soil.

(2) Undrained containers are usually made of glazed pottery or glass (but they may be made of almost anything). They are far more decorative than flower pots—and that is the only good thing you can say about them. Their most serious deficiency is their lack of a bottom drainage hole. Because of this, the soil in them very often becomes waterlogged and sour.

(3) Wooden tubs and boxes used as planters are for the most part larger than flower pots (and lighter than clay pots) and are therefore used for big plants or groupings of plants. They should be made of cypress or redwood to keep them from rotting (whether they are painted or not is immaterial). They should also have about five 1/2-in. drainage holes per square foot of bottom area. And to facilitate drainage and further discourage decay, they should be raised 1/2 in. or more off the surface on which they are placed.

(4) Window boxes of wood, metal or plastic-like fiberboard can be bought ready-made. Or you can build your own of 1-in.-thick redwood or cypress lumber (if you use pine, it must be thoroughly treated with nontoxic-to-plants wood preservative such as copper naphthanate). Use brass screws, not nails, to hold the boards together.

A windowbox can have squared sides or a front that slants out slightly. It should have an inside depth of 8 to 9 in.; a width of 10 to 12 in. The maximum length is 4 ft.: anything longer is somewhat difficult to hang securely and needs a reinforced bottom. Drill 1/2-in. holes at 6-in. intervals in the bottom to provide drainage.

(5) Hanging containers. The most familiar type is a basket of wire mesh or plastic mesh lined on the bottom and sides with sphagnum moss. But almost anything that holds soil and can be hung on wires or chains can be used.

¶ *Soil for container gardening.* The simplest soil mixture consists of two parts garden loam, one part coarse sand and one part peat. If the loam contains a great deal of clay, reduce the amount used by 50%. For fertilizer use a balanced plant food that is scratched into the soil

Plants in window boxes, tubs and pots brighten this small, informal terrace. The main advantage of gardening in containers is that you can shift plants around to change the design of the "garden"; and if you keep new pots of plants coming along throughout the summer, you can replace worn-out plants at any time.

or a concentrate that is applied as a liquid (see Chapter 4). Lime should be necessary only if the loam has a low pH content or if the plants you are growing prefer a sweet soil.

¶ *Potting procedure.* All containers must be scrubbed clean before you plant in them. Use soap and water. The new plants may be infected with left-over diseases otherwise.

Cover drainage holes with one or two shards or stones. If a container does not have bottom drainage, you must place a substantial layer of shards or stones in the bottom. Use about 1 in. in small containers; 2 to 3 in. in large containers.

Fill the containers halfway with soil, and mound it up slightly in a cone. Hold the plant so that the roots drape over the cone, and fill in around them with more soil. The crown of the plant and surface of the soil should be 1 in. below the rim of the container when the potting job is completed. The soil should be lightly firmed for small plants but very solidly firmed for woody plants (professionals pack the soil around potted azaleas with a stick, for example). Then it should be watered until it is moist through and through.

¶ *Watering.* Plants in containers must be watered regularly but carefully. Although house plants are watered either from the top or the bottom, potted plants outdoors are usually watered with a hose or watering can from the top only. If containers have bottom drainage, apply the water until it comes out the bottom holes. If containers are undrained, you must simply trust to luck that you do not drown the plants.

Water should be applied to all container plants when the surface soil feels dry. In very hot, dry weather you may need to water daily. This is particularly true if the plants are in containers made of porous material (red clay pots and hanging wire baskets, for example). You can save work, however, if you mulch the soil with peat. You can also set a fast-drying container in a larger container with a layer of damp sphagnum moss between.

¶ *Other care.* Except for faithful watering, plants in containers do not demand unusual attention. Fertilize them every four to six weeks while they are making growth. Stir up the soil occasionally to admit

Large plants such as these require large containers. Because such containers rarely have bottom drainage holes, watering must be done with care to prevent the soil from becoming waterlogged and sour.

This potted plant is not rootbound; but if and when the rootball becomes covered with an almost solid mat of white roots, then it probably will be. Rootbound plants usually need to be repotted to keep them growing and blooming well.

air. Spray the tops of the plants with water—especially if they are on a terrace where the hot sun strikes them not only from above but also bounces back at them from surrounding walls and paving.

If a vigorous, healthy plant suddenly stops growing and blooming enthusiastically despite good care, it may have become rootbound. This condition is indicated by a heavy mat of small roots on the outside of the rootball. The solution is to move the plant into the *next size larger* container. Do not break the rootball; simply hold it in the center of the larger pot and drizzle fresh soil in around it.

If the rootbound plant is already in the largest container you can find, scrape some of the soil from the sides and bottom of the rootball, trim the roots slightly with a pair of scissors and replant with fresh soil in the same container.

Since soil in containers does not stay in as good condition as that in the garden (for instance, it may become sour or lose its nutrients through leaching), it is advisable to repot perennial plants in fresh soil every year or two just before they start making new growth. Handle them in the manner described in the paragraph above.

Containers that are newly planted every year should be filled with fresh soil every year.

Because potted plants do not have a great deal of resistance to below-freezing temperatures, perennials and woody plants should be stored in a cool basement, garage or porch in winter. They do not need direct sunlight, but should be given just enough water to keep them from drying out completely. In warm climates, plants can be left outdoors but should be covered or moved to a protected spot when frost threatens.

Appendix

STATE AGRICULTURAL EXTENSION SERVICES

WHEREVER THEY LIVE, all gardeners are surrounded by many fine sources of specific information about local gardening conditions and problems and about the species and varieties of plants which grow best locally. None, however, is better than the Agricultural Extension Service maintained by each state. As a taxpayer, you can consider your Extension Service your own private answering service and research arm. Whatever your question about raising plants, improving soil, watering, pest-fighting, etc. (but usually not landscaping), it will try to produce an answer. And a very good answer it will be because the Extension Service, together with the closely affiliated State Agricultural Experiment Station, does continuing research into agricultural and horticultural problems of all kinds.

Address your inquiries to the Agricultural Extension Service at the following locations:

ALABAMA   Alabama Polytechnic Institute, Auburn

ALASKA   University of Alaska, College

ARIZONA   University of Arizona, Tuscon

ARKANSAS   College of Agriculture, University of Arkansas, Fayetteville

CALIFORNIA	College of Agriculture, University of California, Berkeley
COLORADO	Colorado State University, Fort Collins
CONNECTICUT	College of Agriculture, University of Connecticut, Storrs
	Connecticut Agricultural Experiment Station, New Haven
DELAWARE	School of Agriculture, University of Delaware, Newark
FLORIDA	University of Florida, Gainesville
GEORGIA	College of Agriculture, University of Georgia, Athens
HAWAII	University of Hawaii, Honolulu
IDAHO	University of Idaho, Moscow
ILLINOIS	College of Agriculture, University of Illinois, Urbana
INDIANA	Purdue University, Lafayette
IOWA	Iowa State College of Agriculture, Ames
KANSAS	Kansas State College of Agriculture, Manhattan
KENTUCKY	College of Agriculture, University of Kentucky, Lexington
LOUISIANA	Agricultural College, Louisiana State University, Baton Rouge
MAINE	College of Agriculture, University of Maine, Orono
MARYLAND	University of Maryland, College Park
MASSACHUSETTS	College of Agriculture, University of Massachusetts, Amherst
MICHIGAN	College of Agriculture, Michigan State University, East Lansing
MINNESOTA	Institute of Agriculture, University of Minnesota, St. Paul

MISSISSIPPI	Mississippi State College, State College
MISSOURI	College of Agriculture, University of Missouri, Columbia
MONTANA	Montana State College, Bozeman
NEBRASKA	College of Agriculture, University of Nebraska, Lincoln
NEVADA	College of Agriculture, University of Nevada, Reno
NEW HAMPSHIRE	University of New Hampshire, Durham
NEW JERSEY	Rutgers University, New Brunswick
NEW MEXICO	College of Agriculture, State College
NEW YORK	College of Agriculture, Cornell University, Ithaca
NORTH CAROLINA	State College of Agriculture, University of North Carolina, Raleigh
NORTH DAKOTA	State Agricultural College, Fargo
OHIO	College of Agriculture, Ohio State University, Columbus
OKLAHOMA	Oklahoma A. and M. College, Stillwater
OREGON	Oregon State College, Corvallis
PENNSYLVANIA	Pennsylvania State University, University Park
PUERTO RICO	University of Puerto Rico, Box 607, Rio Piedras
RHODE ISLAND	University of Rhode Island, Kingston
SOUTH CAROLINA	Clemson Agricultural College, Clemson
SOUTH DAKOTA	South Dakota State College, College Station
TENNESSEE	College of Agriculture, University of Tennessee, Knoxville
TEXAS	Texas A. and M. College, College Station
UTAH	College of Agriculture, Utah State University, Logan
VERMONT	State Agricultural College, University of Vermont, Burlington

VIRGINIA	Virginia Polytechnic Institute, Blacksburg
WASHINGTON	State College of Washington, Pullman
WEST VIRGINIA	West Virginia University, Morgantown
WISCONSIN	College of Agriculture, University of Wisconsin, Madison
WYOMING	College of Agriculture, University of Wyoming, Laramie

Index